The Familiar Life-Giver

The use of animals for spiritual enlightenment dates back beyond ancient Egypt. Now you can open doors to your secret self and a buried past when you find and befriend animal familiars. Animal Magick shows how to work with animals for your spiritual growth and increased magical power. Familiars are not the stereotyped witch's cat and cohort-in-crime. Real or imagined, familiars make excellent companions: they can warn you of danger, generate healing energy, and love you unconditionally. If you work magick, familiars can aid in augmenting your results with their preternatural power.

Your work with your familiar can take on an even greater purpose, true to the Pagan tradition: that is the remembrance and honoring of our ancestors. Most books on animal magick are written from a Native American viewpoint, but Animal Magick captures the subject of animal familiars from a European Pagan perspective. Now you can investigate ancient European Shamanic traditions—your heritage, perhaps—that were destroyed by Christianity and the Burning Times; you can trace the roots of Witchcraft and the resulting folk magicks still flourishing in the United States; you'll learn to use familiars in your meditations and magick; uncover superstitions about them, and draw associations with ancient Pagan deities. Learn to identify familiars with the descriptions of physical characteristics and magical attributes. Each animal is presented with a special "power chant" to invoke its greatest natural attributes. Through this working magic, you'll not only discover a new source of strength, wisdom, and friendship in your familiar, you'll pay the greatest homage to those who walked the Pagan path before you.

Unearth this buried heritage and breathe new life in the European Shaman and Pagan: all you need is you, your familiar, and Animal Magick.

D0017785

About the Author

D. J. Conway was born on a Beltane Full Moon with a total lunar eclipse, one of the hottest days of that year. Although she came into an Irish-North Germanic-Native American family with natural psychics on both sides, such abilities were not talked about. So she learned discrimination in a family of closet psychics.

D. J. lives a rather quiet life in the company of her husband and her two cats, Callisto and Finnigan, with occasional visits with children and grandchildren. Most of her time is spent researching and writing. "All in all," she says about herself, "I am just an ordinary Pagan person."

To Write to the Author

If you wish to contact the author or would like more information about this book, please write to the author in care of Llewellyn Worldwide, and we will forward your request. Both the author and publisher appreciate hearing from you and learning of your enjoyment of this book and how it has helped you. Llewellyn Worldwide cannot guarantee that every letter written to the author can be answered, but all will be forwarded. Please write to:

D. J. Conway
c/o Llewellyn Worldwide
P.O. Box 64383-K168, St. Paul, MN 55164-0383, U.S.A.
Please enclose a self-addressed, stamped envelope for reply, or $1.00 to cover costs. If outside U.S.A., enclose international postal reply coupon.

Free Catalog from Llewellyn

For more than ninety years Llewellyn has brought its readers knowledge in the fields of metaphysics and human potential. Learn about the newest books in spiritual guidance, natural healing, astrology, occult philosophy, and more. Enjoy book reviews, New Age articles, a calendar of events, plus current advertised products and services. To get your free copy of *Llewellyn's New Worlds*, send your name and address to:

Llewellyn's New Worlds of Mind and Spirit
P.O. Box 64383-K168, St. Paul, MN 55164-0383, U.S.A.

ANIMAL MAGICK

THE ART OF RECOGNIZING & WORKING WITH FAMILIARS

D. J. CONWAY

1996
Llewellyn Publications
St. Paul, Minnesota, 55164-0383, U.S.A.

FIRST EDITION, 1995
Second Printing, 1996

Cover Design by Tom Grewe

Library of Congress Cataloging-in-Publication Data
    Conway, D. J. (Deanna).
    Animal magick : the art of recognizing & working with familiars /
by D. J. Conway. — 1st ed.
        p.   cm. —
    Includes bibliographical references and index.
    ISBN 1-56718-168-6
    1. Animals—Miscellanea. 2. Magic. 3. Animals, Mythical.
4. Ritual. I. Title
    BF1623.A55C66   1995
    133.4'4—dc20   95-10721
                                                                    CIP

Llewellyn Publications
A Division of Llewellyn Worldwide, Ltd.
St. Paul, Minnesota 55164-0383, U.S.A.

To all those who love and honor animals,

To the children who see beauty in every creature,

And to the animals themselves,

Who grace our world.

Other Books by the Author

Celtic Magic
Norse Magic
The Ancient and Shining Ones
Maiden, Mother, Crone
Dancing with Dragons
By Oak, Ash & Thorn
Moon Magick
Flying Without a Broom

Forthcoming

Falcon Feather & Valkyrie Sword
The Dream Warrior (fiction)
Soothslayer (fiction)
Magickal, Mythical, Mystical Beasts

Contents

Part I   **A Familiar What?**   1

   1   Familiars & Humans   3
   2   How to Attract a Familiar   9
   3   Legends & Deities   13
   4   Animal Familiars & Magick   17
       A Meditation for a Familiar. Shape-shifting Meditation.

Part II   **Working Together**   25

   5   Meditations   27
       Learning from the Falcon. Snake Energy. The Spider &
       the Fates. Exploring the Oceans. Riding the Unicorn.
       Into the Underworld. Communing with the Night.
       Pegasus.

   6   Rituals   43
       North Direction. East Direction. South Direction.
       West Direction. Protection Ritual of the Wolves.
       Prosperity Ritual of the Wolves. Love Ritual of the
       Wolves. Spiritual Growth Ritual of the Wolves.
       Cat Magick for Calling Spirits. Dream Work. Opening
       the Psychic Senses. Gaining Wisdom. A Protective
       Mirror.Renewing & Healing Magick. Invisibility Magick.
       New Beginnings.

   7   The Beauty of Friendship   67

Part III   **Animal Allies of Fur, Feather, Fin & Scale**   69

   8   The Cat Family   71
       Domesticated Cats. Cheetah. Cougar. Jaguar. Leopard or
       Panther. Lion. Lynx. Tiger.

9 The Wolf Family   85
  Domesticated Dogs. Coyote. Fox. Jackal. Wolf.

10 Land Creatures   97
  Antelope. Ape or Monkey. Ass or Donkey. Badger. Bear.
  Beaver. Bison or Buffalo. Boar, Sow, or Pig. Bull, Cow,
   or Cattle. Deer or Stag. Elephant. Elk. Ferret. Goats.
  Hedgehog. Hippotamus. Horse. Mongoose. Moose.
  Mouse. Opossum. Otter. Oxen. Porcupine. Rabbit or
  Hare. Raccoon. Ram or Sheep. Rat. Skunk. Squirrel.
  Weasel. Wolverine.

11 Birds & Winged Creatures   149
  Bat. Blackbird. Blue Jay. Cock. Crane. Crow. Dove or
  Pigeon. Eagle. Falcon. Goose. Guinea Fowl. Hawk. Heron.
  Hummingbird. Ibis. Lovebird. Magpie. Nightingale.
  Ostrich. Owl. Parrot. Peacock. Quail. Raven. Robin.
  Sea Gull. Sparrow. Swallow. Swan. Turkey. Vulture.
  Woodpecker. Wren.

12 Amphibians & Reptiles   197
  Adder. Chameleon. Cobra. Crocodile. Frog. Lizard.
  Scorpion. Snakes. Toad. Turtle or Tortoise.

13 Aquatic Creatures   217
  Carp. Dolphin or Porpoise. Eel. Fish. Octopus. Salmon.
  Seal. Whale.

14 Spiders & Insects   227
  Ant. Bees. Beetle or Scarab Beetle. Butterfly. Dragonfly.
  Spiders.

15 Mythical Creatures   239
  Basilisk. Centaur. Dragon. Griffin. Pegasus. Phoenix.
  Satyr. Sphinx. Unicorn. Winged Bull. Wyvern.

Part IV   255

  Appendix: Deities & Their Familiars   257
  Bibliography   269
  Index   271

PART I

A FAMILIAR
WHAT?

Chapter 1

FAMILIARS &
HUMANS

 Webster defines the word *familiar* as "closely acquainted; an intimate associate or companion; a spirit often embodied in an animal and held to attend and serve or guard a person." Our word "familiar" actually comes from the Latin word *famulus*, which means an attendant. The ancient Greeks spoke of personal *daemons*, a type of spiritual helper in either human or animal form. Our present word "demon" was corrupted from this Greek word. The actual Greek word for a familiar, such as will be discussed here, was *paredrii*.

To most people a familiar is a witch's companion, a small animal that helps the witch with magick. The term familiar is usually applied to such creatures as cats, dogs, ferrets, toads, snakes, and some birds. Unfortunately, the word familiar is used in a negative connotation by those who know nothing about the truth and don't bother to separate fact from propaganda.

You don't have to be a witch to have a familiar. In fact you don't even have to believe in familiars to have one. You may already have an actual physical familiar living in your home in the guise of a pet. Do you find yourself receiving mental messages from your familiar/companion? This type of communication is common between sensitive people and their pet/familiar.

You may even have an astral-bodied animal familiar, drawn to you by your enthusiasm for that particular creature with which it is impossible to have contact in the physical realm. Many people collect pictures or little statues of a particular creature and never consciously realize they are subconsciously communicating with that creature, either as a non-magick-working familiar or for the magickal and spiritual powers it has.

My sister, who doesn't work magick and is more than a little skeptical that I do, has collected statues of frogs for years. She also has a large menagerie of living, breathing cats, dogs, and pot-bellied pigs. Her collections, physical and otherwise, are indications of subconscious communication with animals and their powers. She is a nurse and very good at what she does. However, like many healers, she often pours out too much of her own physical energy into her subconscious healings, leaving herself open to illnesses. Being in better contact and communication with her familiars would allow her to avoid this situation.

One never "owns" a familiar. Pet lovers will tell you this in emphatic terms. However, not all pets are familiars, but whether physical pet or familiar, you are allowed to enjoy their company, provide them with care and protection, and love them—but you never own them.

Quite a lot has been written recently about the power animals of Native Americans. However, Native Americans were not the only ones who knew of and used the powers of "familiars," which is what power animals are. Their methods of use differed from that of the Europeans who, at first, called upon animal allies in European shamanism. Later, under Christian domination, this European type of shamanism evolved into Wicca and Paganism, hidden religions.

Native American power animals were held in much more awe and less closeness than the animal allies of the Europeans. The shamans and witches of Europe developed a companionship, both with physical and astral familiars, that carried over into a partnership in magick.

There are four kinds of familiars. The first kind is a physical creature who lives with and has a rapport with a human. These are usually called "pets." The "pets" who are truly familiars are the ones who establish a psychic link with the human of their choice. These physical familiars can communicate their needs without vocalizing. They are usually very good at telepathy. One of our cats is quite adept at sending my husband a mental picture of an empty dish. Charles, knowing there is food in the dish, will send back a picture of a full dish. The cat immediately changes it to an empty dish, meaning he wants something fresh. He will continue to stare at Charles, sending the empty dish picture until he gets what he wants.

The second kind of familiar is an astral creature of animal form which attaches itself to a human for the purpose of aiding her or him. This type of familiar may be attracted by an intense liking for a specific creature that one cannot actually possess in his or her physical life. The familiar may also appear because of a specific need within the human's life. Deceased pets often return in this capacity.

The third category of familiar is an elemental spirit. Ceremonial magicians and witches often call upon an elemental to inhabit an object, such as a talisman, statue, crystal, magick mirror, or piece of jewelry. The genie of the lamp or ring falls into this category. Paracelsus had such a familiar which lived in a large precious stone in the pommel of his ritual sword.

The fourth familiar is a discarnate human being or the spirit of someone who has died. Although a few practitioners of the art will command the appearance of a discarnate being, I'm not in favor of ordering such spirits around. We humans don't like to have others commanding our presence, so why should those who have died? A discarnate spirit that is commanded against his or her desires can be troublesome. Then you are faced with the necessity of getting rid of them, which can often prove more difficult than the original calling. Discarnate spirits, who are willing, take the positions of astral teachers or guides; some people call them guardian angels.

We don't hear much today about familiars, but reading the old records from periods of witchcraft paranoia uncovers some pretty bizarre ideas about familiars. Witches were supposed to have fed them with their own blood, taken their forms to harm people, kept demons in animal form, and other weird things. Of course, if one is trying to suppress a rival religion, one puts out the most grotesque propaganda possible. These tactics are still being used today.

There are definite advantages to befriending a familiar. They make excellent companions. It has been established that those humans who have "pets" live happier, healthier lives.

If you work magick, the familiar (physical or astral) can aid you by augmenting your power. Some physical creatures do this by actually being in the room whenever you work a ritual.

Familiars improve your life by warning you of danger or defending you when danger arises. Few cats will leap on burglars, although I once had one that did, but they will warn you when danger is imminent. Callisto always lets me know someone is coming up the steps to the house by growling and hiding, even though she can't see the visitor. At first I thought this was because she heard footsteps, but this is impossible on the second floor with the stereo going. To her, a stranger means danger. Other cats will hiss, fuzz up, or even refuse to enter a room if someone they consider questionable is there. They have also been known to aggressively awaken their owners during the night to alert them to fires, silent intruders, or other potential disasters. Cats, like several other creatures, will respond with similar reactions to unwelcome, troublesome spirits.

Most dogs will bark aggressively and tackle anyone threatening their human. Sometimes dogs will do this even though they don't "belong" to you. At one time my son temporarily left his dog with me. Buckwheat was very protective of me when my husband wasn't home. I always had to hold his collar if anyone came to the door. If he accompanied my son on a visit, however, he felt no need to be a watch dog. Dogs, like cats, alert their owners to potential troubles, from smoke in the house to refusing to enter an area that has a ghost.

I've seen cats and dogs leave the room when a particular person entered, or avoid a person altogether. Another tactic is to sit and stare at the questionable person until they become uncomfortable and leave. If you pay attention to these actions, and be truthful to yourself about the person in question, you will find that they are people better left out of your circle of friends. In some way they are not compatible or healthy for you.

Animals also are good healers. They seem to know when their human isn't feeling well. It doesn't matter whether the illness is emotional or physical, they get as close as they can and send comforting, healing vibrations to you.

When it comes to augmenting magickal power, there is nothing better than a familiar. Some physical creatures simply can't be kept out of the room when a ritual or spellworking is in progress. The build-up of energy draws them like a magnet. My cat, Flash, could be out in the farthest field mouse-hunting, but when a ritual or trance began, it was only a matter of minutes before he was in the room. You can tell if your "pet" is a true familiar if the power builds even more with his or her presence. A very few pets, like some people, syphon off energy, but this is rarer in the animal kingdom than it is among humans.

A good familiar, especially one who has been with you for a long time, will let you know by telepathy whether or not you are using the appropriate type of magickal procedure. If you aren't, it can become very disruptive until you pay attention to it. Usually, only an adjustment in viewpoint of the desired result is necessary to restore their help.

Having and/or studying a creature, a magician can learn how to temporarily adopt whichever of their traits are necessary to cope with an experience. For example, you are at a gathering and someone comes in that you wish to avoid. By concentrating on the quietness of a mouse or the cunning of a fox, it is possible to leave the room without being noticed. In a way, this is becoming "invisible."

Physical or astral familiars are frequent companions during astral travels or meditations. They are protectors and guides in Otherworld realms. Often, by following them, you are led to new sources of information and understanding, particularly those of a spiritual nature. Physical familiars can remain with you even though they have permanently left the Earth plane.

There is nothing evil about having a familiar, whether they are creatures of the Earth or the astral plane. Non-Pagans do not understand the companionship and working relationship between a Pagan and her or his familiar, therefore they fear the very idea of familiars. However, having a familiar makes one more aware of the connection between humans and all other creatures, and the more intricate connection between all creatures (human and otherwise) and the universal source of spiritual power.

Even if your circumstances prohibit you from having a physical "pet," you are never barred from having an astral familiar. Common sense may tell you that having a panther or bear as a pet is impossible, if not illegal. Allergies may prohibit you from sharing your life with any animal. However, you can enjoy the beauty and companionship of an astral creature safely and completely. The only restrictions are your own desires for a relationship with such a familiar.

Chapter 2

HOW TO ATTRACT
A FAMILIAR

There are two ways to attract a familiar: consciously or subconsciously. Consciously means you deliberately choose a specific animal. Subconsciously means you end up with specific animals even though you hadn't considered the ones who come to you on the astral or physical planes.

Humans are drawn to particular animals as pets. They might say they are a dog-person, a cat-person, a bird-person, etc. Primarily, they choose the same "pet" over and over. They seem to be more comfortable and have a greater rapport with their particular chosen animals.

This may come about because of past lives where they cared for such animals, perhaps even working with them as familiars. The spiritual connection has become so strong that they find communication with their familiar extremely easy.

I love cats, and have no difficulty communicating with most animals. From childhood, I've always found it very easy to get quite close to wild animals. This attraction isn't always a blessing to your everyday life. Our yard is often the munching ground for deer, who have ceased being pets and become pests. We had to cut off all the tree limbs close to our roof to keep the raccoons from trying to get inside, and nearly every cat in the neighborhood suns itself on our little patio.

Sometimes, however, we humans find ourselves the keepers of an animal we never consciously considered. A friend of ours is always on the go and was determined not to be burdened with a pet. He ended up with a parrot that sings opera, and now wouldn't think of getting rid of it. Another friend vehemently declared he would not have a cat. Black Brigit keeps his life full of surprises.

If the creature is one that it would not be advisable or appropriate to possess, or if the person simply could not adjust to a physical creature, the familiar shows up in the astral realms. These creatures come into our vibrations because we subconsciously wish to be near such a being, or because we need the discipline and teaching of such a familiar. These astral creatures can be the astral equivalents of real physical animals, or they can be mythological beings, such as a dragon or winged horse.

Humans, especially those who practice magick, often have both physical and astral familiars. Sometimes these creatures are of the same species as our physical friends, but more often the astral familiars are of a variety of species, many of whom we could not have with us in our physical lives.

Whatever familiar you have, physical or astral or both, be aware that it chooses you, not the other way around. You can open the way for a familiar to come into your life by filling your vibrations with welcoming thoughts. You can attract a specific species by collecting pictures or statues of a creature, by having a deep desire to be friends with them. You can deliberately seek their presence during meditations. Whether these familiars are attracted to you and stay with you, however, depends upon your spiritual and magickal needs and your acceptance of the responsibility of the friendship/partnership.

Sometimes you will find yourself with an astral familiar that you wouldn't allow near you in the physical. I am not a fan of snakes, spiders, or other crawling creatures, yet more than once I have found myself in meditation or ritual work with huge snakes or giant spiders lending their energies. It took me some time to adjust my dislike of such creatures to the point where their energies and appearances enhance rather than detract from the ritual. When these crawling creatures make their appearance, neither of the cats will enter the ritual room. The energies of the feline species and snakes and spiders are evidently not compatible or complimentary.

Obviously acquisition of a physical familiar requires only that you decide what you want, visit the local animal shelters and such, and be patient. Whatever your choice, be prepared for the necessary expenses of routine vaccination, spaying or neutering, and other health care. Provide the creature with the best possible food, potty facilities, a clean warm place to sleep, and plenty of love and attention. I can't speak for those who have fish, turtles, snakes, hamsters, etc. when it comes to the attention category, but providing the other comforts is the same. If you are adopted by a cat or dog, sleeping facilities may be on your bed, so be prepared to share.

In seeking an astral familiar, again you must be patient and accepting. Astral familiars are even more particular about their companions than physical "pets" are. They come and go as they please, may not appear when you call them, and may be a species you think you don't want around. Before you dismiss them, however, have a trial period and do some close observation of their traits and abilities. You may well find they are showing you that you need what they have to offer.

It is highly likely that you will eventually attract a wide variety of astral species, especially if you practice much ritual and magick. Sometimes you will find yourself surrounded by a number of astral familiars. Other times there will be only one or two present. They make their appearances as they are needed.

Some magicians say that you have to see an astral creature three times for it to mean anything. I haven't found that always to be the case. True, sometimes a creature will appear to you in a series of dreams, meditations, statues in stores, pictures, and other unexpected places. In this case there is no doubt that you are being told what creature is coming into your vibrations. Other times the animal will simply appear once in a dream, a meditation, or as a gift of a statue or picture, and the effect on you will be so strong you will know immediately that you have a new working friend.

If you know what creature you would like to attract as an astral familiar, go into meditation and ask for its appearance. Be patient and observant. If your desire is strong enough, the creature will eventually come to you.

If you are willing to accept whatever astral familiar is needed in your life, make yourself extremely sensitive when meditating or doing ritual. Symbolically open your arms and heart in welcome. When a creature makes its appearance, study its movements; listen for its telepathic messages. You may find yourself welcoming more than one such astral familiar in a meditation. Learn about them all and enjoy their companionship.

If you actively fear a certain type of creature, you will likely find yourself with it at some time during a meditation. Persevere in your observation of such a creature until you can at least work with it and perhaps see the fascination in its singular beauty. This doesn't mean you will like it any better in the physical, but you may lose some of your paranoia concerning it.

The most important qualities to cultivate when enlisting the aid of a familiar, physical or astral, are patience, perseverance, a willingness to learn new things, and being friendly and loving.

Part III of this book focuses on the various types of creatures who may become familiars. This list of creatures is by no means complete. You might want to browse through the section to see which creatures would add to your existing powers and which ones would bring you new abilities. If you don't find exactly what you want in this section, study the creature you have in mind and decide how a partnership with it might benefit you.

Familiars are powerful in their own right, aiding you in protection, prophecy, healing, gaining your desires, and finding new spiritual enlightenment. If all this weren't enough, they are also strong friends and loyal companions.

Chapter 3

LEGENDS & DEITIES

Legends and mythologies are full of accounts of animals closely connected to specific deities. These stories are found in almost every culture. The Latin word *anima* means possessing life and spirit, the ability to move, the connecting quality that links all creatures. The ancients applied this word to both human and non-human creatures without distinction.

Ancient cultures knew of and believed strongly in the connection between animals, humans, and deities. This connection was often expressed by statues and pictures showing a god or goddess with an animal head, wearing an animal mask, accompanied by animals, or in animal form. These dual forms expressed visually the specific powers of the deity. By portraying the deities in this manner, spiritual leaders made it easier for less-educated common people to understand and relate to the deities.

In the beginning, the people knew that the deities actually did not have animal heads and therefore did not worship them as animals. In later times, loss of spiritual knowledge and the tendency of some spiritual leaders to withhold information brought about a change in belief. The common people gradually shifted from understanding the symbolism to actually believing that the deity dwelt in a particular creature. For example, later Egyptians kept and worshiped special bulls, crocodiles, and cats.

Certain clans in many cultures around the world had totem animals, their heads displayed on banners, their skins or masks representing these animals worn by warriors and religious leaders. These animals were taboo, so sacred that they were not eaten or hunted.

Much later in history these sacred animals became mascots. Emperors kept live eagles and lions as a sign of their personal connection with a deity and power. Today, we still find sports teams with actual animal mascots, or a person dressed up as an animal and representing a mascot.

The words "mascot" and "mask" come from the ancient Sumerian and Akkadian *maskim* (ancestral ghosts), the Sufi *maskhara*[1] (a reveler with the spirit), and the French *masco* (a masked sorceress), and *mascoto* (witchcraft). In the later period of French history the sacred animal and the mask which represented it had come to be connected with "witches." A witch in this case meant anyone following the old religions.

People once believed that the wearer of a mask could become possessed by the spirit which the mask represented. The Scandinavians called a mask *grim* or *helm* (helmet). The word *grim* is seen in one of the titles of the god Odhinn, *Grimnir*. Many Norse-Germanic legends tell of special helmets that gave the wearer temporary entrance into Otherworld realms. Helmets were closely tied to the powers of the goddess Hel, ruler of the Underworld. Some of the names of helmets listed in ancient legends are Grimhelm (Odhinn's Mask/Hel's Helmet), Hildegrim (Hel's Mask), Helkappe (Hel's Cap), or Tarnkappe (Cap of Darkness).

Today, people wear masks at parties and masquerades, at Halloween and Mardi Gras, without realizing the powerful connection they have with spiritual entities, deity or animal. Most people have forgotten the ancient powers behind the mask and go for the visual effect, rather than the connection with that power. It would be wise to choose a mask carefully, with full knowledge of what powers one is calling upon.

Later legends tell of animals interacting with a hero or heroine. Some stories tell of a misguided person who tried to take advantage of an animal and paid the price for meddling. Several cultures' stories tell of horses that carried away a person to strange and exotic Otherworld realms.

---

1   It could well be that our word "mascara," or eye-makeup, came from this word. Women in India and other countries use kohl to outline their eyes in the belief that this action protects the wearer. It could be the remnant of an ancient goddess custom, taking the place of masks.

Those who were "pure" of heart and acquainted with the ancient knowledge benefited; those who took the journey for greed were punished.

Many favorite children's stories are of animals. Children still subconsciously know how to relate to the wondrous spiritual realms. *Aesop's Fables* and *The Just So Stories*[2] explain in a subtle way the powers and potentials of animals; Kipling was unaware of the ancient beliefs, but the author of *Aesop's Fables* must have been familiar with the concept.

The theme of animal-helpers runs through hundreds of myths and legends. The talking animals of these stories say what they think, often expressing feelings we humans keep bottled up. These animals never try to bend the laws of Nature or rearrange Her to suit their fancies. They are symbolic images which give us glimpses into our true nature and, if we pay attention, point the way to hidden spiritual knowledge.

By studying the myths and legends of the world, one can trace the changes in religious power in any culture. Whenever an animal connected with a particular deity changes from beneficial to evil or malignant, you will find a change from matriarchal to patriarchal religion, or from the ancient religions to a new dominating one.

An example of this is the cat. Originally, the cat was a sacred animal, especially in Egypt. It was a creature of the Goddess, with great power to bless or protect. With the loss of respect for the Goddess, the cat has become a feared and distrusted animal, one that supposedly sucks away your breath and is a companion of the devil. The snake, another Goddess creature, has received the same treatment. Consider how the snake's spiritual connection has been twisted in the story of the garden of Eden.

During the times of the witch trials in Britain and Europe, the names of familiars (the vast majority of them cats) were recorded, along with the details of the grisly tortures and deaths of their owners. In England were Great Tom Twit and Little Tom Twit (two toads); Pyewacket (later a cat's name made famous in the movie *Bell, Book & Candle*), Vinegar Tom; Sack and Sugar, Bunne, Jarmara, Elimanzer, Newes, Tissey, Pygine, Tyffin, Littleman, Lightfoot, Fancie, Sathan, Collyn, Lyard (which means gray), Greedigut, Grissel, Makeshift, Prickeare, and Grimalkin or Grimawkin (which means gray cat).

---

2   This book by Rudyard Kipling (1894-95) is still selling strong, a century after it was written.

Socrates talked of his *daemon*, a spirit that guided him. The Roman Sertorius had an actual white fawn that he said was given to him by the goddess Diana and brought him her messages. Cornelius Agrippa had a black dog which helped him. There is even a story about Mohammed; a pigeon sent by the angel Gabriel was said to whisper information in his ear.

Some familiars' medieval owners probably were witches, or at least versed in magickal procedure. To avoid torture themselves by the witch-hunters, neighbors and witnesses told of seeing the witch stroke the animal (usually a cat) while chanting a curse against someone, followed by a streak of bad luck for the person cursed. In that period of history everything a magician and/or witch did was considered to be of the devil and therefore evil. The accusers themselves may have frequented this magickal practitioner for healing, love and fertility charms, and a little revenge when they felt wronged. Since one could die merely because of association, they were quick to point the witch-hunters' attention elsewhere.

Looking logically at these old records, we immediately see two things missing in the so-called evidence. One, that the person who was cursed very likely was attacking the magician in some way, and two, that there is no mention of using the animal for healing spells. We need to realize we are getting a biased, expurgated version of what actually took place. Evidence was slanted to support the rights of witch-hunters to torture and murder people, and of course to confiscate their property.

The Wiccan community and other magicians today consider all evidence carefully before laying "curses"; they try to find less drastic means of taking care of the problem. We have learned to wisely use the powers of animal familiars for positive solutions.

We humans need to reestablish the spiritual link between ourselves and other creatures with which we live, physically and astrally. Animals and their psychic powers are not evil. As a Pagan and/or magician, this reconnection becomes a necessity if you are to develop to your fullest potential, both in the physical and spiritual worlds.

We are all one family of creatures. Although our outward appearances and lives may be different, inwardly the same spark of life animates us all. Human and non-human were meant to work together. We can learn to relate better through companionship with both astral and physical familiars. Remember, you don't have to be a witch to have a familiar. You just have to be willing to be friends with your new companions.

Chapter 4

ANIMAL FAMILIARS & MAGICK

 So you've decided that you want to have a familiar, physical and/or astral, and you want to work with it on magickal projects. The first thing to consider is freedom of will of the familiar. Physical familiars are often not in the mood. You cannot coerce them into helping. They will come or go, lend or not lend power, during a ritual or spellworking, according to their own agenda. Feel honored if your physical familiar enters your working area and gently sends you energy; but be aware, they don't work on demand.

The best familiars for working magick, in my opinion, are those on the astral plane. They are not limited by physical restrictions or the laws of this plane of existence. They have access to pure spiritual energy for manifestations. Since all magickal results must first be formed in the astral plane before they can manifest in the physical, the astral familiars can more directly influence the building of that planned result.

A magician may have several astral familiars already, although he or she may not be aware of some of them. Before beginning a magickal working and calling upon a familiar, the magician needs to become acquainted with the helpers already present around her or him. You don't wait until you have a fire and then run out to buy insurance. So it is with magick. You accumulate all your tools and get to know them before you practice magick.

This discovery and acquaintance with familiars is best done through a series of meditations. It may take more than one meditation just to relax enough to discover and accept a familiar. Several meditations are advantageous in getting to know more fully those who appear. .

At some time during these meditations, you will very likely encounter a creature that fills you with dread—even hate or fear. When this happens, don't retreat. Ask questions; try to find out the mission it has with you. Sometimes these types of familiars appear because of problems with which we are presently dealing, within ourselves or with our interaction with others. Try to ascertain if this creature represents the problem itself or the characteristics you need to develop in order to solve it. If you find you absolutely can't accept the familiar, politely dismiss it and ask for another. Be prepared, though. The familiar you dismissed will keep appearing until you get the message it brings and learn to work with it.

When preparing for a meditation, it is not necessary to fast, deprive your body, or use drugs in order to get results. If your health is good, and you feel inclined, some fasting won't hurt you. I have never found severe, prolonged fasts did anything except make me feel horrible and irritable.

I am a strong advocate of staying away from drugs that cloud your mind and lessen your control. Large amounts of alcohol, the vast majority of drugs that are declared illegal, and even some prescription drugs will cause flares in the aura which in turn permit the entry of undesirable entities or influences. These drugs also affect the mind and astral body by creating false visions, letting you believe ethical lies, and opening your psychic senses (without protection) to unscrupulous spirits. Remember, not everyone on the spirit side has good intentions.

You want your mind to be totally under your control. It is a scientific fact that the brain produces its own chemicals for a "high" during meditation. In 1959, a researcher at Yale University discovered that the pineal gland (connected with the brow chakra) secretes melatonin. Melatonin is derived from serotonin, which is similar in molecular structure to LSD. Other studies in neurochemistry have shown that the brain produces other consciousness-altering drugs, one of which is dimethyltryptamine. Both dimethyltryptamine and serotonin are produced naturally by the brain, especially during periods of relaxed meditation. The more you practice meditation, the quicker you reach this "high" and the stronger it is.

In choosing a place for meditation, your physical safety and not being suddenly disturbed should be of prime importance. Unless you live alone, this may mean a room with a locked door. Silence the telephone. Nothing gives your body and mind a shock like a suddenly ringing telephone, unless it is someone opening the door and asking if you are okay. Another real nerve-rattler is a pet jumping into your lap.

If you feel best lying down to meditate, be sure you aren't so tired you fall asleep. The best position is in a comfortable chair. A soft, instrumental piece of music playing quietly provides a nice background that filters out small annoying sounds. Burning incense also helps convince your subconscious mind that you plan to participate in something special. If you are allergic to incense smoke or have a condition like asthma, you might want to experiment with essential oils. One of my friends solved the problem of the smoke by placing a few drops of essential oil on a cotton ball. She placed the cotton in a bowl far enough from her that the scent lightly wafted through the room but didn't bother her.

— A Meditation for a Familiar —

The first thing to concentrate on during meditation is the relaxing of the body. Begin with the toes and feet. Mentally tell the muscles to relax. Slowly move up through the body relaxing the muscles as you go. Don't strain at this. Take as long as necessary. Spend more time working on the muscles of the shoulders, neck, and jaw as these are the ones we tense almost constantly.

When you are relaxed, surround yourself with white light. Breathe it in; wrap it around you. Now visualize a well before you; you can also use the image of a pond or river, if you like. Mentally take all the problems, including people, that are bothering you and drop them into the well. If the problems or people won't stay in the well, visualize a lid with a stout lock to keep them inside. Doing this symbolizes to your subconscious mind that these need to be taken care of. You don't want to go into meditation carrying negative feelings with you.

Visualize scenery around you. This can be forests, jungles, deserts, whatever, but picture a place without buildings or other humans. You may be surprised to find yourself in a place you didn't have in mind at all. Accept whatever scenery is shown and begin a leisurely walk around. Be very observant for any creatures that appear.

If a creature approaches you, try to communicate with it. Watch what it does and how it responds to you. Since this is the astral plane, it is possible to communicate with any creature you see. Communication is commonly by telepathic conversations within the mind. You may be told that this creature will be one of your astral familiars or that it has come to make you aware you have need of some of its traits. You may find yourself communicating with several astral beings before you are ready to return to this plane of existence.

When you have wandered through this landscape, and perhaps through others, and observed several astral creatures who show an interest in you, thank them and begin to pull back to your physical body. As you think of your body, slip gently back into it and slowly open your eyes. Move your arms and legs slowly to get the circulation going before you try to stand up.

———

Now is an excellent time to write down brief summaries of each creature you saw and talked with: what was the creature, how did you feel about it, and what did it seem to offer? If you didn't contact any astral creature in this meditation, try again in a day or so. Perhaps fear about what you might see kept them away.

Now that you have contacted an astral familiar you need to make yourself comfortable with it. Pictures or statues of the creature are visual reminders to the subconscious mind to keep the contact point open between the two of you. These can be set out during ritual or spellworking as a physical place for the familiar to come through. Sometimes astral familiars will urge you to use a specific stone to represent them, instead of a statue or picture. The stone may be as simple as one "shown" to you during an excursion into nature, or as elaborate as a polished stone that draws your attention in a shop.

Animal and bird masks have long been used to establish communication between animals and humans. Carved reliefs from Mesopotamia show healers dressed in the full skin of a fish. Skulls and pelts of particular animals were worn in religious and healing rituals. Like present-day shamans, ancient priests and priestesses used these devices to make contact with and call within themselves the needed powers of certain animals.

If you are creative with papier-mache, you could construct a number of masks representing your familiars. These can be painted to physically symbolize the creatures, or they can be abstract renderings. Some Halloween masks resemble various animals. Plain eye-masks, decorated with glitter and feathers, can symbolize more than birds; these don't have to look exactly like a specific animal, just remind you of it.

By wearing an animal mask, the magician can more easily draw into her- or himself certain of that creature's traits that she or he wants to adopt for a short period of time. It also helps in strengthening the psychic bond and communication skills with that particular creature. There are definite times when acquiring temporary traits can help in specific personal matters. For example: you are facing an important meeting with a person who is of an aggressive nature and you are a rather quiet person. In order not to be taken advantage of, you might adopt the confidence and poise of the lion. Filling yourself with lion-power, you go to the meeting and firmly and confidently stand your ground.

Another method of adopting the traits of a particular animal is through shape-shifting, which again can be easily accomplished through the wearing of a mask. Shamanic shape-shifting is not the physical adaptation of an animal's form; it is a mental adaptation of certain characteristics. Ancient priests and priestesses may have learned this skill from Otherworld deities they met during astral travels. There are no oral or written tales to tell us when this ability first surfaced.

By temporarily adopting the consciousness of an animal, the magician can project her- or himself outside normal human awareness and perception. You are then able to look at human events from a different viewpoint, enabling you to make clearer and more accurate decisions. Many times the magician will see information that she or he missed in ordinary human awareness, information that was there all the time but overlooked.

Traits of familiars should only be adopted for a short period of time. For example, if you keep yourself filled with lion-power for long periods of time, you may find yourself becoming arrogant, self-centered, perhaps even predatory.

Shape-shifting is best learned first through meditation. Practicing with various creatures teaches the magician how to relate to those animals, how to adopt their traits, and how to turn off those traits at the end of the procedure. When practicing, the magician is wise to shape-shift into a wide variety of creatures so she or he can broaden her or his understanding beyond just one category of creature. Plan to experience at least one creature from each of the sections in Part III. Some of them you will enjoy more than others, but you will have a wide variety of experiences to call upon later when needed.

— Shape-shifting Meditation —

Prepare yourself as for the last meditation: quiet room, relaxing the body, dumping your problems.

Visualize yourself face to face with a leopard. (You can chose any cat you wish.) Feel yourself slowly merging with the leopard until you can look through its eyes at the scenery around you. The darkness of night is falling around you. You are lying on a limb of a jungle tree. Notice that the way the leopard uses its senses differs from your perceptions. Sniff the breeze; try to sort out the odors that come to you. Feel the breeze ripple through your fur. Be aware of the tree bark beneath you as you flex your claws.

You jump down from the tree and glide quietly through the grass toward a water hole. Your ears turn from side to side as you listen to every noise around you. When you reach the water hole, there is a hyena already there. You challenge it with a snarl. You feel your ears flatten against your head, your lips pull back to expose strong white teeth. The hyena flees.

You crouch at the water's edge and lap the cool water. Even while you are drinking, you are constantly aware of what is happening around you. Your senses are highly alert. The rising Moon shines into the water. Licking the last water drops from your whiskers, you stretch and pad back into the high grass.

Now, pull your consciousness back from the leopard and watch it fade away into the darkness. Become aware of your physical body and slide back into it.

———

When you have completely returned, analyze what you experienced during your joining with the leopard. How did you feel? What was important to you? Did you feel confident in your abilities? Were you more aware than you usually are of little things that happened around you?

This meditation can be repeated with other animals of your choice. Always analyze the meditation when it is over. This helps you to remember exact feelings. Then when you need to call upon an animal's specific traits, it will be much easier to pull them back into your personality. Remember, though, never deliberately *retain* animal traits on a permanent basis. By working with animal familiars in this way, a magician will, however, over a period of time gradually and safely incorporate needed traits into her or his personality in a natural manner.

This shape-shifting, or temporary adoption of traits, is also useful when performing ritual or spellworking. The magician calls upon the powers of an animal or animals at the beginning of the ritual. This has a twofold benefit. The astral animal familiars help with bringing the ritual or spellworking to a satisfactory conclusion, but they also fill the magician with the needed type of power while she or he is performing it. If properly done, this familiar energy can be carried within the magician for hours or days, until there is no longer a need.

With practice, the experienced magician can put on or take off the familiar's powers like a piece of clothing. When you begin a ritual or spellworking, you call upon your familiars to join you. You feel their power flow into your body like a warm tide of energy. Your ritual space is filled with your astral familiars. The magic you are performing becomes infused with it as you perform the spellworking. At the peak of your spellworking you release the power into the spell. The remaining energy flows out of you, back into your familiars, unless you need to keep projecting that energy for an extended period of time. Then you need to ask your familiar to stay near you, infusing you with regular bursts of its particular energy, until your physical requirement for that type of power is ended.

Although you poured energy into the spell, this will not leave your familiars depleted. Magickal energy builds upon itself, multiplying as needed. You thank your familiars for their help and close your ritual or spellworking. Sometimes a residue of power will remain in your body and mind. This may well leave you feeling revved up. The best way to unwind and earth the power is to eat something. Digestion of food brings the physical body quickly back from the "high" of magick.

There are definite ways of knowing if your astral familiars are present when you plan to do a ritual. Some people see them; others sense their presence. If you aren't certain about their presence, begin by calling to them mentally and/or vocally, even before you start the ritual. Ask them to come to your ritual area and help you. You may see movement out of the corners of your eyes, or sense something warm or cold brushing against you. If you still aren't certain, hold up the palm of your power hand (the hand you use most), facing away from you. Slowly turn until that hand has faced each part of the room. You should get a tingling sensation in the palm when your hand faces the astral familiar. It may surprise you to discover that more than one familiar is present.

Bringing familiars, astral or physical, into your life will create changes. Rituals improve; divinations become stronger. You will likely receive sudden inspiration to help you make decisions. In general, your life will begin to improve, according to the personal energy, time, and commitment you put into getting acquainted with your familiars. Naturally, we must remember to thank the familiars for their help.

One way to thank your astral helpers is to give a party for them. Take some cookies and soda to your ritual area and invite their presence. While you sit there, enjoying your soda and goodies, be aware of subtle changes which tell you your helpers have arrived. Mentally communicate with them. Thank them for their help and express your pleasure in their company. There is no ritual here, just an impromptu gathering of friends.

Don't make a bargain or promise with your astral familiars that you cannot, or will not, keep. Treat them like the important friends and helpers they are. Build trust and rapport with them as you would with any physical friend, and enjoy their companionship even when you are not performing a ritual or spellworking. Familiars tend to stay around those humans who make them feel welcome for themselves, not just for their magickal powers.

PART II

WORKING
TOGETHER

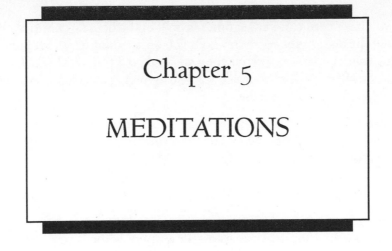

Chapter 5

MEDITATIONS

Practicing meditation is an important part of any magician's personal life. Knowing how to meditate relieves stress on your body and mind, and leaves your thoughts clearer when you need to make an important decision. The only drawbacks in meditation can come from not being truthful with yourself, or deliberately meditating so much that you avoid the reality around you.

If you are not being truthful and open to the truth, you can hear anything you want to hear in meditation. This usually means you are trying to justify what you want to do or have done. Some people spend so much time meditating that they shirk their responsibilities to their family and to life itself. In this way, meditation becomes an escape mechanism, which isn't its true purpose. A real magician will catch her- or himself doing one or both of these things at some time or other, but will see the practice for what it is—an attempt to escape responsibility.

Meditation is not difficult. The only requirements for this spiritual exercise are a quiet, comfortable place to sit and a willingness to do it. Going inward and getting results takes practice and a lot of patience in the beginning. Even if you are experienced at meditation, you will have periods of difficulty in letting go of problems and relaxing. The harder it is for you to meditate, the more you need to do it.

If you have pets, children, or other people in the house, you will want to close the door to the room in which you are meditating. A pet jumping into your lap or someone touching you can give you a real jolt. If there is a telephone in the room, silence it; the ringing can snap you back so fast you may get a headache.

Choose a comfortable chair to sit in. Most people tend to drift off to sleep if they are lying down. Playing soft instrumental music will cover up background noises and help to disengage the active conscious mind. If you want, you can burn incense; but if you do be certain that there is plenty of ventilation in the room. You don't want to start coughing.

There are certain procedures one goes through each time when beginning a meditation. I suggest you follow these without any alteration; they are very important. Begin by mentally surrounding yourself with brilliant white light as a protective measure. Relax your muscles. Start with the toes and feet, working up the body until you finish with the muscles of the head. You do this by silently telling each foot, each leg, and so on, to relax. Imagine them being stroked gently. Spend extra time on the shoulders, neck, and jaw, as that is where tension usually is the greatest.

When you have reached this point, and before you go deeper into the visualization of meditation, you need to mentally unload problems. You can do this by visualizing a method of getting rid of the troubles. This can be in the form of a garbage can, a well, a pond, or a river. See yourself dropping all the problems (this includes troublesome people) into the well, or whatever. Then you walk away and leave them there. This symbolism is a message to your subconscious mind that you don't want the problems and need answers on how to get rid of them. Every meditation should include this "cleaning out" near the beginning. Otherwise you will find yourself thinking about these troubles during meditation.

When the meditation is finished, you need to stretch gently and sit quietly for a few moments. After several sessions, you will realize that you have been astral traveling. You need this quiet time to reorient yourself to both your physical body and the physical world around you. This is an excellent time to make notes of things that happened during the meditation.

The following meditations will get you started in this essential magickal process. It is a good idea to follow the descriptions at first, until you become more comfortable with what you are doing. Then you can change the setting to suit your personal inclinations and desires. Try to vary the types of places to which you go; otherwise you can get bored. Read Chapter 4 in Part I for other detailed meditations.

— *Learning from the Falcon* —

Begin your meditation with the usual preparations—the white light, relaxing, and dumping your problems.

Visualize yourself walking along a path through a thick forest of spruce, fir, and other evergreens. The summer sun slips through the branches now and then to shine upon you with its warm rays. You follow the path to a small stream that bubbles over its rocky bed. Stopping for a few moments, you kneel down and dip up the cold water with your hand. As you drink, a movement on the other side of the stream catches your attention. A warrior-woman stands there, watching you.

This woman wears chest-armor and a winged Viking helmet. At her side swings a heavy sword. She wears deerskin breeches and soft buckskin boots. Long golden braids hang over her shoulders. She motions to you, and you cross the stream to her side.

After talking for a few moments, she leads the way through the forest until you come to a meadow surrounded on three sides by the forest. The fourth side ends abruptly at a cliff. Far below you can hear the roar and pound of ocean waves.

In the center of this meadow is a circle of tall stones. At the entrance of this circle stands another woman, her dignity and power radiating from her. She too wears chest-armor and a helmet, but a long robe covers the rest of her body. Over her shoulders hangs a feathered cloak. On one leather-covered wrist sits a falcon, its bright eyes intent on you as you approach.

This woman is the Norse goddess Freyja, the owner of the falcon cape of shape-shifting. You and your guide follow Freyja into the stone circle. The warrior-woman stands at the entrance while you go with Freyja to the center altar stone. Freyja asks you several important questions that have to do with your life and the practice of magick. If you listen in truth, she may give you helpful advice.

Freyja unclasps the feathered cloak with one hand and hands it to you. She asks you if you are prepared to learn the power behind magick. When you answer yes, she tells you to put on the cloak.[1]

As you fasten the clasp at the neck of the cloak, you begin to feel strange currents of energy pulsing gently through you. The colors in the landscape around you become more vivid; the goddess begins to glow with a golden aura. The falcon cries loudly, and Freyja holds up her arm to allow it to soar into the sky.

"The power behind magick is the will and the mind," Freyja tells you. "What you will can be done. What you visualize strongly will come to pass. You must dare to do these things if you wish to practice true magick."

She steps forward and taps you on the forehead between your eyes. "Fly with the falcon, child of magick. If you can fly and speak with the falcon, it will show you wondrous things."

You spread your arms under the falcon cape and feel yourself swiftly rising to join the circling bird above. The air currents whistle through your feathers as you glide beside it. Everything below you is small but in sharp focus. With your mind you begin to communicate with the falcon, and are surprised to find that you can understand it.

The bird offers to take you to watch other magicians in the world, both in this time and in ancient times. When you agree, it dives suddenly toward the circle below. You follow it, the wind whistling over your outstretched arms. Just before the two of you reach the very top of the stones, there is a gentle pop, and you find yourself in another place.

You are standing in an ancient Persian temple, the falcon sitting beside you on a carved chest. A Persian magi is performing a spellworking. You watch and listen closely. As the old man finishes, there is a sudden gust of wind that lifts both you and the bird toward the ceiling. There is another pop, and you are gliding once more in the sky.

---

1 Obviously, you are interested in magick, or you wouldn't be doing this meditation. However, if you feel hesitant, you can return to your body by thinking of it.

You can now go anywhere and any time you wish. The falcon will be with you as a guide and protector. The choice of your destination is yours.

When you have seen enough for one time, the bird takes you swiftly back to the meadow and the stone circle where Freyja awaits. You gently land beside the goddess and hand her the feathered cloak. The falcon watches you with bright eyes from its perch at the top of a stone.

"Dare to use the will and the mind," Freyja says. "When you are ready, you will be shown more." She taps your forehead again, and you feel yourself quickly sliding back into your physical body.

Freyja's feathered cloak was known for its powers to shape-shift, transport the wearer long distances and through time, and enable the user to gain valuable information. Think about what you saw, how you felt, every aspect of your experiences. There will be clues to help you strengthen your own particular magick.

———

The following may be a difficult meditation, particularly if you aren't fond of snakes. However, understanding how to use and control snake energy is important for healing and divination. The snake is also associated with the kundalini energy force that rises through the chakras.

— Snake Energy —

Begin your meditation with the usual preparations—the white light, relaxing, and dumping your problems.

See yourself standing at the entrance to an ancient Grecian temple. The white marble columns shine in the sun that beats down out of a deep blue sky. Around you is a garden of trees and flowers, intersected by little paths, alongside which are marble benches. A wall separates the temple and its garden from the city beyond. You hear the songs of birds as they flit from tree to tree.

As you climb the steps to the temple door, a priestess comes to meet you. She is dressed in a long white gown with a gold ribbon around her waist. Her dark hair is coiled on her head and held in place by a silver net with ribbons. As she holds out her hands to you, you look deep into her dark eyes, comforted by the welcome you see there.

Taking you by the hand, the priestess leads you into the dimly lit temple. At the far side is a beautiful statue of Athene, goddess of wisdom. Two small chairs sit on either side of the statue. From a tripod burner, the scent of frankincense and bay laurel curls up to hang in the air. The two of you walk across the quiet temple until you are standing at the foot of the statue.

"This is a time for courage and trust," the priestess says. "You must learn to see the beauty and usefulness in all things, however you may feel about them."

She reaches up to the pedestal of the statue and brings down a snake. It is the length of her arm. The snake coils about her arm and up to her shoulder. Its tongue licks gently against her cheek, then her ear. You watch in fascination and perhaps a little dread.

"You will not be harmed," she assures you. "The serpent is not evil in itself, although some men call it so. In this realm you can touch and handle creatures such as you cannot in your world. The extent of your learning and experiencing here will be only what you can accept as truth. The powers of the serpent are many and great to those who know the Mysteries."

The priestess lifts the snake from her arm and gently places it on your shoulders. A shudder goes through you as you feel its weight and the dry touch of its scales against your bare skin. Then a calmness comes over you. You reach up slowly and stroke its muscled body. The tongue flicks against your hand.

"Sit here," the priestess says, pointing to a chair to one side of the statue. "If your heart and mind are open, great Athene will commune with you through Her sacred serpent."

You sit in the chair and watch the woman sprinkle more incense over the glowing coals of the burner. The peace and calmness of the temple flood over you; you relax under the weight of the slowly moving snake. The snake shifts until it is near your ear. Its flicking tongue touches you again and again.

The snake lifts its head before you until it is looking deep into your eyes. The dark, lidless eyes hold your gaze, shutting out all other thoughts. Deep in the base of your spinal column, you feel a warming energy begin to rise. This energy slowly climbs your spine until you feel its power at the crown of your head.

As the kundalini energy flows upward like a fountain, you feel your thoughts and astral body sinking into another place, a place of indescribable beauty. A group of ancient priests and priestesses from many cultures are there. They talk with you about healing and divination—what may be the best paths for you to follow in learning these.

As you prepare to return to the Grecian temple, the goddess Athene appears beside you. She speaks softly, giving you important personal messages. As Her light fades, you find yourself back in the temple.

You gently lift the snake from your shoulders and lay it on the statue pedestal once again. Crossing to the incense burner, you drop a handful of granules on the glowing coals. As you watch them flare and smell the scent rising, you are whirled away. You slide easily back into your physical body in your meditation room.

———

As with the snake meditation, the spider meditation that follows may be a difficult one for you. Most people are not in the least fond of spiders in any form; some are absolutely terrified of them.

— The Spider & the Fates —

Begin your meditation with the usual preparations; the white light, relaxing, and dumping your problems.

You are standing at the edge of a meadow surrounded by a thick green forest. In the center of this open spot is a huge tree whose top is out of your sight and whose branches reach to the very edges of the meadow itself. At the base of this tree is a well, its stones moss-covered. As you walk closer, you see three robed women sitting beside the well.

"Greetings, Earth-child," the one on the left says. "Sit with us and learn, for we are the Norns. I am Urd, weaver of all past, the Sister who hands out the destiny decreed by the Gods."

33

"I am Verthandi, Sister-keeper of the present," says the woman in the middle.

"And I, Skuld, spinner of the future," says the one on the right. "Come learn from us how your life and destiny have been woven together and for what purposes."

You sit beside the Norns as Urd rises and draws water from the well in a wooden bucket. She dips a silver cup into the bucket and brings the water to you.

"Drink from the well of Urd, the mystic well that bubbles up from the roots of the World Tree. It will open your spiritual eyes to the truth."

You drink the cold, clear water. As you turn to hand the cup to the Norns, you see a huge spider web that stretches from the trunk of the mighty World Tree to the well itself. In the center of this web sits a black and white spider.

"Do not be afraid," says Skuld. "She is the weaver whose web-pattern shows us the way to weave each life."

"The red thread in the weaver's web is the pattern of your physical life," Urd explains. "The blue thread is your spiritual life. Look to your past and see where the two ran together, where they parted and you left your true purpose for other things."

The spider clambers about the web, and a red and a blue thread can be seen running through the silk-like spinning. As you see where the threads touch and where they are apart, you think back over your past. You begin to understand where certain choices took you away from the spiritual goals you had when you entered this life.

"Now look at the present," says Verthandi.

The red and blue pattern disappears and is replaced by the colored threads running in new ways through the web. You examine the new pattern in the web and see where you need to make changes in your present life cycle.

"Behold the future," says Skuld pointing at the web as the colored threads once more rearrange themselves.

As you watch this time, the spider is slowly weaving the red and blue strands, your future being made. You think about your future plans and goals and determine where you need to make changes.

"Through your will and determination, if like the spider you listen to the voices of the Gods, you can bring your physical life thread and your spiritual life thread together," says Urd. "Twine them together, Earth-child. When woven apart, you are unhappy and unfulfilled. Woven together, you are content. The choice is yours."

You feel yourself falling suddenly into and through the brightly woven web. You find yourself once again in your physical body in your meditation area.

———

Whenever exploring the Water Element in meditation, you should take care that you are in good health. Colds, chest congestions, and flu often seem to be aggravated by astral traveling through water.

— Exploring the Oceans —

Begin your meditation with the usual preparations—the white light, relaxing, and dumping your problems.

You are standing on a warm sandy beach. The ocean waves roll in toward you, caressing the sand at your feet. Far out in the ocean you see the water spouts of whales as they frolic in the deep water.

There is a yearning inside you to join these mighty creatures of the deep. You walk out into the waves, knowing you will be safe, that breathing under water will not harm you. Quickly you swim out to the whales and float beside them.

A huge whale comes close to you, brushes against you playfully. You run your hands down its side and look into its intelligent eye. Echoing through the water is a strange singing sound, the voices of the whales. Joy fills you as you realize you can communicate with these great beasts.

You float onto the whale's back and cling there as it moves off through the dark waters. Soon you and your guide are moving silently through the ruins of ancient Lemuria and then Atlantis. By your thoughts you can tell the whale where you want to go and what you want to see in these drowned cities. If you get off to explore a building, the whale will wait for you.

When you are finished with your explorations, the whale carries you back to your sandy beach. As you say farewell to your friend, it sings you its song. You swim back to the beach and walk up the sand. When you turn once more toward the ocean, the whale sends up a spout of water and disappears under the waves. You think of your physical body and slide easily back into it.

———

The unicorn is a mythic creature only in physical terms. It is real on the inner planes. With the unicorn by your side in the following meditation, you can journey easily into the realms of faery.

— *Riding the Unicorn* —

Begin your meditation with the usual preparations—the white light, relaxing, and dumping your problems.

You are standing on a hill with darkness all around you. The stars are bright in the night sky. You hear the call of owls, the howl of a wolf. Suddenly, the sky is filled with the blazing colored lights of the aurora borealis, the northern lights. Out of these fantastic lights comes a white form, its delicate hooves treading the night skies. It is a unicorn, the horned horse of the ancients.

The unicorn lands gently beside you and pushes his soft, warm nose against your outstretched hand. His shining horn sparkles in the darkness. In his thoughts he invites you to go with him into the world of faery.

You mount the horned horse, clutching his long silky mane. Like a feather caught in the wind, the unicorn launches himself into the sky. He soars straight into the flickering northern lights and comes out in a bright world of wonder and enchantment.

His shining hooves make no sound as he lands in the flower-studded grass of a little clearing. Tall trees line two sides of this meadow, while a quiet lake lies on the third side. Directly before you is a castle, its towers hung with banners, its gates open.

Near the castle are tables and benches where a crowd of people are feasting. They call to the unicorn who carries you to them. When you reach the feast, you realize that the people are different. Some of the men and women have pointed ears and slant-ed eyebrows, the sign of elves. There are little gnomes and dwarves dressed in Earth colors. Faeries with their delicate transparent wings folded at their backs are drinking from flower goblets. Shy brownies nibble at little cakes, while fauns and cen-taurs smile slyly at you.

A tall man and woman, dressed in forest greens, sit on throne-like chairs near the center of the festivities. The man rises and holds out his hand to you.

"Join us," he says. "We are the Lord and Lady of the Green-wood, and these are our friends. Join us, and be welcome."

"Come, Earth-child," says the woman. "We would have you know us all better. Join the forest feast."

You slide down and walk to a place at one of the tables. An elf brings sweet grass to the unicorn, and several faery children begin to plait flowers in his mane.

A golden plate is placed before you, piled with strange foods. A silver flower goblet is poured full of sparkling yellow wine. You sit beside these wondrous beings and join them in their feast.

Musicians walk about the tables playing a harp, a flute of willow, and a reed pipe. You taste the strange food and find it to your liking. The wine is cool and pleasant. The faeries, elves, and others are willing to answer all your questions.

When the feasting is over, many people follow the Lord and Lady into the meadow to dance. There are slow dances, fast dances, spinning, and walking dances. You can join them if you like.

The unicorn nudges you with his nose. It is time to return to your own plane of existence. Reluctantly, you mount the beau-tiful animal and say goodbye to the faery folk. The unicorn leaps back up to the northern lights. As you pass through the dancing colors, you hear the strains of Otherworld music far below.

The unicorn lands gently once more on the night-darkened hill. As you slide from his back, you feel yourself sliding back into your physical body.

———

The Underworld is *not* hell. It is a resting place for those who die in the physical, a temporary way-station for souls where they can decide to undergo study or reincarnate. The Underworld is also the place of the Dark Mother, the Egyptian Anubis, and the deepest spiritual mysteries.

— *Into the Underworld* —

Begin your meditation with the usual preparations—the white light, relaxing, and dumping your problems.

You find yourself at the entrance to a black cave that leads downward into the Earth. As you wait, undecided about entering, a black jackal comes out of the cave. It comes to stand in front of you, its tongue hanging out.

"Are you willing to enter the Underworld?" the jackal asks. "If you are, then follow me."

The jackal trots beside you as you enter the dark cave. At first you can see nothing, but soon a faint light from an unknown source drifts along with you. You are not afraid of the jackal or the cave.

The cave tunnel makes a sudden turn and you find yourself in a massive cavern. You can't see the ceiling or the far walls because it is so huge. The light in this cavern seems to be filtered from another source. It wavers as light does when it passes through water.

Near the center stands a dark throne set with sparkling gems, and beside it is a cauldron. A woman dressed in a long black gown sits on the throne, while at her side stands the Egyptian god Anubis. Your jackal guide leads you straight to the foot of the throne.

"Welcome," says the woman. "I am Queen of the Underworld. Through me you are born. To me you return at the end of your life. If you are prepared to accept truth, you can look into your past lives and learn from your mistakes." She points a white hand at the cauldron.

"See only truth," Anubis warns you. "If you seek the false, you will repeat the mistakes again."

You step up to the cauldron and look into the dark water within. Pictures begin to form in the water, pictures of the stories of your past lives. Some will be pleasant, some unpleasant. You watch the story of your life unfold, and see the mistakes you made. At last, you turn away from the cauldron and once more stand before Anubis and the Dark Mother.

"Are you prepared for initiation?" Anubis asks.

If you are not prepared to undergo initiation at this time, the jackal will lead you back through the tunnel to your physical body. If you are ready, Anubis and the Dark Mother will initiate you in an Underworld ceremony. There can be no description of this initiation for each person will experience different things, pertinent to their stage of spiritual development and ability to receive.

When the initiation is finished, the jackal leads you back through the tunnel to your physical body.

———

Owls and bats have been symbols of the night and Goddess secrets for centuries. Unfortunately, Christians turned the symbolism of these creatures into something evil. Evil is in the mind of the observer, not in the night or flying creatures.

— *Communing with the Night* —

Begin your meditation with the usual preparations—the white light, relaxing, and dumping your problems.

You are sitting on the ground next to an old oak tree. It is a summer night; a Full Moon rides the skies above. You hear the soft hoot of an owl. Looking up into the tree, you see the white form of a snowy owl perched just above you.

"Come fly with me," the owl says, looking down at you with its huge eyes. "Cast off your fears of darkness and night creatures. Come with me and experience the truth of the night."

You feel strange sensations going through your arms. Great feathers are springing painlessly from your skin, turning your arms into wings. Silently, you rise on the still air to follow the great white owl through the dark.

"Feel the energy streams from the Moon," the owl says as it rises above the trees. "Feel the energy penetrate your body and soul. Feel the Moon's magickal powers."

The owl shows you how to gather the Moon's energy with your feathers as you fly back and forth through the moonlight. The bird tells you how to harness this power for magickal uses.

A swarm of bats passes near you. "All night creatures gather Moon power for different reasons," the owl explains. "Observe, listen, learn, experience."

Your winged arms are sensitive to the different patterns of Moon energy falling about you. You watch the bats and other owls gliding through the skies. Below you you can sense other night creatures going about their business.

"Always be willing to learn," says the owl as it drifts back to the oak tree. "Wisdom lies in knowing that you can never know everything."

You land softly on the grass beside the tree. The owl stares at you with unblinking eyes, then flies away. You slip back into your physical body.

———

Although you may not have realized it, you have been astral traveling through each of these meditations. When some people find this out, they become tense and uncertain that they can do so again. Then they find that productive meditation comes to a standstill. After all, astral travel is supposed to be very difficult. If you can't see yourself from where you are at the ceiling, then you really aren't astral traveling, are you?

Of course, you are. I have never wasted any time looking back to see what my physical body was doing. I know it's sitting in a chair. I'm much more interested in where I'm going. Don't judge your experiences by not finding yourself looking at yourself. To me, this expression always sounds like the Zen question of one hand clapping. Who cares?

— *Pegasus* —

The experience of riding Pegasus is an excellent way to become more comfortable with astral travel. Just relax and enjoy the ride. Begin your meditation with the usual preparations; the white light, relaxing, and dumping your problems.

Visualize the great winged horse coming right into your meditation area. Physical barriers, such as walls, are no problem for Pegasus. The horse comes directly to your side and pushes his soft nose against you.

"Ride with me to other places," he urges. "Time and space mean nothing in the astral realm."

You easily mount the winged horse, twining your hands in his long white mane for support. With a flap of his great wings, Pegasus lifts you above your house. You look down, amazed at the perspective from above. You look out across the surrounding area. Although things look different from this height, you can recognize certain landmarks.

"Where would you like to visit in the past?" Pegasus asks you. "We can go anywhere in any time."

You can choose from your own past or an ancient time you wish to explore. Pegasus will take you there. When you have finished looking into the past, the great horse will once more rise into the air with you on his back.

"Would you see into the future?" Pegasus tosses his head and awaits your answer.

If you agree, Pegasus will take you into future times. This may be the far future or just next week. The choice is yours.

"Have no preconceived ideas of what you will find," he tells you. "For if you do, you will not see the truth, only what you have built in your mind."

When you have finished future exploring, Pegasus takes you back to your meditating body.

"This is astral travel," he says. "You become unaware of the physical body, while your astral body slips quietly away to visit other places. It is a matter of practice and believing that you can."

As you slide from his back, you reunite with your physical form.

———

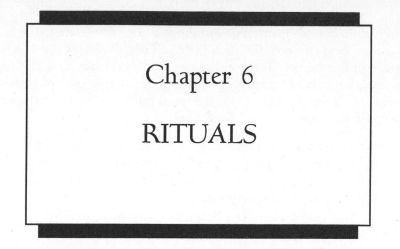

Chapter 6

RITUALS

The following rituals were developed because I like working with the wolves and the other familiars listed. As with any ritual, you can change the animal used, the Element colors, the magickal equipment, herbs, stones, whatever, to suit your particular magickal system and purpose. These rituals also give you examples so that you can write your own. If you need to review information on detecting and using astral familiars, re-read Chapter 4, Part I.

It has been my experience that the wolf's spiritual powers can be used in all magickal systems. The wolf and his power are adaptable to the magickal system of any culture.

The names of the four wolves of the Elements, used in the following rituals, are the names which I have used for years. I have found these names to be quite effective when calling upon these powerful familiars. However, the wolves of the four directions probably answer to other names as well. The names I use work, and that is what matters.

These four wolves and their powers are based on the traditional four Elements: Earth, Air, Fire, Water. In almost all cultures around the world, in one form or another, it is believed that all life is made up of these four Elements.

These Elements also correspond to the four directions, the four winds, and the four quarters of the sacred circle. They are forces and energies which influence our lives, our personalities, and magick. Although there are a number of cultural designations of colors associated with the Elements, I am using those of the European tradition: North, dark green; East, yellow; South, red; and West, blue.

Following are chants and rituals for each wolf and its Element. At the end of these are rituals combining all the wolves and their powers. The four wolves of the Elements are practical beings, so the rituals given are practical for everyday circumstances.

— *North Direction* —

Ice-Leaper rules the northern direction of the magickal circle. He is white with green eyes. Under his domain are winter, night, and old age. He helps with material abundance, and symbolic and actual rebirth of ideas and life. Negative associations with the northern Elements are: rigidity, unwillingness to change, stubbornness, lack of conscience, vacillation. Ice-Leaper is of the Element of Earth, and this Element color is dark green. Ritual tools are: the staff, magickal stones, the drum. If you don't have a drum, you can clap your hands or tap a stick on a block of wood.

Cast your circle if you wish, or place a blanket so you can sit facing North. Burn bayberry or cinnamon incense. With your hand, wave the incense smoke to the four directions, then over yourself. Light a green candle and set it to the North of your position. If you have a wolf statue or picture, put that next to the candle where you have an unobstructed view of it. Lay out several powerful magickal stones in a line between you and the candle.

Beat the drum or clap your hands in a joyous rhythm for several minutes. Then stand facing the North with your staff in your power hand.

Chant

> *Out of the North comes the great wolf Ice-Leaper.*
> *His white fur blends with the snowy hills.*
> *His green eyes see all in the Element of Earth.*
> *I call you with the rhythm of magick, great wolf.*
> *I summon you with the staff of authority.*
> *The power stones of the Earth call to you.*
> *Welcome, great Ice-Leaper, welcome!*
> *Bring to me the knowledge for rebirth in my life.*
> *Send new, fertile ideas that will blossom into prosperity.*
> *Hear my song of summoning.*
> *Enter, and be welcome, Ice-Leaper!*

Lay aside your staff and sit down, facing the North. Visualize the great white wolf, Ice-Leaper, there before you. Open your heart and mind for instruction. Meditate upon the gaining of new ideas that will improve your life. When finished, light more incense in thanks. Extinguish the green candle.

In your meditation you may find Ice-Leaper enticing you to go with him through the snowy forests. I have run with the wolves and been introduced to wonderful Otherworld beings. They have carried me through time to the past and into the future to help me make decisions. Each experience with them will be different, but rewarding.

— *East Direction* —

Dawn-Treader rules the eastern part of the magickal circle. He is light gray with yellow eyes. He rules spring, the dawn, youth. He helps with illumination and wisdom through ideas. Negative associations of this Element are: gossip, fickleness, inattention, bragging, frivolity. Dawn-Treader is of the Element of Air, and this color is yellow. Ritual tools are: the rattle or sistrum, incense herbs, the wand.

Cast your circle or place your blanket so you can face the East. Burn clove, sage, or sandalwood incense, waving the smoke to the four directions and then over yourself. Light a yellow candle in the East. Shake the rattle or sistrum while chanting.

Chant

> *From the Spirit-lands of the East comes Dawn-Treader.*
> *His fur is the light gray of the skies at dawn.*
> *His yellow eyes see all in the Element of Air.*
> *My sacred rattle (sistrum) calls to him.*
> *Through the cool morning he runs.*
> *He smells the sweet scent of the incense.*
> *Come, Dawn-Treader, and show me the way to wisdom.*
> *Lead me on the path of spiritual illumination.*
> *The great wolf of the East comes to me in my sacred place.*
> *He hears my voice and understands my need.*
> *Enter and be welcome, Dawn-Treader!*

Visualize the light gray wolf, Dawn-Treader, sitting before you. His eyes stare straight into yours. He communicates with you, mind to mind. Open your heart and mind to the ancient wisdom of Dawn-Treader. Meditate upon and ask for illumination. When you are finished, burn more incense in thanks. Extinguish the yellow candle. Within four to seven days, you should gain some enlightenment on the questions you had.

— South Direction —

Sun-Chaser rules the southern part of the magickal circle. He is dark gray with red eyes. He rules summer, noon, adulthood. From him you learn trust and growth of character, control of the sexual drive, and the finding of true companionship. Negative associations of the South are: hate, jealousy, fear, anger, war, ego. Sun-Chaser is of the Element of Fire; the color is red. Ritual tools are: a metal bowl, paper and pencil, dark pink or red stones.

Cast your circle or place your blanket so you can sit facing the South. Burn frangipani, rose, or gardenia incense. Wave the smoke to the four directions, then over yourself. Light a red candle and place it in the South. Lay the stones near the candle. On a small piece of paper write either the traits or events that you desire to enter your life, or the negatives you wish to dispense with. Fold the paper, light it from the candle flame, and drop it to burn up in the metal bowl.

Chant

> Sun-Chaser, gray wolf of the South,
> Runs through the bright forests.
> His fiery eyes see all in the Element of Fire.
> The fire in the bowl draws him to me.
> Help me, great Sun-Chaser.
> Help me to find true companionship in life.
> Teach me trust and growth,
> Growth of character that will enrich my path.
> Walk beside me, Sun-Chaser.
> Be my friend and teacher whenever I enter my sacred space.
> Enter and be welcome, great wolf of the South!

Visualize the dark gray wolf, Sun-Chaser, with his red eyes as he sits before you. Meditate upon truth and growth of character, or companionship if you are lonely. When finished, burn more incense in thanks. Extinguish the red candle.

———

— West Direction —

Night-Stalker rules the western section of the magickal circle. He is black with blue eyes. Under his power are autumn, twilight, and middle-age. Through him is gained control of emotions and psychic development. Negative associations of this Element are: laziness, indifference, instability, lack of emotional control, insecurity. Night-Stalker is of the Element of Water; the color is blue. Ritual tools are: any divination aids.

Cast your circle or spread your blanket so you can face West. Have your divination aids near you. Burn jasmine, lilac, or myrrh incense, waving the smoke to the four directions and over yourself. Light a blue candle and place it in the West. Place a small bowl of fresh water before the candle.

Chant

> From the twilight lands comes Night-Stalker,
> Great black wolf of the West.
> His blue eyes see all in the Element of Water.
> All tools of foretelling and divination are under his care
>   and power.

Magickal herbs are in his domain.
Hail, Night-Stalker of the West.
Teach me how to control my emotions.
Instruct me in psychic development.
Help me to walk the straight and shining path of spiritual light.
Enter and be welcome, Night-Stalker!

Pass your divination aids (tarot cards, runes, crystals, whatever) slowly through the incense smoke. Spend a few moments visualizing the black wolf, Night-Stalker. Ask him for gifts of the psychic, development of the psychic. Lay out the cards or runes before you, or set the crystal before you for gazing. Open your mind to Night-Stalker's words of wisdom and guidance. When you are finished, put away your divination aids. Burn more incense in thanks, and extinguish the blue candle.

———

The following ritual is best done during the Dark Moon.

— *Protection Ritual of the Wolves* —

Supplies: incense burner; staff; incense charcoal[1] and appropriate herbs, such as thistle, balm of Gilead, dill, dragon's blood, frankincense, juniper, rue, wormwood; rattle or sistrum; drum; four stones (red, orange, black, purple) or four crystals; four candles and offering bowls; cornmeal and a little salt as offerings. Extra candles: black, purple, and magenta (if you can find it).

Set the Element candles and offering bowls at the four directions: North, dark green; East, yellow; South, red; West, blue. Beginning and ending in the North, and moving counterclockwise, cast the magickal circle. Spread a blanket in the center of the space to sit on.

Put a pinch of herbs on the lighted charcoal. Wave the smoke to the four directions and over yourself. Set the incense burner in a safe place for the rest of the ritual, adding herbs to it as necessary.

---

1   If you don't use incense charcoal in a burner you can choose appropriate incense sticks to burn.

Sit on the blanket and begin to beat the drum in a soft rhythm. Do this at heartbeat rhythm, until you feel the presence of the great wolves within your sacred place. Take the cornmeal and salt to each offering dish, beginning in the North and moving counter-clockwise. Sprinkle a small amount of the mixture into each dish, then light the candle of that direction.

Return to the center and take up the rattle or sistrum in your power hand. Walk or slowly dance around the circle, shaking the rattle. Begin in the North and move counter-clockwise. This action is an exorcism of the area, so mentally drive out all negatives.

Again return to the center and take up the drum. If you don't have a drum, clap your hands in the appropriate places. Go to the North and beat the drum slowly while chanting.

Chant

> *Ice-Leaper of the North,*
> *Come from your snowy winter lands.*
> *Protect me (us).*

Move to the West.

Chant

> *Night-Stalker of the West,*
> *Come from your lands of lakes and rivers.*
> *Protect me (us).*

Move to the South.

Chant

> *Sun-Chaser of the South,*
> *Be here from your sunny forests.*
> *Protect me (us).*

Move to the East.

Chant

> *Dawn-Treader of the East,*
> *Run to me from your twilight spaces.*
> *Protect me (us).*

Move back to the center of the circle and sit down. Beat the drum or clap your hands until you feel the power of the wolves intensifying within your sacred space. Lay aside the drum and add more herbs to the charcoal, waving the smoke to the four directions.

Take up the rattle, shaking it and chanting.

Chant

> *The great wolves protect me.*
> *No harm can come upon me.*
> *I am strong with my spirit animals.*
> *I am strong with wolf power.*
> *The great wolves answer my call.*
> *They protect me.*
> *Their power flows through the rattle to drive away all evil.*
> *I honor the great spiritual power of the wolves.*
> *They are my defenders and protectors.*

Visualize the four wolves, each standing on his part of the circle. See them growing in size until they are huge, filling the room. They turn to face outward from you. With deep challenging growls, they leap away to defend and guard you.

Set up the extra candles in a place where they can safely be allowed to burn completely out. Around them set the power stones. As you light the candles, repeat the following chant.

Chant

> *Flame of the Spirit, hear my desire,*
> *As I light this sacred fire.*
> *Guide me as my thoughts I sow.*
> *True protection let me know.*

Spend several minutes seeing yourself wrapped in protective armor. Also mentally build impenetrable walls of light around yourself, your loved ones, pets, and property. Hold your hands toward the lighted candles and pour your emotions into them. Then release the emotions, keeping only the sense of protection. Clear your sacred area, leaving the candles to burn out. Pour the cornmeal out on the ground.

The next ritual is best done during a waxing or Full Moon.

— *Prosperity Ritual of the Wolves* —

Supplies: incense burner, charcoal, and ground cinnamon, or cinnamon or bayberry incense sticks; cinnamon and mint herbs; four silver coins (50-cent pieces or dollars). Extra candles: green, orange, brown.

If you perform this as part of a magickal circle, cast it as usual. However, this does not need a cast circle to be effective.

Place your blanket in the center. Put a pinch of the herbs on the lighted charcoal, or light an incense stick. Wave the smoke to the four directions and over yourself.

Sitting on the blanket, close your eyes and vocally (or silently) call upon the wolves until you feel their presence within your circle. Take up the silver coins. As you lay a coin at each direction and lightly sprinkle it with cinnamon.

Chant

> *From Ice-Leaper of the North*
> *Comes a rebirth of ideas*
> *Which will increase my prosperity.*

Place a coin at the East. Sprinkle it with cinnamon.

Chant

> *From Dawn-Treader of the East*
> *Comes wisdom and illumination*
> *To better my life.*

Go to the South with a coin; sprinkle it with cinnamon.

Chant

> *From Sun-Chaser of the South*
> *Comes true friends and growth*
> *To make positive changes.*

Lay a coin at the West. Sprinkle it with cinnamon.

Chant

> *From Night-Stalker of the West*
> *Comes intuition and controlled emotions*
> *Which will make me aware of opportunities.*

Return to your blanket and meditate on all the positive aspects of your personality and life. If a negative thought arises, throw it to the wolves. When you feel positive and trusting about your coming improved prosperity, gather up the coins. Put the coins in a pile in the center of your altar or a safe place on which to set the candles. Light the extra candles. Set them around the coins and leave them to burn out completely. Close your sacred circle. After the candles have burned out, put the coins in a small bag, sprinkle them with a little more cinnamon, and carry them with you for seven days.

———

The love ritual that follows is best done during a Full Moon.

— Love Ritual of the Wolves —

Supplies: incense burner, charcoal, and ground orris root or rose petals (incense sticks of rose or jasmine may be substituted); rose petals and yarrow; a pencil; four pink hearts; four pink stones. Extra candles: pink, yellow, blue.

Place the four pink stones at the four directions. Sit on your blanket in the center of the area and breathe evenly until you relax and you feel the room begin to fill with power. You may shake a rattle or sistrum, or softly beat a drum at this time if you wish.

Chant

> *I have a need, great wolves.*
> *I ask your presence and guidance.*

Write the word "prosperous" on one of the hearts and place it near the northern candle.

Chant

> *Great wolf of the North,*
> *Send me a loving companion*
> *Who is prosperous in thought and deed.*

Write "common sense and wisdom" on the next heart. Lay it in the East.

Chant

> *Great wolf of the East,*
> *Send me a true companion*
> *Who is wise with common sense.*

On the next pink heart write "love for only me" and put it in the South.

Chant

> *Great wolf of the South,*
> *Send me a true companion*
> *Who is afire with love only for me.*

Take the last heart and on it write "matching religious thoughts." Place it in the West.

Chant

> *Great wolf of the West,*
> *Send me an intuitive lover*
> *Whose religious thoughts march with mine.*

Now light the extra candles

Chant

> *These are for a lover kind,*
> *Like of soul and like of mind.*

Allow the candles to burn out completely in a safe place. The next day gather up the hearts to put under your pillow. Leave them there at least until the next Full Moon. You will first find your true companion in the astral dream state before he or she appears in your physical life.

The following ritual can be done inside a cast circle for greater psychic protection, but can be performed safely without a cast circle.

— *Spiritual Growth Ritual of the Wolves* —

Supplies: appropriate incense, such as wisteria, lotus, frankincense; four crystals and four stones (white, yellow, brown, indigo). Candles: white, gold (sunny yellow), purple, silver (light gray).

"Wash" the incense smoke over your head and heart areas as you sit in a comfortable position. You can use a chair since you may be meditating for some time.

Set the candles at a safe distance around you and light them. Lay a stone beside each candle. It does not matter which colors are in which direction.

Chant

> By these sacred lights I walk the spirit path.
> Guided by these sacred stones, I know the true way.
> Great spirit wolves, I ask your presence
> As I make my journey in search of wisdom.
> I journey for spiritual growth and enlightenment.
> Walk beside me as I tread the ancient ways.
> Great wolves, my friends and guides, I honor your powers.

Enter a meditation by visualizing yourself in an astral world existence. Try to enter this plane without preconceived ideas of what it will look like or what you will see. Know that you are fully protected by the great wolves; you should be able to feel them, if not see them, journeying with you. The wolves will probably lead you to a temple, an ancient grove where there is a teacher, or an ancient sacred place where you can make direct contact with deities. Pay close attention to what you see and hear. However, don't accept any strange or demanding orders that go against common sense or your own intuition. Take as long as you wish for this meditation. When you return, jot down everything you can remember about your journey.

After the foregoing ritual, you will experience flashes of intuition, prophetic dreams, and other psychic phenomena, so be prepared for this before performing this spiritual-seeking ritual.

The following is not a ritual for those who get jittery at unexplainable noises, movements seen from the corner of the eye, or strange but pleasant odors that suddenly drift through the room. Many people say they want to contact their spirit guides and teachers, but panic when they do.

— Cat Magick for Calling Spirits —

You may make contact with spirits the first time you use this ritual, or it may take you several tries. If you are determined, you will get some type of confirmation of spirit presence: a pat on the head, a hug, the smell of flowers, a feeling of something like spider webs brushing against your face, an ethereal form half-seen in a semi-darkened room, etc. My father makes himself known by the smell of a pipe burning Prince Albert tobacco.

Cats are an excellent indicator of the presence of spirits. Movement on the spiritual plane of existence always gets their attention. Our cats will watch an unseen entity walk through a room or up the stairway until they are out of sight. You can always tell where such an entity is by watching your cat, so calling upon cat energy can help you become more aware of these spiritual visitors.

Supplies: a statue or picture of a cat (domestic or wild, it's your choice); nutmeg oil; a white or silver-gray candle (optional); stones: moonstone, cat's eye, or any stone with a vertical line of light in it; a mirror. Either wisteria incense sticks or dittany of Crete and mugwort to burn on charcoal. If you want to burn wisteria oil by dropping it on charcoal, use only *one* drop at a time. Oils used in this manner tend to produce a lot of smoke and can easily make you cough.

The best time for this ritual is at Full Moon. This timing will give you added energies to draw upon.

Arrange your altar or table with the cat statue/picture to the center back. Set the candle to one side with the mirror at a safe distance in front of it. The mirror needs to be in a standing position so you can look directly into it. For best results, the room should be in semi-darkness. Put a tiny amount of nutmeg oil on the center of your forehead. Light the incense and intone the following chant.

Chant

> Cat-power, come to me.
> Friendly spirits I would see.
> Let me see their face and form,
> Knowing I am safe from harm.
> Cat-power, come to me.
> Friendly spirits I would see.

Place your stones or stone before you, caressing each one as you send vibrations of friendship to your spirit helpers. Mentally call to yourself the cat's ability to see into other planes of existence.

Now gaze into the mirror. At first look directly into your own eyes, then change your focus so you can see behind you. Also be aware of what is happening around you. You may see movement in the corners of your eyes that will disappear if you turn to look at it. Misty blobs of light may hover around you. You may even see faint outlines of spirits behind you reflected in the mirror.

Don't panic if you see these "unusual" things. Greet them as you would any new acquaintance and listen in your mind for communication, for spirits generally speak by sending thoughts. They may send you one of the sensations previously mentioned. Although the hair on your arms and neck may prickle with this first encounter, the spirits will be willing to let you adjust to their presence before making stronger contact with you.

When you finish talking with your guides and teachers, bid them farewell. Snuff out the candle; it can be used for this ritual again.

———

Working with dragonfly-energy for dreams can be done at any time. It is best to repeat this ritual for thirteen days to allow ample time to see the results in your dream journal. Keeping a dream journal is a valuable tool for any magician, as it often reveals a pattern in dream symbols that are a clue to your life, physical and spiritual. A dream journal can be as simple as a spiral-bound or loose-leaf notebook or as elaborate as a blank hardcover book. Date each dream, recording all the details you can remember, even if you don't understand the dream. Prophetic dreams can take as long as nine months or more to occur on the physical plane.

At one time I had a dream about horses dropping out of the sky. Most of them got up and raced off around a track, but several of them were dead. It made no sense to me, but I wrote it down anyway. A few weeks later, there was a pile-up at the local horse racing track. Several horses were killed, but most of them got up and finished the race.

Another time I dreamed of being suspended in the air, looking down at a volcanic eruption. A voice said in my ear, "Alaska." That was all. Nine months later a volcano erupted in southern Alaska. The same thing has happened concerning earthquakes and mining disasters.

I've had many other dreams that were clues to my physical life or mental and emotional difficulties. If I hadn't written them down, I would certainly have forgotten valuable details.

— *Dream Work* —

Supplies: picture of a dragonfly if possible; white or silver candle; mimosa stick incense or mugwort, bay laurel, and hyacinth oil (*one* drop) to burn on charcoal. Optional stones: aquamarine, beryl, quartz crystal, mother-of-pearl.

Sit in a comfortable chair before your altar or a small table. Light the candle and incense. Set your stone or stones next to the candle. If you have a special stone, hold it in your power hand. Look intently at the picture of the dragonfly. If you can't find a picture of a dragonfly on which to focus, try to imagine one.

Dragonflies are beautiful creatures of vivid colors. Imagine your dragonfly coming to land on your hand. See its huge faceted eyes gazing into yours.

Chant

> A key to my dreams, an eye for the truth,
> An ear open to spirit for messages bold,
> Will break down illusions and transform my life,
> So I remake myself in a positive mold.

Now explain to the dragonfly in your own words about your need for help in interpreting your dreams. If you've had difficulty recalling dreams, ask that you remember them. If you've had a series of actions or symbols repeated in dreams, ask the dragonfly to sweep away the illusions of your subconscious mind and present you with an explanation and the truth. If you are looking for answers to a particular situation or problem, tell your spirit creature to send dreams that will help you.

Continue your conversation with the dragonfly as long as you feel a need. Then thank it for its help. Extinguish the candle, saving it for a similar ritual at a later time. Put your special stone, or one of the stones you used, under your pillow when you go to bed. First thing the next morning, write down all the details of your dreams in your journal.

———

This ritual can be the most powerful if done on or near a Full Moon. Opening the psychic senses, and keeping them open, takes patience, perseverance, and practice. This ritual can be used to recharge your psychic attunement with whatever divination aids (cards, runes, etc.) you already use. It is also good when working with a new divination technique.

You can memorize only so much information about a technique; then you must let your psychic senses come through with personal interpretations. For example, good psychic tarot readers will not give the same meaning to a particular card every time they see it in a layout. When they let the psychic kick in, they make the meaning personal to the person for whom they are reading.

— Opening the Psychic Senses —

Supplies: whatever divination tools you plan to use; a statue or picture of a deer; a green or blue-green candle; wisteria, lotus, or jasmine stick incense or dittany of Crete, mugwort, and yarrow to burn on charcoal; nutmeg oil. Stones: amethyst, blue agate, quartz crystal, moonstone, green tourmaline.

Lay out a dark purple, dark blue, or black cloth on which to place your divination tools. Light the candle and incense. Put a tiny drop of nutmeg oil over your third eye, in the center of your forehead just above your eyebrows.

Lay your cards (or whatever) on the cloth before you and cover them with your hands. Take a deep breath and relax, mentally calling upon the mystic white deer to help you.

Chant

> Woodland dreams of intuition come with the graceful deer.
> I greet you, brothers/sisters of the forest.
> Your gift of magick will brighten my life.
> Transformation will come to me.
> Like you, I stand listening to the drum beat of life,
> Poised to follow my guiding spirits.

Perform your card or rune reading as you usually would, but this time listen on the inward planes for tidbits of psychic information in the interpretation. When you are finished, make notes if you wish. Snuff out the candle; it can be used again. Thank the deer for its help.

———

The ibis was always a holy bird in ancient Egypt—so firmly connected with the god Thoth that he was pictured with an ibis head. Thoth is the god of the Moon and wisdom, the teacher of ancient mysteries and the occult sciences. Magick, spells, and all forms of writing are under his direction.

Magicians are always seeking the ancient wisdom that has been lost to us. This is an admirable goal. However, we mortals often need some practical wisdom to guide us over rough places in life. We get too close to a situation or relationship to look at it without bias. The ibis-power of Thoth can give us insight and practical advice.

— Gaining Wisdom —

Supplies: a picture of an ibis or an Egyptian scarab talisman; a yellow or orange candle; lily of the valley or wisteria stick incense or bay laurel, sage, and balm of Gilead for burning on charcoal. Stones: jade, chrysocalla, sodalite, or aventurine, or all of these.

Take a relaxing bath with a little salt and/or lily of the valley oil in it. Dress in a white robe. Go to your ritual area with calm thoughts, leaving any negative problems outside. If this is difficult, sit for a few moments visualizing yourself dropping all these upsetting things down a well.

Set out a candle and incense on your altar or table. Place the ibis picture or the scarab where you can easily see it. The stone or stones can be placed next to the candle.

Light the incense and candle. If you have an actual scarab— either ceramic or metal—hold it in your hands as a contact point with Thoth.

Chant

> Holy ibis, stalking the Nile,
> Hear my call.
> Messenger of Thoth [toe-th], guide me to ancient wisdom,
> Show me the path to take.
> Take me to the secret inner places
> Of deep mysteries and initiations.
> Holy ibis, reveal to me the golden door
> Of forgotten spiritual knowledge.

Tell Thoth exactly what the problem is; explain it in detail. Don't spare yourself if you have been at fault in creating or perpetuating the trouble. Absolute honesty is necessary if you want this god's help. He doesn't waste his time on untruthful people.

Now comes the hardest part. You must be willing to sacrifice something in return. The sacrifice demanded here is mental attitude. This is not a bargain or manipulation, like the techniques orthodox religions use. This is for your own spiritual good, and you decide what it is. Fear is the biggest mental and emotional handicap humans have; we carry a lot of fear around with us daily. So be prepared to sacrifice one of your fears that is adding to your troubles.

I discovered my fear was not pleasing people. I let myself get suckered into a lot of unpleasant and time-consuming situations because I was afraid of what someone would say about me. Ridiculous, isn't it? But when I looked truthfully, there it was. So I sacrificed that fear. At first I sacrificed it on an hour by hour basis, until I learned to catch myself before I got involved. Then I did it for a day. In little bits of time like this, the sacrificing is much easier.

Other people may need to sacrifice the fear of being wrong. These people don't make decisions or take responsibility for their actions or words because they might be wrong. It's always someone else's fault, or they put off making any decision at all until someone else does it for them.

So be brutally truthful with yourself and Thoth. Recognize, hunt down, and sacrifice a fear that is keeping you from growing spiritually. Offer it to Thoth without reservation or regret.

Then listen with your heart and your intuition for answers. You may feel nothing beyond a sense of warmth and comfort at this time, but that's good! It means Thoth has heard you and will send answers.

Extinguish the candle. Carry the scarab or one of your stones with you until the moon turns back to its present position. The answers may come in any number of ways: someone's words, a book you are reading or have recommended to you, dreams, a sudden insight, or even out of a movie or television program. Be aware and listen with your intuition, and be prepared to take responsibility for how you use this information.

———

Sometimes you find yourself under physical, verbal, or psychic attack. Don't be a doormat! Do something about it. Just be careful that you don't specify what you want done or to whom. There is always a chance you have the wrong person. It is better to protect yourself on the psychic level, reflecting the negative energies and letting the chips fall where they may.

If the attack is physical, get in touch with the proper legal authorities and make a complaint. Insist they do something. If the attack is verbal, you must decide whether it can be considered threatening or is gender or religion harassment. This, too, can be taken to the proper authorities. If it is on the psychic level, you're in a whole different ballfield. You have to handle this one on your own.

After you have physically done whatever you can do, it is time to use this ritual. The best time is the Dark Moon, or the waning Moon. A totally different kind of energy flows at this time. Not negative or bad, just different.

— A Protective Mirror —

Supplies: a black or very dark red candle; a picture of a basilisk; pine or patchouli incense sticks or pine, frankincense, patchouli, dill, dragon's blood and/or juniper to burn on charcoal; a mirror with a handle; a picture of you, your pets, and/or your family; tape. Stones: Apache tear, onyx, obsidian, jet, hematite.

Set up your altar or table with the candle to the center back, the stones near it. Lay the hand mirror, reflective side down, over the picture of the basilisk. Have the photo to one side with the tape.

Light the incense and carry it through each room of the house. Return to your altar and take up the mirror and basilisk picture. Keep the picture toward the mirror, but don't look into the mirror! Go to the East of your ritual area, holding the picture and mirror before you.

Chant

> In a mirror, bright, not dark,
> An awesome figure reflects its form
> Into a barrier, protective, fierce.
> I stand behind it safe from harm.
> No threats can reach me, here behind.
> No magick reaches to my heart.
> The mirror sends evil back to source.
> O evil powers, now depart!

Repeat this to the South, West, and then the North. Lay the mirror and picture back on the altar. Take the photo and tape and run them briefly through the incense smoke.

Choose a mirror in the house that you can tape the photo behind. Tape the photo to the back side of the mirror, facing inward. In other words, the photo would face the back of the mirror, so that psychically it would look through the mirror. We have a large mirror in our entry way that faces the front door, an excellent place for a protective spell.

As a further aid, you can place small amounts of the herbs listed above in little cloth bags, hanging one over each door and one near the telephone.

Return to your altar. Thank and dismiss the basilisk. Extinguish the candle and put away your things. Put the basilisk picture in an envelope or some other concealed place until you need it again.

———

Oftentimes, we need renewing as much as we need healing. If you are trying to work for a healing for someone and it hasn't taken effect, perhaps you should consider working with the renewing energy of the phoenix. A healing won't take, or stay, unless we, or the person involved, are renewed in some way.

For centuries, the phoenix has been called a renewing bird, one that arose from its own ashes at the end of a cycle. It is a gentle creature, bringing only positive energies. Any ritual calling upon phoenix-power should be undertaken with the full knowledge that renewing often means dispensing with outworn things. If you have waited to call upon the phoenix until your back is in a corner, the effect often can seem quite traumatic. However, if you are sincere in your desire, even the traumatic will go smoothly.

— Renewing & Healing Magick —

Supplies: picture or piece of jewelry with a phoenix; blue or pink candle; orange or lilac incense sticks or dragon's blood and powdered High John the Conqueror to burn on charcoal. Stones: aquamarine, a holed stone, lapis lazuli, blue tourmaline.

Light your incense and candle. Lay the phoenix picture or representation of it where you can easily see it. Place the stones in an arc above the phoenix. If you have only one stone, place it near the top of the phoenix's head.

Project love as you call to the phoenix. Close your eyes, and feel it draw close, its soft-feathered wings brushing around you in love and protection. In your own words, tell the phoenix why you want to be healed and/or renewed. Be specific. Nothing comes from being vague, except more confusion.

Chant as many times as needed, until you feel calm and renewing energies begin to pour through you. Then sit quietly, absorbing this wonderful power.

Chant

> Phoenix, hear my heart's desire.
> Fill me with renewing fire.
> Renew my body, mind, and soul.
> Loving Phoenix, make me whole.

Relax and drink in the power of the phoenix. You may even feel the soft feathers touching your cheeks, hear the soft sound of an almost cooing voice in your mind.

When the energy begins to ebb, extinguish the candles and put away your things. If you have phoenix jewelry, wear it for the next five days. If you don't, carry with you for that length of time one of the stones you used in the ritual.

———

True invisibility is the mental discipline to project that you are not there. It is learning to temporarily take on characteristics of such creatures as the fox or mouse and pass unnoticed into or out of a room full of people. This is quite useful at times, especially if you would rather not talk to someone like a talkative "friend" or an ex-spouse.

The following little ritual can be used before going to meetings, group gatherings, parties, or any place where you feel you might need the stealthy quality of the fox to make a dignified, but unseen, retreat, if matters warrant it.

Using a particular stone as a power-sink is not a new idea. It has been done with stones, statues, even special places just by the continued and renewing practices of people.

— Invisibility Magick —

Supplies: statue or picture of a fox; any type of stone, and of any size, that you can keep in your ritual area; orange or black candle; magnolia or wisteria incense sticks or nutmeg, galangal, and mugwort to burn on charcoal. Stones: quartz crystal, sunstone.

Prepare for a mini-meditation. Choose a comfortable place to sit. Set out your fox picture or statue where you can see it easily as you open or close your eyes. Place the stones near the picture. Light the candle and set it in a safe place. Light the incense, setting it far enough away that it won't make you choke on the smoke.

Surround yourself with white light, relax your body, and dump your problems. Either hold your special power stone or have it close by where you can put your power hand on it.

Visualize yourself sitting on a log in a little grove of trees. The sun is warm, the birds are singing in the tree above you. Soon a fox trots through the bushes and comes to sit at your feet. Explain to the fox your need to borrow her or his power of invisibility for a time.

As the fox begins to pour this special power into you, you must concentrate on sending it into the stone you are using as a power-sink. When the fox is finished, it may speak to you, mind-to-mind, before it trots away.

When you are finished and back in your physical body again, put the power-stone in a safe place where no one will be handling it. Choose one of the other smaller stones and set it on or near this power-stone for about 30 minutes. As you go off to your meeting or gathering, carry with you this smaller charged stone. This little stone will have a direct connection with the power-stone; if you need added energy, you can use it as a pipeline to the larger supply. When you need to move unnoticed, simply call upon the fox magick. Think of yourself as a fox slipping unseen through the forest. Hold that image in your mind as you move quietly and easily out of a room.

If you are fortunate enough to live near ponds where frogs and toads hatch out each spring, you know how your subconscious mind responds to this seasonal sign of new beginnings. All of us need new beginnings from time to time, and not just in the spring of the year. This little ritual is to open the subconscious mind to the idea that positive new things are needed in your life.

— New Beginnings —

Supplies: statue or picture of a frog or toad; brown or green candle; birch oil; cinnamon incense sticks or cinnamon, bay/laurel, verbena, and squill to burn on charcoal. Stones: jade, green jasper, lapis lazuli.

Dress in greens or earthy colors. Light your candle and place the statue or picture next to it. Place your stones next to the statue or picture. Carry the incense three times clockwise around the room in which you will be working. Stand before your altar or table and raise your arms skyward. Say three times firmly:

"I need new beginnings in my life!"

You can replace the word "beginnings" with ideas, a job, a love, whatever. If you want, you can shout this. The more power you put into this statement, the more effect it makes on your subconscious mind. Hold the statue or picture.

Chant

> A time of wonder and of joy,
> A time of rebirth and of light.
> Like the tiny frog (toad) in spring renewing,
> I joyfully face my new beginning.
> I boldly stand upon the threshold,
> And leave confusion for the light.

Make yourself feel a sense of anticipation of something good coming your way. Revel in that feeling. If you want, dance and/or sing around the room. Tell the frog (toad) how grateful you are that it is helping you.

Since you are likely to feel quite energized after this ritual, I recommend you not do it at bedtime. After cleaning up your altar, this is an excellent time to take a walk or sit watching a Nature scene from the window, if you can.

Make a list of your goals for the next week, month, six months, and year. Just remember that you will be updating them from time to time. Goals that don't change usually die on the vine. Be alert for new opportunities, keeping common sense at hand, of course.

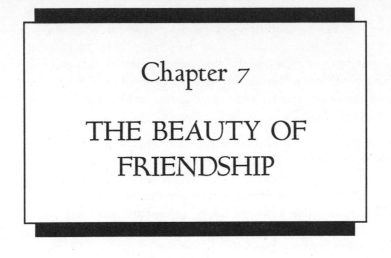

Chapter 7

THE BEAUTY OF FRIENDSHIP

Humans are not the only creatures of intelligence on this planet. Although animals, reptiles, birds, and all the other Earth creatures may not think, behave, or react as we would, that does not make them any less important. If we are to grow spiritually, we must acknowledge their right to exist in their own way, that these beings are loved and important to the Gods and Goddesses, and we must try to understand and appreciate them. In reality, we are all part of one family—the family of this planet Earth.

The cultivation of friendship is an important part of human growth. We need to understand that this friendship can, and should, extend beyond other humans to other creatures. By associating with these creatures through meditation, we learn to be more tolerant of differences in form and thought. This understanding is something which we can put into practice with others of our own species.

Pet owners already know the beautiful relationships that can develop from friendship with another creature. Animals such as dogs and cats and birds give our love back a hundred-fold, without reservation. We are not judged by what we wear, how articulate we are or aren't, or what our social status is. They love us for being us.

Most of us have secret desires to be close to and interact with creatures which could be dangerous to us in the physical. I find all large wild cats fascinating; I've even had the privilege of petting a full-grown cheetah. That doesn't mean I want one as a pet or would really trust one if the trainer were not there. After all, wild means just that—untamed. So I visit any wild cat I want in meditation.

The animals listed in this book, plus hundreds of others, grace our world with their uniqueness, beauty, and raw non-human energy. They can teach us things about ourselves if we listen and observe. Interacting with creatures during meditations is even more rewarding, for in that state of consciousness, these beings can communicate and bring us messages. They cannot physically harm us and usually symbolize traits we need to control or add to our lives.

Astral friendship is a wondrous experience. The most amazing things begin to happen when we make the effort to cross the old barrier-walls and open our hearts to the rest of the Mother's creations. By opening our minds to the beauty of "alien" animals, we expand our consciousness. In the expanding of consciousness, we grow spiritually, and that is exactly the goal to which we should be striving.

PART III

ANIMAL ALLIES OF FUR, FEATHER, FIN & SCALE

By studying the creatures in this section, the magician can learn the physical and magickal traits of specific creatures. This knowledge will enable her/him to better understand a creature and therefore simplify the process of attracting an astral familiar. There will be certain astral familiars already around you; everyone has them. You just must make yourself aware of their presence.

What if you want a very specific familiar? Understanding a familiar and deliberately calling upon it can entice the desired astral creature into your aura.

Astral familiars can appear spontaneously and uncalled in dreams, astral travels, and meditations. When this happens, the magician understands that these are self-appointed personal familiars. Accept them and learn to work with them. Keep the connection strong by visualizing them during rituals and chanting to them.

Sometimes, however, you need the specific powers of a particular creature which has not appeared to you. When this need arrives, you must entice its help. By reading the attributes connected with each creature, the magician can decide which animal she or he should call upon. Then, by the use of the chants, visualization of the animal, and perhaps pictures and/or statues, the magician can intensify the power-connection between her- or himself and the desired astral familiar.

Obviously, most of the listed creatures cannot be kept as "pets," for one reason or another. This need not hinder the magician. You can have as many astral familiars as you can entice to work with you; the neighbors will have no reason to complain. Astral familiars require no physical care, licenses, or permits. Feed them with love and friendship, and always ask politely for their help. All magick doesn't have to be serious—have fun with your familiars too.

Chapter 8

THE CAT
FAMILY

Cat family members come in a variety of shapes, sizes, temperaments, and colors. They are native to most of the world, except for Australia, Madagascar, and some islands. Humans tend to either like or dislike members of the cat family. Unfortunately, much of the dislike springs from propaganda put out in campaigns by the "new" religions in an attempt to dissociate people from Goddess worship. The cat was an animal of the Goddess. The cat (especially the black cat), along with the owl, the bat, and the wolf, was the animal most commonly associated with witches, beginning with the witch-frenzies of the Middle Ages. In Scotland, the Mother of Witches was called the Mither o' the Mawkins (cats). It was said that the gray blossoms of the pussy willow were sacred to witches because they were the souls of unborn cats.

DOMESTICATED CATS

The ancestors of the domestic cat were probably the African wild cat, *Felis chaus*, and/or the Kaffir cat, *Felis lybica*. These two species were tamed and honored by the ancient Egyptians. Through Egyptian influence, domesticated cats were dispersed around the Mediterranean area.

Roman legions and settlers took them into Europe and Britain, where they obviously bred with local species.

A cat once common in Britain and other parts of the continent is the European wild cat, *Felis silvestris*. It looks like a tabby cat in size and general color, but is more powerful and heavily built. It is still considered very savage. No one has managed to tame one. On occasion these cats have cross-bred with the more gentle domestic cats. The European wild cat does not like civilization and today has retreated into the wilds of Scotland, remote areas of Central Europe, and on into Asia Minor.

In ancient cultures, the cat was both a solar and lunar animal. It was said to be psychic and could predict coming disasters. People thought it also could affect the weather, hence the expression "raining cats and dogs."

Many deities were connected with some branch of the cat family. Artemis and Diana were both called the Mother of Cats; the Roman goddess Liberty was portrayed with a cat at her feet. Although the followers of Zoroaster believed that cats were familiars of the evil god Ahriman, the Moslems believed the cat was a good creature given by Allah to help humans. The Hindu goddess Shasti rides a cat, the symbol of prolific fertility and birth.

In Egypt, cats were sacred to Bast and Pasht; this veneration was well established by at least 1570 B.C.E., and by 950 B.C.E. was found in all of Egypt. Bast represented the gentler aspects of the cat, while Pasht signified the more aggressive aspects. Egyptians gave the cat the name *mau*, after the sound it makes. A black cat was especially lucky and was the emblem used by physicians to advertise their services. The temple cats of Bast, upon death, were mummified and buried with great ceremony. Even cats belonging to common people were mourned upon their deaths—the family shaved their eyebrows. Killing a cat anywhere in Egypt brought the death penalty. The idea of the cat and its nine lives derives from an Egyptian belief that the goddess Pasht had nine lives.

In Celtic traditions, cats were associated with Underworld powers, the dead, and prophecy. Often they were portrayed as evil creatures, but this may have been because the wild cats in Celtic countries were untamed. Irish legends tell of a cat called Little Cat, who was a guardian of treasure. In Wales, Great Cat was a powerful being born of Henwen, an enchanted sow.

In Norse myth, the goddess Freyja's chariot was pulled by two cats. After the people converted to Christianity, Freyja became a witch and her cats became black horses possessed by the devil. This new legend said that after seven years the cat-horses earned the right to become witches disguised as black cats. This rewrite of the Norse goddess story may be the origin of the unlucky black cat superstition. Those taught to fear the devil would consider black cats to be his evil helpers.

The Chinese said that the cat was a yin animal connected with evil, the night, and shape-shifting. They believed that the appearance of a strange cat portended a change in fortune and that a black cat meant sickness or misfortune. In Japan, however, the cat was considered to be a positive-powered animal, a creature symbolizing peace and transformation. Cats were popular with Japanese sailors, for they said that the animals had power over the dead and kept away evil spirits that dwelt in the ocean. Although some of their legends tell how the cat was full of trickery and sometimes associated with ghosts, the Japanese still hold the animal in high esteem.

Cats are mischievous and love to play tricks on people. A good example of this was my cat Flash. At one time I temporarily took care of my son's dog. Although Buckwheat never accosted the mailman, the two took a dislike to each other. One day, long after Buckwheat had gone home, the mailman came to the door just as I was letting the cat out. Flash was known far and wide for playing tricks on people. The cat shot out the door, tapped the mailman on the leg, and climbed the closest tree. The mailman (thinking it was the dog) tried to get out his can of pepper spray, sprayed it down his own leg, and trampled up four feet of my herb beds. If cats could snicker, Flash would have. Flash also loved to lie on high ledges and stare at people until they became uncomfortable.

Superstitions: *The eyes of cats shine in the dark; they can see in total darkness.* Cats can't see in total darkness and their eyes do not shine unless there is light to be reflected in them. They can, however, see better than humans or other animals in almost dark conditions because of the reflective coating on the inside of their eyes.

Cats will suck away the breath of children, invalids, and sleeping people, leaving them weak or even killing them. Cats do not suck away the breath of anyone; this erroneous superstition developed during the witch-frenzy of the Middle Ages.

Cats are extremely nervous. Cats aren't nervous; they just have superb reflexes.

In Britain and many places in Europe, a black cat crossing the road or entering your house is considered to be very good fortune.

In parts of Yorkshire the wives of fishermen keep black cats at home to ensure their husbands' safety at sea.

In southern England a black cat crossing the path of a bride as she leaves the church is said to grant a fortunate marriage.

A sneezing cat is said to bring good luck to a bride, as well as being a sign of rain.

Magickal Attributes: A strong protector, especially when faced with a confrontational situation. Knowing when to fight your way out of a bad situation and when to retreat. Independent and self-assured. Searching for hidden information. Seeing spirits.

Chant

> *Littlest lion, panther in miniature,*
> *Help me in my magickal endeavors.*
> *Teach me to see my path through dark places.*
> *Help me to sift the necessary from the unnecessary*
> *And to relax and enjoy life.*
> *Strengthen my magick and carry it to its destination.*

CHEETAH

The cheetah is the fastest animal on Earth. It can reach speeds of 45 miles an hour in just two seconds, but can race for a brief period at 70 miles per hour. It is found in Africa, and at one time also in Asia, from the Caspian Sea to Sumatra. It is as large as a leopard and has long slender legs and a long slender tail. Its fur is very short and coarse; in fact, it feels more like dog hair than a cat's. The pads of its feet and its non-retractable claws also resemble a dog's. The cheetah hunts by sight, even in moonlight. They live in family groups, cooperatively hunting and caring for their young.

At one time, in the far past, cheetahs were trained to hunt gazelles and antelopes in Assyria and Egypt; later they were replaced by dogs. In a record of an Egyptian festival procession honoring Dionysus (circa third century B.C.E.) were lions, leopards, and cheetahs.

Khyam, one of the cheetahs from Wildlife Safari in Oregon, was born at the Safari but taught to hunt for herself in Africa as part of a research program about returning captive-bred cheetahs to the wild. She still poses for pictures with visitors at this large facility but a trainer stands by at all times. Believe me, it's a little intimidating to sit down beside a full-grown cheetah who either stares at you with great dark eyes or totally ignores you. She did allow me to touch her, which was a fascinating experience. Close up, Khyam's dog-like features were quite obvious, but her cat-qualities came out in her deep rumbling purr and her inscrutable stare.

Magickal Attributes: Swiftness, speed. Develop your self-esteem so that you move with a regalness of bearing. Making events occur quicker.

Chant

> Swift wind-runner, beautiful, strong,
> Aid me in success. Take me along
> On your Otherworld journeys to places of light.
> Help me over the barriers. Give me clear sight.

COUGAR

This animal has many names: puma, panther (a misnomer; a true panther is a black leopard), painter, catamount, and mountain lion. It was once very abundant in the Western Hemisphere, from southern Canada to Patagonia. Today, it generally is found only in remote wildernesses in Florida, Louisiana, and the far western states, from British Columbia to Mexico. Cougars are a deep golden brown and have a hair-raising shriek. They are very strong; able to spring twenty feet in one leap. Their curiosity often gets them into trouble with humans.

The cougar was a respected animal among Native Americans. To them it represented leadership, physical grace, and strength. The Algonquins and Ojibways knew the cougar as a form of the "underground panthers," evil beings who lived in an Underworld. To the Cherokees, the cougar, along with the owl, was sacred because of its power to see in the dark.

Although there are no records of cougars existing in the islands of Polynesia, legends are told of a sacred cat, whose description is much like that of a cougar, with flames coming out of its head, legs, and back.

Unfortunately, the cougar, along with the bobcat, lynx, and bear, are still hunted in the Western Hemisphere. On rare occasions, because of injury, extremely bad weather, lack of game, or being run by dogs, a cougar will venture into inhabited areas. Its tendency, though, is to get away from humans as soon as possible. Known for its hair-raising scream, the cougar will also mew and purr like a cat.

Magickal Attributes Savagery, fury, remorselessness. Cunning, hunting and seeking; freedom. Using power in leadership. Balancing power, intention, strength. Self-confidence when facing crowds or troublesome people.

Chant

> *Muscles rippling, free on the mountains,*
> *Great cat of cunning, hunting and seeking,*
> *Teach me quietness and stealth of purpose.*
> *Show me the secrets of quiet magick.*

JAGUAR

The jaguar is the largest member of the cat family in the Western Hemisphere; only the lion and tiger are larger. It is called *el tigre* by the people of Mexico and Central America. It can still be found from Patagonia through South and Central America; sometimes it is seen as far north as Texas, New Mexico, and Arizona.

The jaguar looks much like a leopard, but has a larger head and heavier, broader body. The rosettes on its fur are wider than those of a leopard. Although jaguars are usually a rich yellow or tawny color, black jaguars (sometimes called panthers) are not unusual, especially in the Amazon river valleys.

These cats are extremely ferocious and will hunt humans as well as other animals. They are one of the few members of the cat family that like to swim, and they do this with great strength and agility. Their favorite perches are in trees which, as strong climbers, they have no trouble ascending. They prefer jungle forests where they can leap from branch to branch as they track a victim.

Mayas and Aztecs considered the jaguar a very magickal animal, capable of shifting its shape in order to cause fear and kill people. They had a Jaguar God to whom they made sacrifices. Mayan priests wore jaguar-skin tunics and headdresses representing the animal during certain rites. This creature holds a prominent place in the myths of these cultures.

In Aztec society, the warrior class was symbolized by depictions of jaguars and eagles eating human hearts. The special god of the warriors, Tezcatlipoca, was often pictured as a jaguar. The Toltecs associated the jaguar with rain and thunder (which was called his "voice"). His yellow skin represented the Sun; during eclipses they said that the jaguar swallowed the Sun. However, the Toltecs believed that the Sun God became a jaguar when he went underground at night. On rare occasions, a pure black jaguar will be seen. These black cats are sometimes called panthers by the natives. Jaguars are fiercely independent, cunning, and distrustful of humans. Like leopards, the jaguar will hunt single humans or dogs, which it especially hates.

Magickal Attributes: Developing the ability to walk without fear in Otherworld realms. Releasing fear.

Chant

Shape-shifting jaguar, fearless and bold,
Reveal to me doors to the Otherworld lands.
Teach to me courage, self-confidence strong,
That I may be firm in conviction of plans.
Let me ride with the thunder, that energy great,
And walk with the jaguar, a path of true fate.

LEOPARD OR PANTHER

For pure malice and savagery, the leopard outdoes even the lion and tiger. It is extremely fierce, treacherous, and, although it is wary, has little fear of human civilization. The leopard has been known to repeatedly come into compounds to kill and eat dogs, goats, cattle, and sometimes children. The leopard is very intelligent and quick to learn anything that is to its advantage. It climbs trees and can leap ten feet or more into the air. It is most active in darkness. It is generally a golden brown color with black rosettes.

The leopard can be found over a large area, from the Black Sea in Europe east to Burma and the Malay Peninsula, including all of India and Sri Lanka. It even ranges north as far as Siberia. In Africa it can be found everywhere except the Sahara Desert. The black leopard, called a panther, is fairly common in Ethiopia and the East Indies. The Siberian leopard, which has a better disposition than most, is different in coloring; this cat has bluish-gray eyes and long-haired spotted fur that is almost pearl-gray in color. The so-called snow leopard of the Himalayas is not really a leopard at all, although it does have the rosettes or broken black rings. Its coat of deep, soft fur is a pale gray or creamy buff.

In Egypt, Osiris and his priests were sometimes pictured wearing leopard skins. In Africa, it was a sacred animal to the Ibo and at times was considered to be inhabited by the souls of the dead. The Chinese said it represented bravery and intense ferocity. The Arabs called it *Nimir*, which means courage, boldness, and grace.

The leopard was the traditional mount of the god Dionysus in Greece; sometimes it walked beside him or pulled his chariot. His priests often wore panther skins. In the Greek language, the panther's name meant "all-beast." The word panther and all-beast also connected it with the god Pan. The Greeks equated this animal with Argus of the Thousand Eyes.

Superstitions: *Thought by the ancients to be the offspring of a lioness and a male pard (possibly a leopard), or a lion and a female pard. The pard was often described as the panther (another name for leopard).*

Leopards have babies only once, because the young tear their way out of the womb.

Magickal Attributes: Swiftness, cunning, strength, perseverance, boldness, beauty. Gaining confidence for astral travel and Otherworld journeys.

Chant

> Leopard gliding, through shadows sliding,
> Intent on its plans in the dark of the night.
> Like the leopard I go with the energy flow
> On the pathway to Otherworld light.
> I journey for growth, for creating true worth,
> For the learning of wisdom and might.
> With wisdom I'll burn, while I confidently turn
> All darkness about me to conquering light.

LION

Most of the lions today are in Africa, although at one time they ranged in India from Sind in the northwest to Bengal in the northeast. They live in prides, or family groups. A lioness can be distinguished by her lack of a mane; on rare occasions, however, a female will sport a mane. Lions are very strong and use a cooperative hunting technique to supply the pride with food.

Lions once inhabited Turkey, Iraq, Palestine, Iran, Greece, Asia Minor, and Syria; in fact, throughout the Middle East. Some ancient rulers trained them for hunting. Egyptians placed portraits of lions on doors, or their statues before the gates of their temples, as protectors and guardians. In Egyptian art, a lion with the solar disk represented the god Ra; if shown with a crescent it represented the god Osiris. The statues of two lions facing opposite directions symbolized the past and the future.

Male lions were associated with solar gods, especially in Greece, Rome, and Persia, while lionesses were companions of Great Mother goddesses, often drawing their chariots. Representations of these goddesses with their companion lionesses have been found in Crete, Mycenae, Phrygia, Thrace, Syria, Lycia, Sparta, Sumeria, India, and Tibet. In connection with the Great Mother, the lioness symbolized both maternity and the capacity for vengeance.

In Egypt, the goddess Sekhmet was associated with the lioness. She was shown with a lioness-head, representing the devouring heat of the Sun. She was a deity of fertility, protecting the young; fate (because she ruled over the Tablets of Destiny); and also a goddess of war and destruction. The Egyptians believed that the lion presided over the annual Nile floods.

The goddess Ishtar of Babylon was often shown standing on a lion or with two lions. For Marduk, a Sumerian god, the lion symbolized sovereignty and strength. In Chaldea, Nergal, the god of war and death, was often pictured as a lion. Among the Hittites, their weather god's chariot was pulled by lions and their Great Mother rode a lioness. At different times in Babylonia and Assyria, the lion was connected with Ningirsu, Ninlil, Ninurta, Ishtar, Inanna, and Damkina.

Strangely enough, Babylonians and Sumerians also considered the lion to be a member of the dog family. In their literature, the lion is a metaphor for a war-king or fierce deity. Stone lions guarded the temple entrances of the god Enki at Eridu and of Ishtar at Kalhu.

In Mediterranean cultures, the goddess Cybele and her son/lover Attis rode in a lion-drawn chariot. Early Arabs had a deity called Yaghuth, a lion-god, and considered the lion a protector against evil.

The Persian religion of Mithraism used a lion head surrounded with a mane of Sun rays as their emblem. One grade of their initiates was called the Lion. The Greek Sun God Apollo Chrysocomes (He of the Golden Locks) was sometimes identified with the lion and its flowing mane.

In alchemy, the lion, when shown alone, corresponded to sulphur. If balanced with three other creatures, the lion symbolized the Element of Earth or philosophical Fire. It also represented gold and the Sun.

In India, the goddess Durga was represented by a lion in her capacity of destroyer of demons, but Hindus also considered the lion to be a Guardian of the North. This animal represented strength, courage, and energy to the Chinese; they even had a lion dance during their Feast of Lanterns festival.

In England, the city of Caerleon is the "Lion's Place." Cornwall's old name, Lyonesse, means the country of the she-lion. "City of the Lion" is a translation of the name Singapore. The Lion Throne of Buddhism is still sacred.

The fur of young lion cubs feels like coarse, rough wool. The adults will call to each other in a sawing, cough-type roar.

Superstitions: *Several countries believe that a lion will not attack or injure a royal prince.*

He disguises his spoor from hunters by swishing his tail behind him.

A sick lion will eat monkeys to be cured.

Lions fear a white cock. They are also frightened of creaking wheels.

Lion cubs are born dead and stay that way for three days until the father licks them into life.

Lions sleep with their eyes open.

Magickal Attributes: Learn to relax; don't carry the stress of one situation into another. Strengthen family ties. Strength, courage, energy. Releasing stress and tension.

Chant

> *Creature of the Sun Lord, beloved of the Lady,*
> *Reveal to me the ancient methods of magick.*
> *Walk beside me as I grow in strength and courage.*
> *Show me when to keep ties strong and when to break them.*
> *Help me to understand the times for work and the times for rest.*
> *Mighty lion, lend me your energies.*

LYNX

Also called the wildcat or bay lynx, the bobcat (*Lynx rufus*) exists throughout the Western Hemisphere, from southern Canada to Mexico, in a variety of climates from forest to desert. It is a medium-sized feline that can weigh up to forty pounds. The bobcat is a reddish-brown, streaked with dark brown; the white under parts are spotted with black. It has a short tail and black tufts on its ears.

The Canadian lynx, *Lynx canadensis*, has large feet (useful in snow), prominent ear tufts, and a ruff on the sides of the head. It can weigh up to forty pounds and be three-and-one-half-feet long. It occurs in large numbers in the Canadian spruce forests. The European lynx is extinct in western Europe, but can still be found in sections of northern Asia.

To Native Americans, this creature was a keeper of secrets and occult knowledge; a powerful and silent animal, they said it had the ability to unravel mysteries.

The lynx or bobcat always seems to smile in a secretive way, making one think of the expression "the cat that swallowed the canary." In their natural setting, they will sometimes play like kittens. Like the fox and coyote, the lynx is a natural predator of rodents.

Superstitions: Europeans during the Middle Ages had a strange belief about the lynx. *It was said that its urine could harden into precious stones called Ligurius (lynx-piss), a carbuncle.*

Magickal Attributes: suspicion, vigilance, keenness of sight. Can lead you to understanding mystic mysteries and occult secrets. Can help with divination skills and developing the psychic senses. Discovering secrets about either yourself or someone close to you. Sometimes a lynx is seen when one needs to look within the self and see the truth of what one actually is. At other times, it signals the approaching ability to move through time and space in astral travel. Seeking to find and understand ancient mystical and secret mysteries.

Chant

> *Keeper of the ancient secrets,*
> *Teacher of the hidden skills,*
> *Open my heart and mind to wisdom.*
> *Fill my days with strengthened will.*
> *Reveal the fearful truth of being,*
> *The part of us we fail to see.*
> *O lynx of smiling, hidden secrets,*
> *Bring aid and wisdom now to me.*

TIGER

A typical big cat of Asia, the tiger ranges as far north as Siberia and as far south as India and the Malay Peninsula. The closest it gets to Europe is the Caucasus area and the Caspian Sea. It has a yellow-brown coat striped with black, but has no mane. It is one of the few members of the cat family that likes to swim. It climbs with great speed and can leap 15 feet in a single bound. For brutal savagery and feats of power, the tiger easily outdoes the lion.

In India, the goddess Durga often rides a tiger and the god Shiva, in his destructive aspect, wears a tiger skin. To these people the tiger represented royalty, power, and fearlessness.

In Greek art, the tiger is sometimes substituted for the leopard in depictions of the god Dionysus. Legend isn't too clear about whether the newborn Dionysus was placed by Hermes on the skin of a leopard, a tiger, or a fawn.

The tiger symbolizes courage and warrior qualities to the Japanese. In China, where the animal is considered Lord of the Land Animals, the mythologies are full of tigers. Sometimes it is pictured with wings, a symbol of its supernatural powers. This animal represents authority, courage, ferocity, and military might.

Tsai Shen, the Chinese god of wealth, rides a tiger, who guards the money chests; in this aspect the tiger becomes an emblem of gamblers. The goddess of wind also rides upon a tiger.

The most interesting application of the tiger symbol by the Chinese is in their representation of the four Elements, or directions. A white tiger is in the West and symbolizes Autumn, the Element of metal, and frightens away evil spirits and guards graves. A blue tiger is in the East, standing for plant life and Spring. In the South is a red tiger, who represents Summer and life. A black tiger symbolizes the North, Winter, and Water. In the center space is a yellow tiger, emblem of the Sun and the ruler.

The most hilarious thing I ever saw was a baby tiger that was brought to a television studio for a program. This five-month-old terror on claws suddenly decided he didn't like any of the camera crew. He tore loose from his trainer's hands and immediately went full-tilt after the cameramen. He wasn't satisfied until he had treed the entire camera crew and the show host.

Superstitions: *That a tigress, pursuing one who has stolen her cubs, can be distracted by a reflective glass ball.*

Magickal Attributes: Power, energy. If action is called for, don't analyze it to death; just do it! Unpleasant but necessary action only gets worse if you procrastinate. Finding strength and will-power to tackle an unpleasant situation.

Chant

Striped terror of the jungles,
Walker of secret paths and ancient ways,
Give me the strength and courage to do what is necessary.
Teach me not to cringe from actions that may cause pain,
*   but must be done.*
Tiger of action, lead the way that I may know how to go
*   confidently through my life.*

Chapter 9

THE WOLF FAMILY

The dog is a member of the family *canidae* and the genus *canis*. Other wild members of this group are the wolf, coyote, fox, dingo, and jackal. This canine family has five toes on the front feet and four on the back; their claws are non–retractable. Their teeth are formed for shearing crushing action.

DOMESTICATED DOGS

Domesticated dogs come in many sizes and colors. They have been with humans for a very long time. One of the earliest recorded stories of a dog's devotion to its master is the tale of the dog Argus who waited years for Ulysses to return.

Originally, dogs were the companions of the Goddess. They guarded the gates of Her Underworld realm and aided Her in receiving the souls of the dead. In Babylon, the goddess of fate and healing, Gula, had a dog as her symbol. The dog was also associated with the Middle Eastern goddesses Belit-ili, Astarte, and Ashtoreth. In Egypt, the dog was a symbol of Amenti, the Great Mother. Several of the ancient Middle East cultures placed the lion in the dog family, along with dogs, wolves, and jackals. Dogs or hounds accompanied Cybele, Artemis, and Diana. Ancient Greeks called dogs psychic, saying their howling carried away departing souls. Hecate had her dogs of darkness and the Underworld. Dogs and hounds were often portrayed with Celtic Mother Goddesses, such as Epona, who rode with a dog in her lap. They could be either lunar or solar creatures.

Frescoes and seals from the Minoan civilization portray a goddess called the Life-giver, the Mistress of Animals. This deity was a forerunner of Artemis Eileithyia and is flanked by winged dogs. In Thessaly, the goddess Enodia was another name for Artemis. She was a divine huntress whose companions were hounds; dogs were sacrificed to her. When Athene took her aspect of death-goddess, her priestesses would howl or sing at the Moon. There are vague hints in ancient records that these priestesses, either actually or figuratively, ran in packs to hunt down a soul. The three-headed dog Cerberus guarded the gates of the Greek Underworld.

Among Scythian tribes, Artemis was called the Divine Huntress and the Great Bitch. Her priestesses were known as the Alani (hunting dogs) and sacred bitches; they hunted and sacrificed the stag-gods. Son of a bitch originally meant a follower of the Goddess.

In Irish mythology, the dog Dormarth was said to guard the gate of death; mourning too loudly could make the dog attack the approaching soul. In Celtic myths, devoted hounds are often mentioned. An example of these are Bran and Sceolan, the hounds of Finn mac Cumhail. In Wales, the Cwn Annwn (Underworld Hounds) of Arawn, Lord of the Underworld, were always white with red ears. They ran down and punished those who broke the laws of men and the gods. Nodens, the god of springs and healing, was able to shape-shift into a dog.

The Moon dogs of the Norse people are very similar to the Cwn Annwn of Wales; these dogs were connected with the goddess Hel and were said to run with Odhinn during the Wild Hunt. The Wild Hunt, or the Ride of Death, appears in many stories all over Europe. Norse and Teutonic literature tell of Odhinn, or the Erl King, riding with a pack of phantom hounds (great black beasts with eyes as big as saucers) during storms. This ride was supposed to happen on New Year's Eve, storm or not. Folklore says that to hear the sounds of this hunt was an omen of death and disaster.

There is a wide variation in the names and descriptions of this Wild Hunt, depending upon the European lore from which it is taken. Later Teutonic lore says that Dietrich of Berne led it, while the French state that the Grand Huntsman was from Fontainebleau. There is even an English tale that King Arthur leads one group. The Irish call the hunt's hounds the Hounds of Hell; in England they are the Gabriel Hounds, the Yeth Hounds, the Whistlers, the Dartmoor Pack, or the Wisht Hounds. Norse tales speak of the *Lusse,* a witch who becomes a bird of prey and leads the Wild Hunt (the *Lussiferd* or *Lussireidi*) on the longest night of the year in December.

In India, ancient Vedic records speak of the Moon as the gate of death; the Moon was ruled by the goddess Sarama and her two dogs. Yama, god of the dead, had two fierce, four-eyed dogs; they were his messengers to humans. A companion of the god Indra was a faithful hunting dog.

In Mithraism, the dog beside the sacrificed bull symbolized the Mother Goddess and resurrection.

In Chinese lore, there is the red Celestial Dog, T'ien Kou, who has dual purposes. When he helps Erh-lang chase away evil spirits, he is yin and represents fidelity and devotion, but when he becomes guardian of the night, he is yang and symbolizes destruction and catastrophe. T'ien Kou is connected with comets, meteors, and eclipses. The dog is a protector and guardian in Japanese lore. The Buddhists have a Lion-Dog which they say is the defender of the law.

In Slavic legend, the three goddesses, called Zorya, chained a dog to the constellation of the Little Bear; when it breaks free, the world will end.

Dogs have been associated with Moon goddesses around the world. The Mongols, Chiquitos, and Balkan peoples all have mythologies connecting the Moon and dogs. Quetzalcoatl, the Aztec god, was said to have entered the land of the dead in the shape of a dog; some legends say that the Dog god Xolotl was his twin brother.

Although the dog is said to cause eclipses in some places, in other cultures it is considered a protector against evil. The Berbers of Northern Africa still consider one who kills a dog unclean for the rest of his life, the same as if he had killed a human. Because dogs were associated with the ancient

Mother Goddesses, however, the Semitic and Islamic cultures made the animal "unclean," evil, and demonic. Women and dogs were not allowed to approach Islamic shrines. The word "dog" became an insult.

During the persecution of witches, the dog was considered to be a demon lover of the witch and one of her powerful familiars. At one time magicians used a black dog to pull mandrake root from the ground, believing that the root's scream would cause a human to go insane. In alchemy, a picture of a dog being devoured by a wolf symbolized the purification of gold by antimony.

Superstitions: *Some people believe that dogs will howl when there is a death.* This idea comes from a Semitic tradition that dogs can see the Angel of Death approach and will howl. The belief is found throughout Europe. *It is said that a dog howling is a sure sign of death, because dogs can scent death and see the ghost of the departing person.*

The Irish said that curses could be laid with a dog's help. In fact, the Celtic word cainte *(dog) meant a Bard who could speak a true curse.*

The custom of lifting a bride over the threshold may have come from the ancient Assyrian burial of an image of a dog at that spot in a house; lifting the bride would show the guardian that the newcomer was welcome.

An old Gypsy belief states that if a dog digs a hole in your garden there will be a death in the family. If a dog licks a human's wound, it will heal.

Magickal Attributes: Tracking skills; the ability to scent a "trail" through conflicting or confusing situations. Companionship, keen hearing, loyalty, willingness to follow through. Using intuition to find new ideas and solutions. Seeking a teacher within by going into the silence. If seen in meditation, you will be guarded from approaching danger and threats. Protection. Finding out the truth.

Chant

> *Goddess-companions, we trail the truth.*
> *Understand our night-cries!*
> *We guide and protect Her children.*
> *Heed our warnings!*
> *We sing to the Moon to show you the way*
> *To ancient Moon magicks!*
> *We stand at the gates between the worlds.*
> *Follow us!*

COYOTE

This animal, a small wolf (*Canis latrans*), is sometimes called the prairie wolf or brush wolf. It is found in the western sections of the United States. It is less than four feet long and weighs about thirty pounds. It looks much like a small German shepherd, but has a bushier tail. It has a sharp, yapping bark.

The coyote has learned to adapt itself to human civilization, often living within the outer boundaries of cities and towns. It is intelligent; sometimes a female will deliberately lure a domesticated dog out where the rest of the pack can kill it. The coyote can run for short distances at a speed up to forty-five miles an hour. These creatures are best known for their howling at night.

To Native Americans, the coyote was the archetypal Trickster Hero, who stole fire for humans, but also could bring floods. Coyote was a spirit of the night, with great magickal powers. Although he was said to be able to lead one out of danger, he was more often associated with death, pain, and evil.

Magickal Attributes: Take care as Coyote is a Trickster! Cunning, shape-shifter, stealth, opportunity, dark and light magick, illumination, truth, creativity, new life, experience. Don't be foolish or you could trip yourself up. Seeking opportunities.

Chant

> Trickster, Shape-Changer, keep me from danger.
> Cunning magician, teach me your ways
> Of magickal fire, powers much higher.
> Lead me to new life. Brighten my days.

FOX

This creature belongs to the dog/wolf family, Canidae. However, the pupil of its eye is elliptical when contracted, not circular as with dogs and wolves. There are about nine different kinds of American foxes, four European and Asiatic species, and four that live in North Africa. The red fox is the best known.

The common red fox is found in most areas of Europe, Asia, and the Americas. The American species, *Vulpes fulva*, is very similar to the European species, *Vulpes vulpes*. The European red fox is larger than its American cousin: fifteen to twenty pounds; foxes average up to forty inches long.

The fox has a variety of colors: the typical red with splotches of white, especially on the tip of its tail; jet black; black with white tips on the hair. I have seen a fox that was red with a white-frosted look to its fur.

The fox has a long bushy tail, short legs, and long ears. Although at birth their eyes are a bluish-gray, this changes to amber in adulthood. They are nocturnal creatures and usually mate for life. They are very cunning and intelligent, their senses sharp. Primarily, their diet consists of rodents, but they like fruit, as in the fable of the fox and the grapes.

The gray fox, *Urocyon cinereoargenteus*, of the southern United States is the only tree-climbing fox. The kit or swift fox, *Vulpes velox*, lives on the western plains; it is very small and yellowish-gray. The white or "blue" Arctic fox, *Alopex lagopus*, is found in the far northern regions; it is white in winter, blue-gray in summer, and is the only fox to migrate.

The Indian or Bengal fox, *Vulpes bengalensis*, lives in tropical and subtropical areas; it is a deep red and leaves no scent. In Russia, Siberia, China, and central Asia is found the corsac, which is a sandy color; this fox also leaves no scent. The desert fox, *Vulpes vulpes leucopus*, of southwestern Asia is a rusty red-gray with a dark stripe across the shoulders. Africa has two species of foxes: the pale fox (*Vulpes pallia*), a pale yellow, with a thinner, black-tipped tail and longer ears; the ass fox (*Vulpes chama*), also yellow but with much longer ears. The smaller Rupell's fox (*Vulpes ruppellii*) is found in the Nubian Desert, Syria, Afghanistan, and parts of Persia, and is fawn, red, and gray.

If pursued by hounds, the fox can lope along at about six miles an hour, but can speed up to forty-five miles an hour for short periods.

The Sumerians said that the fox was connected with the Trickster god Enki. Those who followed Zoroastrianism believed that the fox, with his supernatural powers, was capable of frightening off demons.

In Greece and certain other ancient Mediterranean cultures, the god Dionysus was called Bassareus when he was in his fox form. His priestesses wore fox skins and were called Bassarids.

A Trickster figure in the West, the fox is considered even more powerful in the Far East where they say it has supernatural powers as a shapeshifter. China and Japan have many legends of fox spirits taking human form just to cause trouble. If a fox-human's reflection was shown in water or a mirror, however, the true form could be seen. They also believed that if the fox was treated with respect and the proper attention, it could be persuaded to bring good fortune. In Japan the rice god Inari had a fox as one of his symbols. Seeing foxes in Japan had special significance; a black fox was good luck, a white one misfortune, and three together meant disaster. In China, the fox symbolized craftiness as well as long life.

For many centuries fox fire has been associated with foxes. Fox fire is the phosphorescent light that comes from decaying wood and can be seen at night as an eerie glow. The Japanese associate this light without heat with the will-o'-the-wisp, as do other cultures. In Scandinavian countries, the aurora borealis was known as "the light of the fox." During the Middle Ages, the fox was used as a symbol for the devil.

Superstitions: *In Wales it is still said that to see one fox is lucky, but to see several together is unlucky. The Welsh also say that witches transform themselves into foxes.*

When hungry, the fox will pretend to be dead, then grab the curious birds that come near him.

Magickal Attributes: Cunning, slyness; the ability to make fools out of those who aggressively pursue you. Remaining unobserved while watching the actions and motives of others. Stealth, wisdom, invisibility. Cunning when needing to deal with possible troublesome people.

Chant

> *Stealthy messenger of the gods,*
> *Cunning and wise, reliable friend,*
> *Guide my steps through this maze of deception*
> *And see this problem to its end.*

JACKAL

This is the most common wild dog in the warmer parts of Africa, India, and the Far East. It looks much like a wolf, but is only slightly larger than a red fox. Jackals are nocturnal animals, hunting only at night, usually in very large packs. However, the African black-backed jackal, *canis mesomelas*, is a solitary species, hunting alone. Their strange cry can be even more frightening than that of the hyena.

In Africa the jackal has been called the "lion's provider," in the belief that it acts as a scout for hunting lions. It is a scavenger, a stealthy creature that has been known to enter villages at night to kill domestic animals. Today, we sometimes use the term "jackal" to describe a person who does sordid work for someone else, a person who feeds off others.

In parts of India there still exists an old belief that the leader of the jackal pack has a horn in the middle of its forehead; they say that any human who manages to get this horn will receive great benefits, rather like the legends of the unicorn horn. In the Hindu belief, jackals and ravens accompany Black Kali in her aspect as destroyer. Shiva, in his aspect as consort of Kali, was called a jackal.

Anubis, an Egyptian god who presided over the tombs as Lord of the Dead, had the head of a jackal. Anubis, called the Opener of the Way, was a psychopomp who guided the souls of the dead to the Judgment Hall of the Otherworld where the souls were weighed for truth on the scales of Maat. His presence was considered essential in the rituals of Isis and Osiris. As the child of Nephthys (an Underworld and death goddess), Anubis had a holy city called Canopis (Eye of the Jackal or Dog); the canopic jar was used in mummification of the entrails of the deceased. Roman processions honoring Isis always had a priest wearing the Anubis mask walking before the image of the goddess.

To the followers of Zoroaster, the jackal was another animal of the demon Ahriman, and was, therefore, evil.

Magickal Attributes: seeking mystical knowledge, particularly knowing your past lives. Astral travel into Otherworld realms for spiritual teaching and initiation.

Chant

> *Silent jackal of the night,*
> *Thoth [toe-th] of sacred mysteries deep,*
> *Instruct me in the ancient ways,*
> *While awake or while asleep.*
> *Guide my steps in mystic paths,*
> *That lead to rebirth of my soul.*
> *In initiation stand beside me*
> *While I seek my highest goal.*

WOLF

The gray wolf once ranged over the entire Western Hemisphere, from the plateau of central Mexico to the Arctic regions, except in extremely dry, desert areas. In Asia it prowled as far south as the northern sections of India. It disappeared from Britain and most of Europe hundreds of years ago.

The wolf is quite large for a member of the canine family, *canis lupus*, and is strong and highly intelligent. Most wolves resemble German shepherd dogs, but with shaggier fur, shorter ears, and a bushy tail. They range in size from 175 pounds in Alaska to the fifty-pound red wolf of Texas. The most common color is a mixture of black, white, and gray fur, giving a grizzled effect.

The wolf hunts in small family packs. It can out-smart hunters, even to the point of urinating on traps to show its disdain. It does not give slavish attention to humans like a dog, but prefers its freedom. At times, particularly in eastern Europe, the wolf will attack humans.

At one time wolves were so common and dangerous in Britain that the month of January was set aside for hunting them. January was called *Wolfmonat*, or Wolf Month. An outlaw of that time, a man with a price on his head, was known as a "wolf-head." Although wolves were exterminated in England in 1509, they could be found in the mountains of Scotland until the middle of the seventeenth century, and in Ireland until the beginning of the eighteenth century.

The Egyptian god Wepwawet was either pictured as a wolf or with a wolf head. A banner bearing his image was carried before the pharaoh in victory processions. However, both the Hindus and the followers of Zoroaster considered the wolf to be evil and the symbol of evil in human nature.

Plato and Pausanias both wrote about the wolf cult in Arcadia; the initiates of the cult worshiped Zeus Lycaeus, called themselves Lukoi, and sacrificed and ate wolves. The wolf was also associated with Apollo (who had a bronze wolf image at Delphi), Ares/Mars, and Silvanus. The Roman festival of Mars was called the Lupercalia.

As with the goddess Artemis being called the Great Bitch, so was the Great Goddess, under the title of Lupa or Feronia, called the Great She-Wolf in early Rome. The Lupercalia (Festival of the She-Wolf), honoring her, lasted well into later Roman times. The Romans considered this aspect of the goddess to be the mother of their ancestors, the foster-mother of Romulus and Remus.

Among the Celts, wolves were considered to be powerful, but helpful animals. Legend says that Cormac, king of Ireland, was always accompanied by them. The god Cernunnos was pictured with a wolf, bear, and otter.

Odhinn had two wolves as constant companions in Valhalla. They were called Geri and Freki. They may have been the offspring of the Hag of the Iron Wood, or Hel's Mother. One of Loki's children, the great wolf Fenrir, was chained by the gods because of his viciousness. It is said that Fenrir will break free at Doomsday, the Day of the Wolf. The wolves Skoll (repulsion) and Hati (hatred) chase the Sun and Moon; when there was an eclipse it was said that the wolves temporarily swallowed the globe.

The Valkyries were sometimes shown riding wolves, in their aspect of soul-collectors. This idea may have survived in the belief during the Middle Ages that witches in the form of werewolves rode wolves through the night.

Several heroes and founders of nations had wolves for foster-mothers: Cormac of Ireland; Tu Kueh, founder of Turkey; Ataturk, or "the Gray Wolf," of Turkey; Zoroaster; Romulus and Remus, founders of Rome; Siegfried of northern Germany, whose oldest name was Wolfdietrich.

In pre-Christian Europe, the wolf was a very popular clan totem. This can be seen by the prevalence of certain names during that period: Wolfe, Wulf, Wulfstan, Wolfram, Wolfburg, and others. Many clans were accused of turning themselves into wolves at certain times of the year; the reality behind this was probably that these clans dressed in wolf skins and masks for certain religious rites.

Native Americans said that when the wolf howled, he created wind. If he continued to howl, fog came. They considered the Moon its power ally.

Wolves have long been misunderstood. Fortunately, today there are several groups in the United States that are raising and studying wolves, with a goal to stop their extinction. There is a large wolf preserve in Washington state that offers guided tours through its facilities. If you arrange to go there near a Full Moon and just at dusk, you are treated to the most wonderful symphony of wolf calls by the entire population.

Superstitions: *In Britain it was believed that if a wolf saw a man before the man saw it, the man would be struck dumb and couldn't cry out. If the man sees it first, the wolf loses its ferocity and can't run away.*

In many parts of Europe they believe that if you say the word wolf in December you will be attacked by one.

The French at one time hung a wolf's tooth about a child's neck to protect it from evil spirits.

Wolves give birth only in May and during thunderstorms.

Hair taken from a specific area on the rump of a live wolf is aphrodisiac in nature.

The eyes of a wolf will glow in the darkness.

Magickal Attributes: Cunning, escaping hunters, ability to pass by dangers invisibly, outwitting those who wish you harm, fighting when necessary. Sometimes an astral wolf will lead you to a spiritual teacher. Wisdom, hunting and seeking, magick, dreams, introspection, intuition, listening, death and rebirth, transformation. Strong protection. Spiritual guidance in dreams and meditations.

Chant

> The mournful cries rise in the night.
> We are seeking!
> Wolves' song greets the Moon so bright.
> We are brave and wise!
> Sleek, muscled bodies beneath the Moon.
> We help turn the wheel of death and rebirth!
> By our magick we send a boon
> Of true dreaming!

Chapter 10

LAND
CREATURES

Rather than try to divide the following creatures into more, and perhaps confusing, categories, I have chosen to put them all under the above title. This should make the creatures listed in this chapter easier to locate in the book.

ANTELOPE

Antelope are found in the plains, jungles, or inaccessible mountain regions; they appear to bridge the gap between sheep, goats, and cattle. Their horns are permanent and their hooves like those of cattle. True antelopes live only in Eurasia and Africa. Africa has more species than the rest of the world; the African hartebeest is typical. Antelopes are swift, agile, and usually have cylindrical horns. The largest antelope is the eland, which is five or six feet at the shoulder. The *saiga* of Asia and *nilgai* of India are also called antelopes, although they more closely resemble goats. The European chamois is really a goat-antelope.

What is known as the American antelope is not really an antelope at all, but a pronghorn (pictured on the following page). Originally its territory extended from the provinces of Saskatchewan and Alberta in

Canada down through the region west of the Mississippi River valley and into central Mexico.

Second only to the cheetah in speed, the antelope is very curious by nature. Anything blatantly human will cause them to run, but other unusual movement will entice them to cautiously approach. The pronghorn have hollow horns, a novelty among antelope, and shed them every year.

In Sumerian mythology, the antelope was both a lunar and solar animal. As a solar creature it was sacred to the god Ea who was sometimes called Ea-Oannes ("the antelope of Apsu and of creation") and the god Marduk. In its lunar form the antelope or gazelle was sacred to the goddess Astarte.

In Egyptian lore, this animal represented Osiris and Horus, but was also sacred to the goddess Isis. It was sacrificed, however, to the desert god Set.

In most of Asia Minor the antelope was considered to be a lunar animal and associated with the Great Mother. In India it was an emblem of Shiva. The chariots of Chandra and Soma were drawn by antelopes or gazelles.

The gazelle, a type of antelope, was considered to be an animal of the Egyptian god Set, along with the oryx and goat. This creature represented the sign of Capricorn in the Hindu zodiac. The gazelle was a creature of Artemis/Diana in Greece and Rome, and the chief storm god in Sumeria.

The oryx was especially revered by ancient Egyptians as a sacrificial animal.

In the flat areas of the western states, herds of antelope are common. They are beautiful graceful creatures who either bound away in springy leaps or run at great speeds if startled. Usually, one has to observe them through binoculars, since getting close is nearly impossible.

Superstitions: *It was once believed that antelope in Middle Eastern countries cut down trees with their horns.*

Magickal Attributes: Swiftness, gentleness, being in touch with the Earth. Strength, dangerousness. Caution when approaching something new. A strong survival instinct through understanding yourself and the cycle of life. Sometimes a message that you should seek a higher purpose instead of dwelling totally on the physical. Developing a strong survival instinct in yourself or another, especially if living in abusive or threatening circumstances.

Chant

> *Swift-footed antelope, teach me survival instincts.*
> *Make me aware of intuitive warnings.*
> *Let the aggressor be brought low by his or her own actions.*
> *Dispel his or her power to harm others.*
> *Show me the path to safety, peace, and harmony.*

APE or MONKEY

The term ape is used to describe the tailless anthropoids. The great apes of the world include the gorilla, chimpanzee, orangutan, the long-armed gibbons, and the siamang. Much of their behavior is almost human. Their arms and shoulders are greatly developed in comparison to their legs, which are much shorter. They have long fingers, short opposable thumbs, and lack a tail; their feet can be used for grasping as well as walking. They also have well-developed brains.

The ancient Egyptians considered the baboon to be sacred to the gods Thoth (deity of wisdom) and Hapi (god of the Nile). Images of Thoth show either an ibis-head or a baboon-head; this baboon-head is sometimes mistaken for that of a dog. In paintings, Thoth is often portrayed as a baboon as he stands in the Judgment Hall of Osiris in the land of the dead. Ancient records say that four apes sit beside the Lake of Fire near the throne of Osiris. These creatures listen to all appeals of the soul and judge it before it can pass into the lands of Osiris.

In the Hindu cultures of India, apes and monkeys represent benevolence and gentleness. Because of their monkey god Hanuman, who rescued the kidnapped Sita, the

99

Hindu people consider these creatures sacred. However, in Buddhism the monkey signifies greed.

The monkey is revered in Japan. There are legends of what are called the Three Mystic Monkeys; the names of these are Mizaru (hands over the eyes), Kikazaru (hands over the ears), and Iwazaru (hands over the mouth). The Greek Eleusinian Mysteries had an initiation formula which reminds one of these three monkeys: things seen, heard, and tasted. In China, the monkey was said to have the power to grant good health, success, and protection.

Several West African tribes consider the monkey to be a sacred animal and the servant of Ogugu. Even the Mayan god of the North Star was pictured with a monkey-head.

Several ancient writers of the Mediterranean cultures, such as Pliny and Aesop, used the ape to symbolize foolishness and the kind of mother love that smothers.

Superstitions: *The expression to "monkey around" means to do useless things that can be irritating to others.*

Monkeys are depressed during the waning and New Moons.

Magickal Attributes: Ingenuity when dealing with problems. Care and protection of family. Don't "monkey" around, but get on with what you have to do. Putting a "monkey wrench" into a situation or plans where the outcome would be harmful in some way.

Chant

> Help me to see truth in all situations
> With my spiritual eyes.
> Teach me to hear Otherworld messages
> With my spiritual ears.
> Bring to me food for the soul from the gods
> That my spiritual body may be nourished.

ASS or DONKEY

The domesticated ass has served humans for thousands of years. Egyptians used the ass as far back as 3000 B.C.E.; they didn't use the horse until about 1900 B.C.E. The ass probably originated with the Abyssinian or Somali wild ass. The word "ass" likely comes from the word *athon*, which is Hebrew for she-ass. The word "donkey" comes from the animal's dun color. Sure-footed, it is stronger than a horse and has greater endurance. The ass or donkey is noted for its stubbornness and irascible temper. At one time it was found wild in Mongolia, Tibet, Iran, India, and Africa. The Kiang, of Tibet, and the Ghorkhar, of India, are examples.

The ass is also related to the zebra and horse. It has very long ears, a black back stripe, and upstanding black mane. They generally live in small family groups or bands in arid regions, where they feed on herbs, grass, and shrubs. In the wild, the ass is a swift runner, extremely alert and wary.

The animal pictured on ancient Egyptian and Assyrian monuments is the wild onager, a much larger creature than the donkey. In Egypt, it was sacrificed to Set, god of the desert regions. To ancient Egyptians, the ass was a symbol of desolation, wariness, and speed. There is evidence that Set was a god of the conquering Hyksos, who came out of the desert to overrun Egypt. Set's Greek name, Typhon, was derived from the desert wind that brings such diseases as typhus.

In Chaldean engravings, the death goddess was shown kneeling on an ass which stood in a boat; the boat was being ferried across the river that separates the Underworld from the physical world.

The donkey in Greek myths was sacred to the gods Dionysus, Priapus, and Cronus/Saturn. Typhon (the Greek version of Set) was portrayed with the head of an ass. Therefore, the Greeks considered this animal to represent sloth, infatuation, and disastrous upsets. The Roman deity Pales (sometimes called male, other times female) had a human body and the head of an ass; her or his priests wore ass masks. She or he was considered to be the guardian of flocks and herds.

The Chinese Immortal Chang Kwo-lao, who brought children, had a marvelous magickal donkey. When he didn't need it, he could change his mount into paper and fold it up.

In Hindu legends, the demon Ravana drove an ass-drawn chariot when he abducted Sita. Because of this, the Hindus consider the ass to be a malevolent creature. The Norse, who were of Aryan origin, used the word "ass" to denote both an Asian and a deity. Muslims also say it is cursed and constantly pray for misfortune to befall its owner.

Superstitions: *If a donkey brays and twitches its ears, rain is coming. The wild ass will bray twelve times on the eve of the Spring Equinox.*

If a child with whooping cough is put on a donkey and the beast walked in a circle nine times, the child will be cured.

Magickal Attributes: Use with caution! Finding the means to provide for physical needs even in the most trying circumstances. Extreme stubbornness; obstinacy; digging in your heels when others are trying to push you into something you don't want. Doing the opposite of what you know you should. Pretending to know or be something you are not. Use if you are indecisive or never seem to take a stand, but need to.

Chant

> Muscles tight, feet dug in,
> A stubbornness to fight and win.
> Right or wrong these traits may be
> The choice, of course, belongs to me.
> May I be true to the light within
> When determination shows the need to win.

BADGER

A member of the weasel family, this is a tough, wedge-shaped animal with long, sharp claws and strong teeth. The common badger, *Taxidea taxus*, is found only in North America, but there are badgers on all the large land masses of the world except Australia and Madagascar. An adult is two to three feet long, a foot high at the shoulder, and weighs over twenty pounds. It has long, shaggy gray hair tipped with black; its eyes are small and its muzzle pointed. A nocturnal animal, the badger lives in burrows.

The Eurasian badger was the subject of a bloody sport in England in the early part of the last century, when it was thrown into a pit full of dogs; this "sport" was ended by law in 1850. The badger has a stump of a tail and looks rather like a small bear. Its claws make it a superb digger. The Eurasian badger has a white head with a black line that runs from the nose over and around the eyes, then over the ears.

To the Chinese, this animal is a lunar yin creature, both playful and full of mischief, with the supernatural power of shape-shifting. In Japan, the badger is a rice spirit like the fox; the wind-badger Tanuki provides rice crops and helps their growth. In European countries, the badger is considered to be a weather prophet.

A tenacious and courageous animal, the badger is unyielding in the face of danger. To do this, it backs into a hole or a corner where it is protected from attack at the rear. In this way it can face down much larger adversaries. Many of the more powerful medicine women called upon the power of the badger for healing. To Native Americans, the badger symbolized the healing of children and was connected with herbal magick, roots, and herbs because of its digging ability. Some tribes considered the badger's spiritual powers stronger than the bear.

Superstitions: *There is an old tale that the badger has holes in its tail, one for each of its years.*

If you carry a badger's tooth in your pocket, you will be lucky at cards, gambling, or any wager.

Magickal Attributes: Can teach you to fight for your rights and spiritual ideas. Revenge, wisdom, cunning, perseverance. When faced with a crisis, don't panic but act, even get angry, in a creative, productive way. Earth magick and wisdom. For knowledge in how to protect yourself in a specific situation.

Chant

> *Cunning badger of the forest,*
> *Guide me to wisdom, truth and light.*
> *All injustices against me,*
> *Wipe clean the slate and set them right.*

BEAR

One species of bear or another is found from subtropical climates to the polar regions. They are generally large mammals, with coarse fur, a very short tail, and flat soles on their paws. Their non-retractable claws are used in digging and climbing. Although they eat almost everything from fruits and berries to fish and small animals, they are fond of honey. They tend to semi-hibernate in colder regions.

The black bear ranges over much of the United States and Canada. The grizzly frequents the wilder areas of the western United States and Canada; it does not climb like most bears. The huge Alaskan brown bear is the largest flesh eater in the world; some of them reach as much as 1,400 pounds. They are unpredictable in temperament like the grizzly. The white polar bear is found in all arctic regions.

The European brown bear is found in both Europe and Asia. The shaggy sloth bear is native to India. The short-haired Malay bear is a small, tropical species. The Himalayan bear has a white crescent on its breast.

The bear usually minds its own business, but will protect its young with great ferocity. It is so attuned to the seasons that it knows when to prepare ahead for Winter. When attacked, it will often stand on its hind legs so that it towers above its opponent.

Countries as far apart as Finland, Siberia, and Japan consider the bear to be a sacred animal, an animal Master who teaches shamans. Siberian tribes always call the bear the Old Man, the Grandfather, the Chief's Son, or Crooked Tail. In the Finnish *Kalevala* this animal is referred to as the Honey-eater, the Fur-adorned, and the Forest Apple. As the Dog of God, it was thought to be ten times as powerful as a man and twelve times more intelligent. In parts of Japan, the bear represents benevolence and wisdom; in China, strength and bravery.

The Arcadians of the Mediterranean area considered themselves to be descended from bears. In Cretan myth, the two bears sacred to Artemis cared for the infant Zeus and were later changed into the constellations of Ursa Major and Minor.

Young girl-priestesses in the cult of Artemis were referred to as "cub bears." Once a year during the festival of Brauronia in Athens, they dressed in bear-skins and paraded to the Goddess's temple. Callisto, a companion of Artemis, was called the Beautiful She-Bear; she was said to be the guardian of the Pole Star.

The continental Celtic goddess Dea Artia of Berne was called a she-bear and was portrayed with a bear near her. Even among the Norse this creature was sacred; it belonged to Thorr, god of thunder and lightning, to Odhinn, and to Norse lunar water goddesses. The famed Norse berserkers originally followed the bear cult of Freyja; Odhinn later took over the role of the bear god. The word *berserker* comes from the words *bear sark*, or bearskin shirt. It is quite likely that these special warriors were initiated into an exclusive Mystery cult, one that taught them how to use trance or hallucinogens to produce the bearlike strength and extreme bravery they exhibited in battle.

In the Celtic myths, the bear was considered to be a lunar creature. Although now extinct in Britain and Ireland, the bear lives on in legends. The word *arth*, which means "bear," is the root word for the name Arthur. The phrase "Son of the Bear" often appears in Irish and Welsh names.

Alchemists used the bear to symbolize prime matter and the dangerous aspect of the subconscious mind.

Into the 1900s, Eastern Slavs had a ceremony for a newborn baby; the grandmother laid the child on a bearskin to bring it good luck and health. Porphyry, in the third century C.E., mentioned the same practice.

In Native American lore, the bear was chief of all animals when it came to herbal knowledge. This creature was connected with healing and the underground earth energy of roots and herbs.

Superstitions: *The bear breeds only once in seven years, according to back-woodsmen in the United States. These same people also say that a child can be cured of whooping cough if it rides on a bear.*

Bear cubs are born formless and licked into their shape by the mother.

A sick bear will eat ants or mullein to be healed.

Magickal Attributes: Strength and stamina; can help you to find balance and harmony in your life. Patience, defense, revenge, wisdom, dreams, intuition, listening, introspection, death and rebirth, transformation. Seek quiet places for answers and harmony in your life. A creature of dreams, astral travel, visionaries, mystics, and shamans. To bring balance and harmony.

Chant

> Deep in slumber, dreams unending,
> Wise old bear, patient, strong,
> Send me dreams of transformation.
> Grant me intuition along
> With introspection of my life,
> Inner listening, no more strife.

BEAVER

The beaver is the largest rodent in the Northern Hemisphere of the New World. It is found also in Europe and northern Asia. The beaver generally weighs from thirty to sixty-eight pounds and can reach up to forty-three inches in length, including its broad, flat tail. It is a skilled, fast swimmer with a remarkable lung capacity. The beaver spends its time cutting down trees to dam up water for ponds. When working, one beaver will cut the tree while another keeps watch. They also eat the bark and twigs of trees. Beaver fur formed the bulk of the early fur trades, particularly in the New World. The original beavers of the Oligocene Age were land-burrowing animals.

Ancient European cultures believed the beaver symbolized industry, vigilance, and peacefulness.

Two naturalists, husband and wife, decided to take a pair of beaver home with them to observe their behavior at close range. They got more than they bargained for. While they were out to dinner one evening, the beavers proceeded to cut the legs off all the tables and build a dam in one corner of the room.

Superstitions: *More than one culture believed that when pursued the beaver would bite off its testicles and throw them at the pursuer.*

The folk saying "busy as a beaver" comes from the way this creature works.

Magickal Attributes: Concentrating your energies into a job that needs doing. Being persistent. Using available resources to make your life more pleasant. Team work, sense of achievement. Have alternative solutions planned. For harmony in group work. To get a job.

Chant

> *Busy, busy, as the beaver,*
> *Persistent in my work and fun,*
> *I plan and labor toward my goals*
> *Until appointed tasks are done.*
> *Beaver, show me how to use*
> *The things at hand to reach my goal,*
> *Balancing my work and pleasure,*
> *My mind and body, and my soul.*

BISON or BUFFALO

The name bison is applied to the American bison (buffalo), the European bison (wisent), and at times to the wild ox of India (the gaur). The water buffalo of the Far East also plays a part in mythology.

The American buffalo has a large head that it carries low, a short neck, and heavy, humped shoulders. Except for the dense curly mane around its neck, the buffalo's hair is short. It can stand six feet at the shoulders, and a large bull can weigh up to 2,000 pounds. Both bulls and cows have short, sharp horns. The old cows, not the bulls, act as leaders of the herd.

Larger than the American buffalo, the wisent, or European bison, was once at home in many of the forests of Asia and Europe, including England. Today there are very few of them left. In the United States and Canada, buffalo roamed over most of the country, except for the arid deserts

and the Pacific Coast. They were almost exterminated by the hunters who supplied the railroad crews with meat. Naturalists have, today, provided the buffalo with preserves where their numbers are increasing once more.

As far back as the Upper Paleolithic times, the bison was honored. In a cave at Ariege, France, there is a painting of a man dressed in a bison head and skin.

Vana, the Vedic god of the dead, was pictured riding a buffalo, as was the Taoist deity Lao Tzu. Legend says that Lao Tzu rode a green buffalo when he disappeared into the West. The Hindu goddess Durga was sent by the gods to kill a buffalo monster; the buffalo is still sacrificed to her. Even the Romans knew of buffalos and used them in the amphitheater in Rome.

Native Americans, especially the Oglala Sioux, considered the buffalo the chief of all animals and said it represented the Earth. The buffalo was a sacred animal, particularly if it was the rare white buffalo. The story of White Buffalo Woman is one of their legends.

The largest herds of North American buffalo today exist in Yellowstone National Park and in Canada.

Magickal Attributes: Social life, fertility, courage, abundance, prosperity, knowledge, sharing, work, challenge, survival. Visions of a buffalo show that prayers are heard, reminding you that nothing is achieved without the help of spirit. Formulating plans that will benefit you.

Chant

> Rumbling like thunder o'er the prairie,
> Great herds of abundance, sharing with man,
> I need your knowledge to meet life's challenges,
> To survive and move on with my plans.

BOAR, SOW or PIG

The largest of all wild pigs, the wild boar originally roamed over all forested areas of Europe, east across Asia and Siberia to the Pacific Coast of the United States and south into North Africa. In this country, there are still a few of them left, ranging in the mountains of California and into Mexico. The European wild boar, *Sus scrofa*, is a rugged, sinewy creature, dusky or grayish brown in color. Its large, sharp tusks can be up to a foot long. The ancestor of the domesticated pig, a male can stand three feet at the shoulder and weigh up to 400 pounds. If cornered, the boar is courageous and ferocious, attacking humans, dogs, horses, even tigers, without quarter.

The Sumerian deity Tammuz, as a symbolic figure of Winter killed by Spring, was slain by a boar. Any myth that tells of a hero/god being gored in the groin refers to ritual castration. The Greek Adonis also was slain by a boar; therefore, the boar was a sacrifice made to Aphrodite, lover of Adonis. The priests of Adonis probably wore boar skins during these specific rituals where they sacrificed boars as substitutes for the god. Homer wrote that the teeth of boars were used as a decoration on the helmets of Greek warriors. The boar was also considered sacred to Ares/Mars, who was the god of war, destruction, and strife.

Piglets were sacrificed at the Eleusinia and Thesmophoria celebrations to Demeter and Persephone. In the figurines and wall paintings of ancient Greek shrines can be seen sow-masked priestess-dancers.

The Romans offered pigs to Mars, Ceres, Tellus Mater, and Proserpina. Pig blood was often used as a purifier. Because the cowrie shell reminded the Romans of the white sow, they called it *porcella* ("little sow"); our word porcelain comes from this. Ceres and Tellus Mater received the sacrifice of a pregnant sow and flat grain cakes during the day of sowing, known as Sementiva.

On Crete, the Crone aspect of the Goddess was represented as a sow. The Greek Demeter was sometimes known as Phorcis the Sow; the goddess Circe was connected with pigs as seen in the legend of turning Odysseus's men into swine. Tantric Buddhists still worship Marici, the Diamond Sow.

A clear connection between the sow and the Moon is found in a carving on Malta; this engraving shows a sow with thirteen teats, which represent the thirteen lunar months of a Goddess year. The number thirteen came to be an unlucky number simply because it was originally associated with the Goddess.

The Hindu god Rudra was known as the "Boar of the Sky." Vajnavrahi, goddess of the dawn, was symbolized by a sow as the source of all life. Vishnu, in one of his aspects, was called the Boar; he had three boar sons who were sacrificed.

To Egyptians, the pig was an evil animal and belonged to the god Set, yet they allowed this animal to trample seeds into the ground during sowing. To both the Egyptians and the Phoenicians, the pig was an unclean animal and taboo as food, although the Egyptians ate it once a year at a Full Moon. In Zoroastrianism, it was associated with the Sun.

A white boar in China and Japan represented the Moon, courage, conquest, and the qualities needed by a warrior. The Chinese considered the pig to be greedy and dirty and only useful if tamed. The Pig Faery, Chu Pa-chieh, was a half-man, half-pig entity.

In Scandinavian and Teutonic lore, the boar was a funerary and storm animal, also symbolizing fertility and the harvest. At Yule, a boar was sacrificed to the god Freyr; this deity also rode a golden boar called Gullinbursti (Golden Bristles). Northern Germans swore by Gullinbursti, as this creature could reveal secrets and detect lies. Freyr's sister, Freyja, rode a sow whose name was Hildisvini (Battle Pig); one of her names was Syr (the Sow). Swedish kings once wore boar masks to show their spiritual marriage with this goddess. The Norse-Teutonic god Heimdall was said to have been fathered by boar's blood.

Norse and Anglo-Saxon invaders of England brought with them the custom of offering a boar to the god Freyr and a sow to the goddess Freyja at the Winter Solstice. They worshiped the boar or pig as a symbol of fertility of the land. In Old England this custom survived in the killing of a wild boar and serving its head at Christmas. The apple in the mouth of the boar represented the charmed apple of immortality.

Pigs were considered by the Celts to be the food of the gods and were sacred to the god Manannan mac Lir. Boar images were frequently used to adorn helmets (where they represented protection from danger) and artwork. To the Celts, the boar, and pigs in general, symbolized war, the warrior, hunting, protection, and fertility. The black sow was considered to be an evil animal, symbolizing death, cold, and great evil.

The goddess Brigit owned the boar Orc Triath. The name "Airc" (which comes from Orc) means "battle sow." Arthur had a terrible foe, the boar Twrch Trwyth. The White Boar of Marvan brought its master inspiration to write music and poetry. In Welsh tales, Pwyll was given a gift of pigs by Arawn, and Merlin spoke with a little pig in visions.

The Welsh goddess Cerridwen, a Great Mother and lunar deity, was known as the White Sow. The sow was a lunar animal connected with the Underworld and the Sacred Cauldron, a symbol of divine inspiration. This animal also represented death and rebirth to the Celtic peoples. Several later Welsh saints built their monasteries on specific spots because they had been led there by a magickal white sow.

In the cultures of the Pacific Ocean, pigs were a chief sacrifice to the gods. The tusked boar was a very important sacred object in some of the men's secret societies.

Superstitions: *The people of Scotland and Yorkshire say that it is unlucky for a pig to cross your path, especially if you are a fisherman.*

A pig carrying straws in its mouth is a prediction of a coming storm.

An old superstition known as far back as Pliny says that the touch of a pregnant or menstruating woman will cause curing pork to spoil. Old misogynist Pliny also wrote that such a woman would turn wine to vinegar, kill seedlings, blunt razors, and spoil food.

In Ireland, they say the pig can see the wind.

A pig can get hair balls like a cat does. This happens to be true.

Magickal Attributes: The ability to set up an ambush for an attacker and not give up until the aggressor has been sent on his way; concealing oneself when in danger; cunning, intelligence. A symbol of the spiritual food necessary for the developing magician. Boar: Courage and protection, the Earth Lord. Sow: Crone Goddess, deep Earth magick, knowledge of past lives.

Chant

> Boar—
> *Golden Bristles, friend of Freyr,*
> *Expose the traps laid for my feet*
> *By cunning aggressors secretly.*
> *Join with me in their total defeat.*

111

Boar of courage, Earth Lord guide,
Protect me always. Be at my side.
Sow—
Battle-Sow, companion of Freyja,
Lead me to knowledge of lives long past.
Instruct me in the deep Earth magick
That strong may be the spells I cast.

BULL, COW or CATTLE

Domesticated cattle are the descendants of wild species of the family Bovidae. Fossil remains of one species found from western Asia to continental Europe were six to seven feet at the shoulders. The aurochs, or uri, were the first domesticated European cattle and were described by Caesar. Most modern breeds are traced back to either the urus or the Celtic Shorthorn, or both. The humped cattle of Asia and Africa, *Bos indicus*, are not suited to wetter climates, and evolved from an entirely different ancestor.

Cattle are ruminants with a four-compartment stomach, split hoofs, and non-shedding horns, if they have horns at all.

The bull protects its herd of cows and young. If danger approaches, the bull will bellow and paw the ground in warning, then charge. Once enraged, this animal will continue to fight until either the aggressor is dead or retreats from the area.

The bull Nandi was ridden by the Hindu god Shiva, while both Agni and Indra could take the form of a bull. White bulls were sacrificed to represent him as Kali's consort. Sometimes the god Yama is portrayed with a bull-head. To the Hindus, the bull represents strength, speed, and the reproductive powers of Nature.

In Hindu belief, the cow is particularly sacred and rarely sacrificed. The *Rig-Veda* firmly states that the cow is not to be killed. Because of this injunction, the people of India treat it with great respect and care, ritually painting the animal and decorating it with garlands during festivals. Since Lakshmi, goddess of fortune, is associated with milk, the Hindus say that such a drink should not be refused. The goddesses Aditi and Prithivi are both connected with cows in their fertility aspects. This animal is also a symbol of Kali. The root word of cow is the Sanskrit *gau* and the Egyptian *kau*. Thus, such Hindu goddesses as Gauri and Kauri are connected with this animal.

In ancient Egypt, early kings called themselves bulls. The Memphis Apis bull (known to the Egyptians as Hap) belonged to the god Ptah, but was sometimes connected with Osiris. Egyptian paintings show the body of Osiris being carried by a black bull. The later rulers, the Ptolemies, combined Apis and Osiris to derive their deity Sarapis. The Bull of Mentu was sacred to Menthu, and the white bull to Min. *The Book of the Dead* describes the ancient practice of wrapping the dead in a bull's hide for magickal purification.

Several Egyptian goddesses were associated with cows: the Great Mother Hathor from whose udder came the Milky Way; Nut, the Celestial Cow with stars on her belly; and Isis who sometimes wore a cow-head or horns. The Egyptian word for cow was *kau*, a title accorded both Isis and Hathor. However, a single white hair on a cow disqualified it as a sacrifice to Isis.

Astarte and Ishtar of the Middle East also were portrayed as cows with lunar horns. Ninhursag of Mesopotamia was sometimes called Nintur ("cattle pen").

In other ancient Middle Eastern cultures, the bull also played an important religious role. Although it was usually a solar animal, when it was ridden by a goddess such as Astarte it became a lunar beast. The sky god Enki was known as the "savage bull of the sky," but the Moon god Sinn could take the form of a bull. The Sumerian deity Dumuzi, consort of Inanna, was titled the "wild bull" and wore a beard of lapis lazuli. The god El, Ba'al or Bel of Canaan, Syria, and Phoenicia was represented as a bull. El was believed to be consort to the goddess Asherah, who was called the sacred cow.

The people of Crete held the bull in high regard. The bull dances there (called the *Taurokathapsia*), so vividly portrayed in their temples, were to honor the bull and what it represented. The bull-leapers were probably the forerunners of the modern bull fighters. In Crete, all the kings inherited the title Minos, wore bull-masks, and were considered to be spiritually tied to the bull during this special festival. The Cretan Moon bull was sacrificed in place of the king at the end of the ritual. The sacred *labyrs* ("lip"), an extremely holy Cretan Goddess symbol, was used in the bull sacrifice.

Perhaps the best known bull sacrifices were held by the followers of Mithras. Initiates were bathed in the blood of a sacrificed bull to symbolize death and resurrection. Both this ritual and the underground place where it was performed was known to the Romans and followers of Mithras as the *taurobolium*.

In Greece, the goddess Hera could take the form of a cow; these animals were sacrificed to her and to Hercules. Homer called Hera *boopis*, which means "cow-faced," while at Argos she was worshiped as the Goddess of the Yoke; sacred herds were kept at her temple there. In Greek legend, Io and Europa, who were both turned into cows to satisfy the lusts of Zeus, were said to have been of the three sacred Goddess colors: white, black, and red. Artemis Tauropolos (Bull-Slayer) was the feminine form of Mithras. The birth of Dionysus (called Bull-Faced and Bull-Horned) was celebrated by a Spring festival and a bull-driving ritual.

Italy means "calf-land," a designation that ties it to Hera, the Great Mother, in her form as a cow. The cornucopia used by the Romans to symbolize the good things given by the Great Cow is still called the Horn of Plenty.

The bull was an important symbol in Celtic mythology; it symbolized strength and potency. Certain divination rituals required that a red and white bull be sacrificed and the diviner wrap himself in the fresh hide for the night. The word "cattle" was often used to distinguish between the domestic and wild stock. In Celtic mythology, as told in the Welsh *Triads*, the Underworld cows of the faeries were said to be red with white ears. Manannan mac Lir of Ireland had two cows, one speckled and one dun; these beasts with their twisted horns were always in milk.

Scandinavian legend tells of Audhumla, the Great Cow, who licked the giants and gods into existence from the ice. Nerthus, the Earth Mother, had sacred cows that drew her cart in a yearly journey across the land. The Chinese viewed the cow as a lunar animal representing the earth principle.

It is amazing to learn that in a certain area of England during the seventeenth century the people were still celebrating the day of Diana in August with a bull sacrifice.

Superstitions: *The Irish believe that if hares and cows are in the same field on May Day, witches are stealing the milk. They guard their cattle against witches and the faeries by hanging rowan or mountain ash boughs over the stable door.*

The Scots tar behind the cattle's ears and at the root of the tail to prevent witches stealing the milk.

In some sections of Scotland they still make bonfires of rowan and ash wood; the cattle are then driven through the smoke of these fires to protect them against the faeries. There was also an old Scottish superstition against white cows; they were said to give inferior milk. Red cows were preferred.

Carry the tip of a calf's tongue in your pocket to protect you from danger and see that you always have money.

Cattle turn to the East and kneel at midnight on Christmas Eve.

If a cow lows in your face, it is a death omen. If one breaks into your garden, someone in the family will soon die.

If a cow carries her tail upright, rain is approaching. If she slaps it against a tree or fence, it is a sign of coming bad weather.

Cows eat buttercups to help them produce better butter.

Magickal Attributes: Knowing when to be aggressive. Defending yourself and your family. Being content where you are, but also being aware of what may be going on around you. Being alert for danger. Performing difficult work in a conscientious manner. Bull: Earth Lord, fertility, strength. Cow: Great Mother Goddess, love, abundance.

Chant

> *Bull—*
> *Powerful bull of heaven and sky,*
> *Mighty beast of wisdom ancient,*
> *Bellow your warning to my enemies.*
> *Trample the evil-doers under your hooves.*
> *Frighten them with your tossing, sharp horns.*
> *Shelter me in the shadow of your muscled might.*
> *Protect me with your unlimited powers.*

Cow—
Horned Isis, Great Goddess Mother,
Fountain of wisdom and deep powerful magick,
Open my mind to my own inner power.
Grant me the wisdom to use it wisely.
Let me be bold in spell-casting.
Give me a sense of responsibility
To protect the helpless and abused,
To bring to justice those who do evil.
Teach me to hear your voice and follow your will.

DEER or STAG

Deer are even-toed, hooved animals of the family Cervidae. They also chew a cud, like cattle do. Most males have antlers which are shed every year. However, the female among the caribou have antlers like the males. The coats of deer are of a neutral color in shades of red, brown, or gray; the fawns in some species are temporarily spotted with white.

The species of deer come in all sizes, from the tiny deer of Africa to the now-extinct Irish elk which had an antler-spread of eleven feet from tip to tip. Some type of deer is found in nearly every area of the world. The deer can go a long time without water and still maintain its strength.

The deer has long been considered a magickal creature. This animal was sacred to such Greek goddesses as Artemis, Aphrodite, Athene, and the Roman Diana. At an Attica festival, Artemis was presented with a sacrificed deer and honeycakes in the shape of a deer. This goddess was also called Elaphaia ("She of the Red Deer") and Elaphebolia ("She Who Strikes the Red Deer"). The Etruscan version of Artemis is shown winged, holding a deer in one hand and a lion in the other.

Fawn skins were worn by the Greek Maenads and the Bacchant and Orphic devotees. The fawn skin was also a sacred garment of the lower initiates of some of the Greek mystery religions. Dionysus was said to wear the magickal skin of a fawn, tiger, or leopard and had been placed on a fawn skin by Hermes when he was born from the thigh of Zeus.

However, the stag was also a creature of Apollo at Delphi. The Greeks believed that the stag could identify medicinal herbs and plants. In early Egyptian temple paintings the deer is shown with Isis.

On a Minoan seal is shown the figure of an antlered stag dancer with large breasts. Stag dances were performed by men dressed as women at the New Year in England, Romania, and Germany into the nineteenth century.

In India, the deer was the mount of the god Vayu, deity of the wind. In China, Lu-Hsing, god of salaries and employees, rode a deer; to the Chinese the deer represented high rank, official success, and wealth.

Among the Celts, the stag was an animal of Cernunnos, the hunting god Cocidius, and the hero Ossian. When connected with these deities, the stag symbolized the virility of the warrior, the Sun, and fertility. Deer were sacrificed as a substitute for the Horned God in goddess rituals. In Celtic myth, a white doe or white stag was often sent by the Otherworld deities to guide some human into their realm. The animal god Cernunnos wore an antlered headdress. The Irish goddess Flidais was associated with deer; they drew her chariot. Sometimes deer were called faery cattle and messengers. Stories tell of nymphs and faeries changing into fawns to escape capture. The skin and antlers of deer were used as ritual garments.

From earliest times the stag was a sacred animal in the Black Sea and Anatolia areas, and among the Hittites. In some Sumerian rituals the statue of their fertility god was clothed in the skin and antlers of a stag.

In both China and Japan the dragon is often called the Celestial Stag. Chinese also have a god of immortality, Shou-Hsien, sometimes pictured as a white stag. In certain cultures of Asia and pre-Columbian America the stag was associated with regeneration because it shed and renewed its antlers each year. It was also believed to be an enemy of the snake.

Amulets made of deer skin parchment were preferred by ceremonial magicians of the Middle Ages. Some of the magickal power of the deer was believed to remain in such parchment.

117

To Native Americans, deer and all forked-horned animals represented dangerous psychic and spiritual powers that had a double nature. By observing this creature, humans learned to hide when being hunted.

Superstitions: *If deer feed on the herb dittany, they can become immune to arrow wounds.*

Deer, especially stags, can be charmed by the music of pan-pipes.

After eating snakes, a deer can shed its coat and old age with it.

To heal, use the right antler. To keep snakes away, burn either antler. Ointments made from stag bone marrow will cure fevers.

Magickal Attributes: Keen scent, grace, swiftness, gentleness. Using other methods to reach your goals than force. Being alert for any danger. A white deer in meditation often bears a message or will lead you to someone or something that will reveal spiritual knowledge. Hunting and seeking, abundance, dreams, intuition, introspection, listening, death and rebirth, transformation. Accept others as they are and don't try to change them. Deer: woodland Goddess, psychic powers, alternative paths to a goal. Stag: Lord of the Underworld, messages from guides, better understanding of the cycle of death and rebirth.

Chant

> Woodland dreams of intuition come with the graceful deer.
> I greet you, brothers of the forest.
> Your gift of magick will brighten my life.
> Transformation will come to me.
> Like you, I stand listening to the drum beat of life,
> Poised to follow my guiding spirits.

ELEPHANT

Elephants are the largest and most powerful land animals alive. There is one Asiatic or Indian species, *Elephas maximus*, and one, *Loxodonta africana*, in Africa. They are huge, with a thick gray hide, leathery and tough. They have massive heads, a long rope-like tail, small eyes, large fan-like ears, and ivory tusks. An elephant may weigh from three to four tons, with the average life span at eighty years.

The Indian elephant has a high domed head, moderate-sized ears, a concave forehead, four or five nails on each hind foot; the tip of the trunk has one finger-like protuberance. The African elephant does not have a domed head, but has large, broad ears, an arched forehead, and three nails on the hind foot; the tip of the trunk has two finger-like protuberances.

Because of the slaughter for their ivory, the elephant stands in danger of becoming extinct. Although they have an acute sense of smell, elephants possess only fair hearing and poor eyesight. They are very intelligent and keep learning all their lives.

In Africa, the elephant is found in areas where there is sufficient water and trees for food. The Asiatic elephant lives in India, Sri Lanka, Burma, Indo-China, and the Malay Peninsula. After the cow, the elephant is the most venerated animal of the Hindu people.

The rulers of India trained and used the elephant in war. In 280 B.C.E. King Pyrrhus waged the first war using elephants against the Romans. Hannibal employed them in the battle between Rome and Carthage in 218 B.C.E.

Sometimes a "white" (really a slate-gray color) Asiatic elephant is found; it is especially sacred and is usually presented to the ruler of the area or to a temple. In the East, the white elephant is said to bring extremely good fortune.

The Hindu god Ganesha (Lord of Hosts) has the head of an elephant and is very popular with the people as the god of removing obstacles. The god Indra rides a white elephant whose name is Airavata. Sometimes the deity Shiva wears an elephant skin. Krishna, whose highly sexed wife was Radha ("She-Elephant"), could assume an elephant form also. To the Hindu people, the elephant symbolizes royalty, intelligence, might, long life, sexual prowess, and the strength of the sacred wisdom.

The Buddhists class the elephant with the dove of peace, saying it represents wisdom, strength, prudence, and sovereignty. In Buddhist fertility rituals, the elephant is a symbol of the Sacred Marriage. The Chinese Buddhist deity P'u Hsien was said to ride a white elephant.

The Greek Dionysus and the Roman Bacchus were sometimes pictured as riding in a chariot drawn by elephants. In this aspect, the animal represented victory over death, immortality, and long life.

The symbolism of powerful magick in the elephant extended to its ivory, particularly during the Middle Ages. The hero Roland was said to have a war horn made of such ivory; it was called an "oliphant."

Superstitions: *The folk saying of a "white elephant" originally meant something of great spiritual value; now it has come to mean an object that has no practical use and is expensive to keep.* The white elephant bought by P. T. Barnum to exhibit in his circus cost him $200,000 just to get it to New York.

Elephants never forget. Elephants don't have the fantastic memory with which they are credited, although they are intelligent.

Elephants only get pregnant once and live for 300 years.

Elephants are afraid of mice.

Magickal Attributes: Removal of obstacles and barriers. Always being willing to learn new things. Building confidence. Patience and confidence to tackle a new job, schooling, or learning situation.

Chant

Before the power of Ganesha
All barriers and obstacles are removed.
Through the wisdom of Ganesha
I draw confidence and new opportunities.
Under the love of Ganesha
I learn and grow stronger in all ways.

ELK

The biggest deer alive today is the American elk, *Cervus canadensis*, called Wapiti by the Shawnee Native Americans. It is the American cousin of the European red deer, *Cervus elaphus*.

The American elk can stand five feet at the shoulders and weigh from 500-1000 pounds. It is brownish gray with a large orange-yellow rump disk. The neck is covered with long dark hair.

The bugling of the males in the autumn attracts the females. Although its antlers are massive, the elk can travel through the thickest of forests. To Native Americans an elk tooth represented long life. The elk knows how to pace itself so it can outlast its pursuers.

The great horns of the prehistoric Irish elk, *Mega-ceros giganteus*, are the largest recorded of the species. This elk was related to the fallow deer.

In ancient sites in Lithuania and northwestern Russia, staffs have been discovered with either elk doe heads or elk antlers on them. Similar staffs have been found among ancient grave goods.

To both Native Americans and Siberian people, the elk symbolizes the strength of the warrior, supernatural power, and, strangely enough, the whirlwind.

Magickal Attributes: Stamina, strength, speed, sensual passion. Like the elk herds, that for most of the year stay with their own sex, honor those of your gender. Developing strength and stamina to get a job done. Learning to pace yourself instead of pushing too hard and losing energy in a short time.

Chant

> *Majestic forest king with antlers high,*
> *Mighty strength belongs to you.*
> *Fill my mind with common sense*
> *To do the things that I must do.*

Lead me in paths of quiet calm
Where I connect with other minds,
Whose souls, like mine, yearn for the Truth
And worship higher powers divine.
Where paths to spirit are unique
To every woman and each man,
And all respect each person's way
Of following an unvoiced plan.

FERRET

This animal is a member of the weasel family, Mustelidae, and has been domesticated for many centuries. The ferret goes through a white and brown phase as the seasons change.

The common ferret is known as the European polecat, *Mustela putorius*, in some countries. It is well known in Europe, and for several centuries in the past was used in hunting. It was also common among the Romans and others who kept it to kill rats and mice. The ferret has a long slender body and a very keen desire to kill.

Several years ago, the keeping of ferrets as pets was quite popular. People either didn't know, or didn't care, that these animals were related to weasels. After being bitten several times, or the other household pets being attacked, the ferret was either destroyed or let loose, which presented another problem for the whole neighborhood.

Magickal Attributes: Ferreting out information as to the motives of others, especially when you suspect they might be harmful to you in some way. Gaining hidden information to benefit and/or protect yourself. Learning the real intent of others with whom you must interact. Seeing truth behind the facade.

Chant

Silently peering, truth I'm nearing,
Ferret-like I seek truth and light.
Lies uncovering, motives discovering,
To expose trouble-makers, make things right.

GOATS

The domesticated goat is a descendant of the Chetan ibex or pasang that ranges from southeastern Europe to southwestern Asia. For centuries they have been giving milk, cheese, and meat for food, especially in the Middle East. True wild goats are found in Europe, Central Asia, and North Africa.

The mountain goat is not really a goat, but an antelope. It is found in the Rocky Mountains of the western United States and has close relatives in Siberia. It is sure-footed, lives in high rugged areas, and can be a deadly fighter.

In Arabic lore, the goat mentioned was really the ibex. The Arabs considered that it symbolized lawlessness, straying from the correct path, and independence. Male goats were connected with the Hindu god Agni, deity of fire.

In Sumeria, the goat often appeared with hunting goddesses or as a companion to the god Marduk. Ba'al Gad, the Goat God of Palestine, was believed to be a redeemer of his people's sins. The Mesopotamians called the goat the "man-substitute," meaning it took the place of human sacrifice.

It was sacred to Dionysus, the satyrs, Faunus, and Pan, and sacrificed to Artemis at the Athenian festival of Munichia. In Lybrian rites, a goat skin (*aegis*) was draped on the statues of Athene. Dionysus Melanaigis ("black goatskin") was honored at the festival called Apaturia. The Romans considered it an unclean animal to the priest of Jupiter, who could not touch it.

Norse legends tell of magickal goats, such as the two that pulled Thorr's chariot. Heidrun was a nanny goat that lived in Valhalla and supplied mead to the heroes there. Scandinavians still make a Yule goat out of straw for the Winter Solstice; this effigy is then burned, a reminder of the ancient sacrifices.

Some country people still like to keep a few goats around. These animals are death on blackberry vines; unfortunately, they will also eat almost anything else they can get their teeth into.

Superstitions: *In Wales black goats are regarded as the keepers of treasure and friends of the faeries. If a black goat is seen on a mountain path it means treasure is hidden nearby.*

In ancient England, the corn spirit was considered to be a goat. This idea still remains in the Isle of Skye where farmers pass around a sheaf of wheat at harvest; this sheaf is called the goabbir bhacagh *(crippled goat). In Scotland this sheaf is named the lame goat.*

One superstition found in Scotland and England is that goats can never be seen for twenty-four hours straight. This is because they must take one trip a day to the devil to have their beards combed.

The devil can take the form of a goat, but the hairs of a goat's beard are a talisman to ward off the devil.

A goat skin hung from the mast was believed by sailors to ensure a calm voyage.

If injured or wounded, the goat will eat the herb dittany and be healed.

Magickal Attributes: Abundance. Removing guilty feelings of the past or present. Independence. Getting in touch with the wilder Nature energies and beings.

Chant

> *All guilt from the past, my fault or others',*
> *I release!*
> *All insecurities and uncertainties of the present,*
> *I release!*
> *I remember the painful lessons,*
> *But I no longer dwell on them.*
> *I will not deliberately hurt others,*
> *Nor will I hurt myself.*
> *I am a beloved child of the God and Goddess.*
> *My new life begins now!*

HEDGEHOG

This small mammal is not found in the western hemisphere at all, but is widespread throughout most of the old world, except for Australia and Madagascar. In Europe, the common hedgehog is best known. Its territory extends from England and Ireland all the way east to Siberia, Manchuria, and Korea. In countries where the Winters are cold, the hedgehog hibernates. In certain areas of China, this animal is considered sacred and treated with respect.

Hedgehogs are generally small enough to hold in your hand. They are usually chocolate-brown in color with yellowish-white tips on the spines. Although their spines are sharp, they are not barbed like the porcupine. With care, you can pick up a hedgehog without hurting yourself. When threatened, they curl up in a ball, spines outward, until the enemy goes away. They generally eat slugs, worms, insects, frogs, and snakes.

The hedgehog's reputation depends upon what culture you study. In China it was considered sinister. Aristotle wrote that it could predict the weather. It was an emblem of the Sumerian goddess Ishtar as Great Mother.

Small figurines of hedgehogs have been found in Minoa and Mycenae, along with their pictures painted on vases. In Greece, Rhodes, and Etruria before the sixth century B.C.E., vases shaped like hedgehogs were used for infant burials. This suggests a connection with the Goddess and her regenerating womb.

Superstitions: *The Irish said the hedgehog was a witch in disguise who sucked cows dry.*

In Europe, the hedgehog is considered to be a weather prophet. If it comes out on February 2 and stays out, the worst of Winter is over. In the United States, this is applied to the woodchuck.

The hedgehog will roll in dropped grapes, sticking them on his spines to carry home with him.

Magickal Attributes: Less defensiveness and seriousness in life. Appreciate life more. Building defenses and protective barriers that discourage negative people. Reconnecting yourself with the Crone aspect of the Goddess.

Chant

> Little hedgehog, spines atremble,
> The Mother's child, what do you fear?
> Like the hedgehog I feel defenseless
> Until I feel the Goddess near.
> Trust in Her, that's what I'm learning
> As I live life day to day.
> Mother, help me be more trusting.
> Show to me your loving way.

HIPPOPOTAMUS

Known in some places as the water horse, the hippo at one time frequented most of the large lakes and rivers of Africa. This huge mammal can weigh up to four tons. It is ten to twelve feet long and about four feet tall. The hippo has a great square head, short legs, four-toed feet, and a short tail. It is a powerful, but slow, swimmer. It spends much of its time in or near water as drying out will cause its bare, thick gray skin to crack and bleed. The hippo can float or sink and run along the bottom at about eight miles an hour. It can stay under water for as long as thirty minutes without resurfacing for air. The word hippopotamus is actually a Greek word meaning "river horse."

The Egyptian goddess Amenti was sometimes portrayed as a hippo, while the goddess of birth, Ta-Urt, was shown as an actual hippo standing on its back legs. When Ta-Urt entered her avenging aspect, she was pictured with a hippo body and a lioness's head. The hippo represented the Goddess in the water as the cow did on land. A red hippo represented the evil god Set. The Greeks and Romans knew the hippo as the beast of the Nile.

Superstitions: *Hippos will overturn boats and eat humans. They will attack humans if they are wounded or attacked themselves, but hippos only bite humans. They don't eat them.*

Magickal Attributes: Pregnancy or birth of new ideas. Righteous anger when threatened, cheated, or taken advantage of. Seeking new ideas. Justice. Mother-fury when necessary. Protection of yourself, children, family, pets.

Chant

> *River-Horse, arise in anger.*
> *Children are threatened!*
> *Great Ta-Urt, the little ones are crying.*
> *They are afraid!*
> *Cruel humans stalk and hurt them.*
> *Avenge them, Ta-Urt!*
> *All the helpless seek your aid.*
> *Protect them, great Ta-Urt!*

HORSE

The horse is from the species *Equus caballus*, which distinguishes it from the ass and zebra, who are from the same genus family. There is a great number of breeds of horses, each possessing distinctive characteristics not common to the others. The modern horse has descended from three basic stocks: the Libyan horse of northern Africa; the common horse of Upper Asia and Europe; and the Celtic pony.

This animal was known to the Babylonians as far back as 2300 B.C.E. and was used by them to draw war chariots beginning in about 1700 B.C.E. The horse was used for riding by the Greeks, Alaric, Attila, and Genghis Khan among others. It was brought to the New World by Cortez.

Because the horse was such a valuable animal, only the rich could afford to sacrifice it. This creature symbolized the Sun and the Moon, the sky and the Underworld, according to its color and the deity with which it appeared. The white horse was connected with the Moon; red, white, or golden ones with the Sun. Black horses, such as the one ridden by the Wild Huntsman, accompanied deities of death and the Underworld. The horse in general symbolized power, swiftness, wisdom, prophetic abilities, magickal powers.

In Persia, Greece, Rome, and Scandinavia the white horse was especially sacred. The Chinese Cosmic Cloud Horse, an avatar of Kuan Yin, was white, as was the horse of the Japanese deity Kwannon. The Celestial

Charger, the Horse King Ma-wang of China, was considered to be the ancestor of all horses. The Chinese Ancestral Horse was always accompanied by a dragon, a phoenix, and a crane. The Middle Eastern goddess Anahita drove a chariot pulled by four white horses that represented wind, rain, cloud, and sleet. In India, the horse signifies the cosmos, wind, sea foam, fire, and light itself.

The Romans had an annual horse sacrifice called the October Horse, or Cut Horse (*Equus curtius*). The severed bleeding tail was taken to the Temple of Vesta where the blood was allowed to drip on the altar (the closest the Vestals ever came to blood sacrifice). The chariots of Apollo and Mithras were drawn by white horses.

The Muslims call the horse a "god-sent" animal, believing it can prophesy, foresee danger, and see the dead. The *Atharva Veda* of the Zoroastrians tells of a snake-killing horse, Pedu, who was the enemy of Ahriman and the protector of the pure animals. In India, the Sun god Surya had seven red mares to pull his chariot.

Among the Norse and northern Germans, the horse was sacred to Odhinn; he had an eight-legged gray horse called Sleipnir that could run on land, sea, or in the air. The Skalds used the kenning "high-chested rope-Sleipnir" to mean the gallows on which sacrifices to Odhinn were hung; the Old Norse word *drasil* meant both horse and gallows, while *Yggr* was one of Odhinn's names. The *Eddas* mention special horses with golden manes, such as Freyfaxi.

Gray cloud-horses were said to be an alternative method of travel for the Valkyries. In the ancient festival called May Riding, a woman representing Freyja rode on a white horse, while a man representing Freyr rode on a black one. Very ancient Swedish kings were sacrificed by being ritually torn apart by horse-masked priestesses of Freyja; these priestesses were called Valkyries in the texts. The *volva*, a priestess of Freyja, was said by medieval writers to be able to transform herself into a mare. They believed the volva took on the personification of the death-goddess who rode the Valraven, a winged black horse.

Sacred to the goddesses Epona and Rhiannon, the horse was thought by the Celts to be a guide to the Otherworlds. This animal was an emblem of war and solar deities. Epona was a version of the Cretan Leukippe (White Mare), an Amazon horse goddess. The ancient Welsh horse god was called Waelsi or Waels, whom the Slavic cultures knew as Volos.

Superstitions: *Some of the older houses in Jutland still bear a double-headed horse carved into the rafters for luck. Horseshoes are widely believed to avert evil and bring good fortune; this belief is also held by the Jews, the Turks, and many others around the world. Ornaments woven from horsehair are said to protect the wearer.*

In Wales, a gray horse is considered to be a death omen, as is dreaming of a white horse in England and Germany. If you meet a white horse, you can break the spell if you spit on the ground. Gray horses and horses with four white feet are considered unlucky in racing. Non-racing horses that have spots or patches of color are said to have magickal talents.

It is a general superstition that horses will tremble and refuse to go on if they come near a dead body, even though they can't see it.

The herb moonwort is supposed to cause horseshoes to fall off the horse's feet. However, if the rider happened to be at the stones of Wayland Smithy in Berkshire, England (near the famous White Horse), he could place a coin on one of the stones. Leaving the horse there, and withdrawing out of sight, he could then expect the horse to be magickally shod.

A holed stone (known as a hogstone in England) was hung over the stable door to protect horses against witches and faeries riding them to exhaustion at night.

Originally, the tail was plaited with ribbons to keep the horse safe from witches.

Horse brasses were considered to be magickal in such far-apart places as China and Scandinavia. They were used to protect horses from witches and the evil eye.

The deeper a horse dips his nostrils while drinking, the better sire he will be.

When its master dies, a horse will shed tears.

At one time there were groups of horsemen who passed along secret words. It was believed that if these words were whispered in a horse's ear it gave the person immediate command over the animal.

Magickal Attributes: Stamina, endurance, faithfulness. It symbolizes freedom when it runs free; when it works with humans, it represents friendship and cooperation. Travel, journey, swiftness, friends, loyalty. Astral traveling. Companion and guardian when taking a trip. Guide to overcoming obstacles. Checking a situation for possible danger.

Chant

> Pounding hooves, tossing mane,
> Take me swiftly on my life's journey.
> Loyal friend, carry me to a place of safety.
> Lift me over the obstacles in my path.

MONGOOSE

The mongoose, a carnivore related to the civet cat, is of the genus *Herpestes*. This gray-brown animal lives in India, Africa, and southern Spain. It has a sharp nose, narrow body, and short legs. Its three-foot length is about half tail. This creature is easily tamed. Very agile and intelligent, the mongoose is valuable for its destruction of lizards, insects, and snakes, especially cobras.

The mongoose, or palm-rat, is found throughout the Middle East, including Egypt and India. In some legends listing the weasel, the actual creature meant is the mongoose.

The Mesopotamian goddess Ningilin was connected with this animal; this goddess was invoked in spells repelling snakes.

Superstitions: *The mongoose will always kill a cobra and is immune to the venom.* This is not true; sometimes the mongoose loses the fight and dies.

Magickal Attributes: Defense, protection, destroying evil. For the capture and conviction of criminals of any kind.

Chant

> Swiftly leaping, danger keeping
> In a corner, impotent.
> Mongoose-power, come to our
> Defense. Destroy all ill intent.
> Corner, cage, with righteous rage,

All those who threaten, harm, or kill.
Imprison, bind, those of dark mind,
Beneath the mongoose-power and will.

MOOSE

This creature is known in Europe as the "elk," *Alces alces*. There are three kinds of Old World moose which are found in the Scandinavian peninsula, Germany, Siberia, and Manchuria.

The moose is an immense black-brown or dark brown deer, which can stand as high as seven to eight feet at the shoulder and weigh up to 1,800 pounds. Its antlers can have a spread as large as seven feet. The cow doesn't have horns, and the bull is further identified by a hanging pouch of skin under the throat. Both sexes have long legs, humped shoulders, and large muzzles.

Three or four varieties of North American moose range from the Rocky Mountains in the west to Maine and north through Canada and Alaska. The moose is the giant of the deer family. It has huge flattened antlers with numerous points.

In Native American legend, the moose is thought to represent a balance between gentleness and strength.

Magickal Attributes: Wisdom, strength, shared joy. Building your self-esteem. Creating a balance between giving orders and doing things. Knowing when to say something and when to keep silent. Guidance and wisdom when approaching any touchy confrontation.

Chant

Giant dweller of forest and marsh-land,
I face a time of uncertainty.
Fill me with your confidence, your wisdom.
Teach me when to speak and when to be silent.
Help me find a point of balance and harmony
That success may be mine in honor.

MOUSE

A small rodent belonging to the genus *Mus*, this creature is usually a soft brown color. They have twitching whiskers on each side of a slightly pointed muzzle and sharp gnawing front teeth. They have keen hearing and eyesight.

Some type of mouse can be found in nearly every area of the world. The most beguiling is the American harvest mouse, which is found in fields searching for seeds and grass. It has a very long tail, builds its spherical nest in tall grasses, and swings like an acrobat on the grass.

The common mouse of older European traditions was not always held in low esteem as it is today. It was believed to be the form taken by a soul when it escaped from the lips of a dead person.

The white-footed mouse is an appealing creature with a strong curiosity. It lives in the woods and eats berries and nuts. It has a very musical voice (totally unexpected in a mouse) and often chirps.

Ordinarily a very shy rodent, the mouse can move quietly and inconspicuously through its surroundings; it can also move extremely fast if necessary.

The ancient Greek cult of Apollo Smitheus evolved from an earlier cult of the mouse; this creature is also associated with Zeus/Sabazius.

In C.E. 77, Pliny the Elder wrote that roasted mice mixed with honey would cure measles, colds, sore throats, and fever.

In Celtic folklore, the mouse is mentioned several times, as in the tale of Manawydan and Pryderi where a mouse was the shape-shifted wife of a magician.

Some people have had excellent results in getting rid of mice by slipping a note in their hiding places, asking them to leave. They only ate my note.

Superstitions: *Since mice are underground dwellers, they were thought to be connected with the Underworld and in touch with the dark powers of the deities there. However, some cultures believed that the soul took the form of a mouse at death or during astral travel.*

There are several superstitions pertaining to the origin of mice. *One is that the devil created the mouse to cause trouble in the Ark. Another says they fell to Earth from special clouds during a storm. In Germany, the people said that witches made mice.*

A mouse is considered a sign of bad luck in most places, especially if it eats your clothing.

In the Highlands of Scotland, some people wear the teeth of mice as good luck charms. They also make charmed water for cattle diseases by putting the skin, backbone, or teeth of a mouse in it.

In Germany, a white mouse is thought to be lucky and to kill one brings misfortune.

The liver of mice gets large at the Full Moon, and smaller at the New Moon.

Magickal Attributes: Secrets, cunning, shyness; the ability to remain inconspicuous; invisibility. Often, its appearance signals the need to watch small details, the fine print in contracts, or the double meaning in words. Watching for deception. Stealth, initiative, trust, innocence, change, discovery, balance, harmony. For guidance before signing any papers or making any promises.

Chant

> *Quietly creeping, accomplishing his purpose without attention,*
> *The wise little mouse trusts the Creator.*
> *Help me, small one, to trust and to find initiative*
> *So that wonderful changes come my way.*

OPOSSUM

The opossum is the only marsupial found in the United States; it is generally at home from South America to New England. Opossums can now be found even in the colder Western states.

The common opossum, *Didelphis virginiana*, of the southern United States is about the size of a cat, with a scaly, prehensile tail. It is a gray color, its fur mixed with coarse white hairs. Civilization bothers it very little. It looks rather like an oversized rat. It is bad-tempered, unresponsive, and indifferent to company, greeting nearly everything with a snarl. However, the opossum carries its young around with it until they are almost grown. When confronted with danger, it gives the appearance of being dead, even to the odor it excretes.

Native Americans considered the opossum to symbolize strategy and diversion from its ability to play dead.

Magickal Attributes: Finding yourself in a corner and creating a diversion. Dealing with the unexpected; planning strategies for protection. Are you playing 'possum and not dealing with distasteful situations? Wisdom for getting out of distasteful or dangerous situations, relationships.

Chant

> Cunning possum, Trickster changeling,
> So alive, yet seeming dead,
> Teach me wise old possum magick
> That reacts from instinct, not from head.
> Show me the way to slip past danger.
> Fill me with earthy wisdom great,
> That I might be secure and happy
> Living life and trusting fate.

OTTER

Otters are of both the fresh water and sea species. They are mainly fishermen and are skilled swimmers. They love to frolic in water, often sliding down banks into streams or ponds in play. They are playful, friendly, curious about everything, and enjoy life.

The American otter, *Lutra canadensis*, is about three and one-half-feet long and can weight from ten to fifteen pounds. It is a rich brown with lighter under parts. The otter has a broad flattened head set on a long stout neck, small ears, and a heavy tapering tail. Its short legs have webbed toes.

The otter was an important cult animal in ancient Peru and, for some reason, paired with the ocelot. The Ainu of Japan, however, think the otter is forgetful and wasteful.

To the Celts, the otter was a very magickal creature; it accompanied the god Cernunnos. Native Americans said the otter symbolized female energy because it lived in both the Earth and Water Elements. This energy could be used by both men and women. However, they also called it a Trickster being.

Magickal Attributes: Finding inner treasures or talents; faithfulness; gaining wisdom; the ability to recover from a crisis. Be sensible, but not overly suspicious, when something or someone new enters your life. Its appearance points to a need to enjoy life rather than just endure it. Social life, friends, happiness. Guidance to uncovering talents, psychic or physical.

Chant

> *Slipping, sliding, soft fur gliding*
> *Through the forest water bright.*
> *Friendly otter in tumbling water,*
> *Lead me to happiness and light.*

OXEN

An ox is really what Americans call a steer, a castrated bull. They are descended from the Old World Aurochs, or Urus, which was once found in parts of Europe and North Africa from Egypt to Morocco and Algeria. The wild species disappeared in Britain before the Romans arrived. Both sexes usually have horns.

The Egyptians and Babylonians were among the earliest peoples to use oxen. They milked cows as early as 3000 B.C.E. The ancient Chinese harnessed the ox but never milked it. However, humans have kept oxen since the earliest domestication of the animal for sacrificial purposes. In Attica and Peloponnesia in Greece, an ox could only be killed for sacrifice. This act was considered to be a murder and the knife used had to be thrown away. In both Greece and Rome the ox was connected with agricultural deities and the laying of foundations. When Roman generals returned victorious, they made an offering to Capitoline Jupiter of white oxen.

The Chinese used the ox instead of a bull in their Spring festivals and fertility rites. The god of oxen, Niu Wang (the golden-haired buffalo) was said to protect against cattle epidemics; the Chinese placed his image in stables for this purpose. In Buddhism, the white ox was considered to symbolize contemplative wisdom.

Superstitions: *If bad weather is coming, the ox will refuse to leave its stall.*

Magickal Attributes: Working patiently, strength for the long haul, prosperity. A symbol of sacrifices made or needing to be made. Gaining patience and stamina for a project that will take time.

Chant

> Like the sacred oxen at the altar,
> I have paid what price was asked.
> Now I move beyond sacrifice,
> Reaping benefits from my tasks.
> No man shall tell me what is sin.
> The Mother's judgment is between us two.
> No other's word has power o'er me,
> For under Her hands I start anew.

PORCUPINE

The porcupine is a large rodent with sharp, barbed quills mingled with the hair. Their food is primarily bark, buds, and foliage of trees. The Old World variety, *Hystrix*, and the New World ones, *Erethizon* and *Coendou*, are not closely related. The Central and South American tree porcupine, *Coendou*, has a prehensile tail. Fossils of porcupines have been found in Argentina, Europe, and Asia.

The name porcupine means "pig with spines." The Crested or Old World porcupine is found over most of Africa, all of south Asia, and throughout southeastern Europe. It is unlike its New World counterpart, although they both have quills. When disturbed, the porcupine rattles its quills on the tail in warning.

Among the Native Americans, the porcupine represents the South direction and represents faith and trust.

Porcupines can seriously damage or kill trees by eating off the bark. This is a continuing problem of orchardists whose land borders on wild areas.

Superstitions: *The porcupine shoots its quills at attackers.* Not true; the barbed quills are driven in by a sharp swing of the tail.

Magickal Attributes: Mind your own business, but be prepared to sharply defend yourself if threatened. Trust in the guidance of spirit. Creating your own path in life. Learning what to say and what not to say when caught in an argument, yours or between others. Learning to be prickly if others overstep their bounds.

Chant

> *Prickly, stickly, do not push*
> *Into my life without consent.*
> *Unasked advice has no price.*
> *Control is not good intent.*

RABBIT or HARE

Hares and rabbits are not the same animals. Rabbits bring their babies into the world naked and sightless, while those of the hare are better developed with a coat of fur and good vision. Hares also run faster than rabbits. Rabbits move in short quick spurts and are very adept at dodging. When there is danger present, the rabbit will remain motionless until the last moment before dashing away.

The rabbit, a member of the order Lagomorpha, is found in Europe, Asia, North Africa, and North and South America. In North America, the cottontail, genus *Sylvilagus*, is identified by the white underside of its short tail.

The hare, a large rabbit of the genus *Lepus*, can weigh as much as eleven pounds. They are fast-moving and can leap in great bounds. The ears and tail are much longer than those of the rabbit. The most common hare in the United States is the snowshoe hare, which changes from brown in the Spring to white in the Winter. It is generally called a jack rabbit.

The domesticated rabbit was introduced into England at an early date, probably by the Romans. Strabo wrote that ship cargoes of rabbits were brought to the Roman markets in Spain.

There is an old Teutonic legend that the hare was once a bird and was transformed into its present form by Eostra, the goddess of Spring. In gratitude for this, the hare laid eggs during the April festival of the Goddess. Our Easter customs are survivals of this ancient tradition. The North Germanic goddess Holda was said to be followed by hares carrying torches.

This creature was also sacred to the British Moon goddess Andraste; its movements were used as a form of divination. Queen Boadicea's banners were said to have the image of a hare on them. In Scotland, the word *malkin* or *mawkin* means both cat and hare.

It is also associated with other deities around the world, such as Freyja (who was accompanied by hares), Hermes (who used a hare as a messenger), Aphrodite, and Eros. The American folk tale of Brer Rabbit comes from the African Trickster deity who always outwits other animals.

Some Native Americans said that the Great Hare was the original creator of the universe; they said that the face of the Full Moon was the reflection of the rabbit in his own eye. The magickal Great Hare of the Native Americans figures strongly in many of their legends. The Egyptians knew of the story of the world-creative hare and used its picture to symbolize elemental existence.

The Hindus say the outline of a hare can be seen in the spots on the Moon. Sanskrit calls the Moon *cacin*, which means "marked with the hare." An old Sanskrit fable tells of a hare that lived on the Moon and was king of all the earthly hares; thus, the Moon deity Chandra is often shown carrying a hare. Certain European cultures said the hare was the spirit of the corn. The last sheaf of corn was called "the hare"; the peasants shaped it into the rough form of a hare and used it in rituals. To the Japanese, the hare is a very ancient symbol of long life.

The Moon Hare in China symbolizes long life and is the guardian of all wild animals. Various colors mean different things: white, divinity; red, good fortune, peace, prosperity; black, good fortune, a successful reign.

Superstitions: *The saying "Mad as a March hare" refers to the ferocious fights between male hares during the March mating season.*

During the Middle Ages in Europe, the hare came to be associated with witches and black magick; they believed only a silver bullet could kill a hare.

The left hind foot of a rabbit is thought to be a powerful charm against all evil. To work properly, it should be carried in the left pocket. If an infant at birth has its feet brushed with a rabbit's foot, it will not have accidents.

A rabbit's foot for good luck is used by many actors to apply make-up. If this is lost, disaster follows.

It is a general belief in England that a hare crossing your path brings bad luck, probably because hares are said to be witches in disguise. This idea about witches and hares is known throughout Wales, Scotland, the Isle of Man, and Ireland also. The farmers of these countries will burn the brush each year and kill all hares that they find for this reason. This connection is carried so far as people digging up, turning over, and burying the tracks of hares in the hopes of suffocating a witch.

A local witch is said to show the wounds of any maimed or killed hare.

If a hare gets aboard a ship in Scotland, the vessel is considered witch-ridden. No one will get on it until a clergyman blesses the ship again. In fact, they will not even mention the word rabbit but call it a coney instead.

The Cornish hold a belief that must strike fear into the heart of any man thinking of dumping his sweetheart. They say that if a maiden is forsaken and dies broken-hearted she comes back as a white hare. This hare is invisible to all except the guilty party who is plagued by its appearance everywhere he goes.

In the northern part of England, there is a charm used to dream of a sweetheart. Nine pins are stuck into the blade-bone of a rabbit, and the bone put under the pillow.

If a pregnant woman sees a hare, her child will be born with a harelip.

The hare never closes its eyes and changes its sex once a year.

In many parts of Britain, it is believed that saying "white rabbits" very quickly three times on the first day of the month will give you good luck for the rest of that month.

To see or kill a black rabbit is bad luck.

Poachers once believed that carrying a rabbit's foot would keep them from being caught.

Magickal Attributes: Transformation; receiving hidden teachings and intuitive messages. Quick-thinking when necessary; don't push yourself on others. A fear of disaster or illness. Sometimes the appearance of this creature signals that you need to stop worrying about your future; just take what steps you can to protect and provide for yourself. Strengthening intuition.

Chant

> Scurry, scurry, worry, worry,
> Like the hare I run about,
> Busy, busy, in a tizzy,
> I only hear the voice without.
> Quiet, hare. Do not despair.
> The voice within is strong and sure.
> If you just listen, you'll learn your mission,
> Be confident and self-assured.

RACCOON

This creature is strictly North American, ranging from the southern border of Canada all the way down to Florida. The raccoon, *Procyon lotor*, has a black facial mask running across its eyes, a bushy ringed tail, and dense grayish fur. Large adult males can weigh up twenty pounds or more. The raccoon is a very curious animal and an adept climber, making its home in hollow trees.

Native Americans called the raccoon the "black-masked little bear." It is ingenious, curious, and playful. Its home is usually around water courses, lakes, and marshes where it hunts at night. It likes to dip its food in water before eating it. Its long, extremely sensitive fingers make it possible for the raccoon to work simple catches on doors or take lids off cans of food.

The Ainu of Japan have a story that says the raccoon was created as a servant to the bear. They also have a raccoon deity called the Cook of the God of the Mountain.

Raccoons adapt quite well to city areas if they have a wooded place to which they can retreat. There are several groups of raccoons in the outlying areas of Portland, Oregon, for example. Even in our town of under 20,000, raccoons come down to the houses on occasion.

Magickal Attributes: Creativeness when faced with new problems. Be curious about the world around you. Seeking guidance and confidence for a new job or schooling. To be presented with new ideas.

Chant

> *Black-masked little bear,*
> *Show me how to be curious and open to new ideas.*
> *Introduce me to new wonders each day.*
> *Fill my mind with creativity, an insatiable thirst*
> *For learning and expanding on all levels.*

RAM or SHEEP

Rocky Mountain bighorn sheep have extremely sharp eyesight and long-range vision. They have an acute sense of smell and sharp ears. Their habitation is the rugged, dangerous terrain of the high mountains, where they gallop at breakneck speeds and negotiate nearly impossible places. Excellent climbers, these sheep can balance on the narrowest of ledges.

Sheep as a whole are considered to represent placid stupidity, unthinking conformity, and timidness. The ram, however, represented virility, fertility, and sexual prowess. The Moon was often called a shepherd, his flocks the constellations.

Sheep in general have been sacrificed to many deities; rams were particularly sacrificed to phallic deities. The Greeks and Romans sacrificed them to Zeus, Hera, Mars, Silvanus, Terminus, and Cyprian Aphrodite. They are evil to the Hindus but sacred to the Muslims. Shepherds in China have a god of sheep, Huang Ch'u-Ping, who can give them large flocks.

The ram, on the other hand, has been a symbol of virility and procreative force. In its solar attributes it was often associated with sky gods, but its horns sometimes connected it with lunar deities.

The Phoenician god Ba'al-Hammon wore rams' horns. In Babylon, Ea-Oannes was often represented by a column with a ram's head on top. In Egypt the sacred ram of Mendes was believed to embody the essences of Ra, Osiris, Khepera, and Shu. Amen-Ra was called a ram, and Khnemu was ram-headed.

In Greece, the ram was sacred to Zeus/Sabazius, the fertility god, and Dionysus, the generator of life force. The followers of Attis would bathe in ram's blood as part of certain rituals during their Mystery rites. The god Pan was closely associated with flocks and rams. Hermes, as Lord of the Flocks, carried a lamb. A ram was sacrificed to the house god Lares in Roman purification rites.

In ancient Crete, Anatolia, and the Aegean, rams having wings or three horns were often portrayed on seals and wall engravings. Three horns may associate the ram with the Triple Goddess, while the wings symbolize an animal acceptable for sacrifice to the gods.

It is the main sacrificial animal in the Islam culture, and in India it represents the sacred fire of Agni.

To the Celts, the ram was of chthonic power and connected with the Otherworlds. It was an attribute of war deities, but also accompanied the Horned God. Engravings show ram-headed serpents and rams with human heads. Ewes and their milk were associated with the Celtic goddess Brigit and her Spring festival of Imbolc, which means "ewe's milk."

The Norse god Heimdall's name meant "ram"; he was in charge of a special horn that he would blow at the end of the world.

Superstitions: *The term "black sheep of the family" has come to mean a person who is different or troublesome and goes their own way.*

Except in places like Shropshire, England, the black sheep is considered lucky. To many shepherds, a black sheep or lamb in the flock is a good luck sign. In Shropshire, though, if black twins are born it is a sign of disaster.

In many areas in England, it is believed that if you take a certain small bone from the head of a sheep and carry it you will have good luck.

In Scotland, sheep are driven under rowan hoops at Halloween and Beltane to keep away the faeries.

Sheep bow three times to the East on Christmas morning.

Some shepherds are still buried with a tuft of wool in their coffins. This is so they can be excused from attending Judgment Day and not have to leave their flocks.

Magickal Attributes: Being able to keep your balance in precarious or dangerous situations. Being confident of your abilities. Ram: fertility, courage to remain in balance in an unstable situation. Ewe: abundance, pregnancy, new beginnings.

Chant

> *Ram—*
> *Great horned ram, filled with life force,*
> *Teach me to be a "black sheep,"*
> *Going my own way, following my inner path,*
> *Not walking in the rut made by the narrow-minded.*
> *Help me to balance harmoniously in unstable places,*
> *Keeping my freedom to be me.*
> *Ewe—*
> *Little lambs are new beginnings.*
> *Let my life be full of new beginnings.*
> *Little lambs leap for joy of life.*
> *Let my life be rich with spontaneous joy.*
> *Little lambs believe wholly in the love and protection of their*
>   *mother and father.*
> *Teach me to believe in the love and protection of the Great*
>   *Mother and Father.*

RAT

The Old World rat, of the genus *Rattus*, is a smaller ground-living rodent with a long slender tail. In the United States, the most common rat is the large Norway rat. Fleas that infest rats are the principal carriers of bubonic plague. Rats have long slender bodies, pointed muzzles, a long hairless tail, and sharp incisor teeth. They can be black, brown, gray, and occasionally white.

To the Japanese, the rat is the first sign of their zodiac, a symbol of fertility and wealth. A white rat is the companion of the Japanese god of happiness and symbol of Daikoku, the god of prosperity. The Chinese, though, believe the rat represents timidity and meanness.

These creatures were sacred to the people of Phrygia, and in Egypt they symbolized wisdom. A rat is the steed of the Indian elephant-headed god Ganesha and considered to be the most powerful of all demons; even with this designation, the Hindus say that the rat represents prudence and foresight.

Superstitions: In Celtic lore, rats are not mentioned favorably. *An old Irish belief says that rats can be killed if one recites rhyming spells.*

Rats will desert a ship that is going to sink.

Rats leaving a house means the building will collapse.

Magickal Attributes: Cunning; moving silently and unnoticed; tracking down what you seek; defending yourself with aggressiveness when necessary. To gain foresight in any coming situation in order to avoid problems.

Chant

> *Cunning rat of silent creeping,*
> *Friend of Ganesha, lord of might,*
> *Guide me through mazes by your foresight,*
> *For all good things are mine by right.*

SKUNK

The skunk, *Mephitis*, is known in both Europe and the United States. They have long, thick black fur, with two white stripes running from the neck to the back legs, and a bushy tail. They are about the size of a house cat. Ordinarily, skunks are peaceable, friendly creatures. They are slow and deliberate in their movements.

When menaced, however, the skunk can emit a nasty spray that can be smelled for half a mile. Deodorized skunks are sometimes kept as pets and are very much like cats in their habits.

Friends of the family had two deodorized skunks which they kept indoors. One day the more adventuresome little male escaped and waddled off down the ditch bank before anyone knew he was gone. When Ray came home from work, he was sent to find the escapee. There on the ditch bank stood a skunk, who let Ray pick it up. Wrong skunk! Ray had to burn his clothes. Their pet skunk did come wandering back when he got hungry and lonesome.

Superstitions: *The skunk sprays its odor on its tail and then flips the droplets at the aggressor.* Not true; when that back-end faces you with the tail raised, watch out! The glands at the root of the tail have strong squirting power.

Magickal Attributes: For courage and will-power to raise a "stink" if you are being harassed or threatened. Radiating self-respect and self-confidence. Become aware of the type of people attracted to you and repel the undesirable. Sifting out and getting rid of "friends" who do not want you to succeed.

Chant

> I will not tolerate abuse in any form.
> I have power!
> I will not let others use me.
> I am a divine child!
> I will sift out friends, keeping the good.
> That is my responsibility!
> Like the skunk, I will learn when to be disagreeable.
> That is my right!

SQUIRREL

There are a wide variety of squirrels in both the United States and Europe. The word squirrel, a rodent of the family Sciuridae, is used to mean such creatures as chipmunks, ground squirrels, prairie dogs, and woodchucks. However, the word usually refers to the tree-dwelling species. Squirrels are often quite intelligent when it comes to eluding hunters. They have been known to move slowly around a tree trunk, always keeping the hunter on the opposite side.

The tree squirrel has a long bushy tail and hoards nuts for Winter. It is known for its nervous movements, rapid flight, sudden appearances and disappearances. The expression "bright-eyed and bushy-tailed" comes from the characteristics of this squirrel.

The squirrel was an emblem of the Irish queen Medb. There is an old Scandinavian legend that the squirrel is a messenger of the gods and carries news of what is going on in the world to animals in distant lands. The squirrel Ratatosk was said to dwell in the Scandinavian-Norse World Tree. Ratatosk was a mischief-maker, carrying gossip from one place to another.

Squirrels are quite clever when it comes to handling hunting cats. Several squirrels live in Rod's yard and enjoy tormenting his cat Brigit. One or two of the squirrels will keep her busy while the others continue to pack off his walnuts. They seem to take the whole affair as a game.

Superstitions: *In some parts of Europe it is said you will lose your hunting skill if you kill a squirrel.*

Magickal Attributes: Preparing for the future by storing up time, resources, and energy; resting during unproductive times. Moving to a higher level of consciousness to avoid harassment. Sometimes its appearance means changes or the approach of adversaries. Warning, wisdom, change, trust, discovery, truth, balance, harmony. Use as a spiritual watch-dog to warn you of danger on any level.

Chant

> Chatter, scold, creature bold,
> Warning all by your call.
> Discovery, change, bring within my range.
> Warnings as free, send to me.

WEASEL

The weasel is the smallest of all flesh-eaters. It is found all over the world, except in New Guinea and Australia. Weasels are relentless killers, exceedingly wary and alert. Quick and bold, they will attack animals considerably larger than themselves. Their fur is called "ermine."

A small, slender carnivore of the family Mustelidae, the weasel has a small head, long neck and body, and a slim tail with a black tip. Its fur is dark brown with white or yellowish under parts. In northern areas, the weasel's fur changes to white in the Winter. There are many species, which vary in size from that of a chipmunk to that of a mink.

Although almost universally feared and associated with evil, Egyptians considered the weasel to be a sacred animal. To the Chinese, it was one of the Five Animals, able to hear everything said and see below the surface intentions. Medieval scholars wrote that the weasel was the only other creature, besides the cock, that could kill a basilisk.

Superstitions: *If a weasel approaches a house and makes a squeaking sound, a death is near.*

If a weasel crosses your path, the day will be bad. If it is white, the day will be even worse.

In parts of Europe, they say it is impossible to catch a weasel asleep.

Magickal Attributes: Revenge, dark magick, cunning, stealth, ingenuity. The temptation to look for hidden reasons behind everything. Revenge against evil.

Chant

> *Deep, old magick of the dark,*
> *Warrior balance of the light,*
> *Teach that evil lies within,*
> *Never in the day or night.*

WOLVERINE

This is the largest member of the weasel family. The wolverine stands about a foot high at the shoulder and weighs twenty-five to thirty pounds. Its long shaggy fur is blackish-brown, with a paler brown band running on each side from behind the shoulder to the rump. It is ferocious, cunning, daring, powerful, and a thief. Even the bear, wolf, and cougar will not challenge it. It fights to win and knows no fear, regardless of the size of its opponent. The wolverine has very poor eyesight. Its scent glands emit a foul odor.

The wolverine is also known as the carcajou or skunk-bear, and a glutton because it has a ravenous appetite. Even the ancient writers Linnaeus and Pallas knew of the wolverine. Its fur is prized in the far north because one's breath will not freeze on it in sub-zero weather.

Fur trappers and backwoodsmen in Canada and Alaska know firsthand the damage and mischief a wolverine can make. These animals will break into cabins and food caches, eating all they can and urinating on what is left.

Magickal Attributes: Revenge, cunning, dark magick. Protection against attackers, on whatever level they use.

Chant

> *Muscled revenge out of the night*
> *Comes swiftly against transgressors.*
> *Beware, all those who evilly work against me,*
> *For I am a wolverine of deep magick.*
> *You cannot hide from my wrath.*
> *Stay clear of my trail and my life,*
> *And revenge will not follow you in the darkness.*

Chapter II

BIRDS &
WINGED CREATURES

All around the world birds and many other winged creatures have much the same mystical, spiritual connotations: that of spiritual messengers from the gods, higher states of being, and/or the soul itself. The fact that this universal symbolism of birds, as well as the symbolism of other animals, is similar in widely diverse cultures that have had no contact with each other points to the ancient ability to contact, understand, and use the vast reservoir of total human understanding, the collective unconscious mind.

The Egyptian hieroglyph of a bird with a human head represented the *ba*, or soul, which flew away from the body at death. This same type of "bird" was used in Greek and Roman art and had the same meaning.

The Greek writer Euripides said that birds are the "heralds of the gods," a symbolism repeated in many cultures that had never had any contact with the Greeks. The practice of divining through the songs, movements, or flight of birds probably began as a consultation of the dead, because many cultures thought birds to be vehicles for departed souls.

In Latin, the word *aves* meant both "birds" and "ghosts." Shamans from such places as Siberia, Indonesia, Central Asia, and even into the Pacific believe that communication with the dead for reasons of prophecy can be done by turning themselves into birds and flying to the Otherworld. Mayan and Aztec priests wore feathered capes, which were probably symbolic of their secret knowledge of "flying" to the Otherworld.

Eating certain birds was thought to give the consumer the bird's magickal powers. The heart of an eagle gave courage; flesh of crows and owls wisdom; the flesh of hawks keen vision. Some bird bones were made into magickal flutes used for rituals.

Celtic faeries, or fays, are associated with this ability to assume bird-form and communicate with the Otherworld. They are described, and still pictured, as having wings.

Certain seers, such as the Greek Cassandra, were given the understanding of bird language (language of the Otherworld); usually this happened after serpents licked their ears. The Teutonic hero Siegfried gained this power after tasting dragon's blood. In Germanic languages, the word for bird and magickal formula are both the same.

In alchemy, a bird swooping downward represented condensation; several birds together symbolized dissolution.

Some wild birds can be enticed to eat from your hand if you are patient. During the Winter when they are searching for food is the best time to try this. Mountain chickadees are extremely shy; I was told they would never eat from your hand. However, the children and I hand-fed them for four years before we moved. Chickadees need high quantities of protein and love peanut butter and sunflower seeds. We learned why there were some sunflower seeds dropped on the ground around the feeders. These little birds will give the seed a quick shake. If the seed is not ripened properly or the shell is empty, they throw it out.

Superstitions: *The old saying "A bird in the hand is worth two in the bush" comes from Plutarch.*

Several superstitions have to do with birds in general. *If a bird taps on a window or flies into a house, it is a message of death, especially if the bird is white.*

It is considered unlucky to have wallpaper with birds on it.

If you start a journey and a flock of birds flies on your right, it is a lucky omen; if they fly on your left, postpone the journey or it will go badly.

If a bird uses some of your hair to make a nest, you will have a headache.

BAT

Although a bat is a mammal and not a bird, I have chosen to place it in this chapter as a winged creature. There are eight families of bats peculiar to the Old World, six to the New World, and three in common to both. The most common bat in North America is the little brown bat or mouse-eared bat. It lives as far south as Mexico and as far north as trees grow. It is quite common around human habitations.

The bat is the only mammal with the power of true flight. Although they are found worldwide, bats are most abundant in semi-tropical and tropical climates. Some bats hibernate during the Winter months, while others migrate to a warmer climate. They feed during dark hours, usually spending the daytime hours in caves, hollow trees, or old buildings. Bats roost by hanging upside down, gripping a perch with their clawed feet. There are approximately 2,000 different kinds of bats. The majority of bats are harmless and beneficial as they eat large amounts of insects. Only the vampire bat feeds on blood, human or animal.

Some ancient cultures believed that bats were once a kind of bird that was changed into part human-looking in answer to their prayers. Finnish people believed that during sleep the soul often took the form of a bat, and that violent death turned the soul into a bat condemned to remain on the Earth.

Contrary to superstition, bats do not become tangled in women's hair. Nor will they stay in the hair until it thunders. This idea is probably a collective unconscious memory of the connection between bats and the Great Mother Goddess. Their high-pitched squeaks enable them to avoid the tiniest strand of wire, even in total darkness.

Bats were considered to be unlucky and unclean in some cultures, fortunate and edible in others. Because they are creatures of the night and dark places, bats are often symbolic of desolation and the Underworld.

In China, the name for bat is *fu*, which means happiness; the Chinese believe that the bat brings happiness and good luck. A drawing of two bats represents Shou-Hsing, god of long life; this symbolizes good wishes.

A drawing of five bats signifies the five blessings of health, wealth, long life, happiness, and peace.

In Japan, however, the bat symbolizes unhappiness, unrest, and chaos. To the Buddhists, it means incomplete and dark understanding.

The ancient Mayans worshiped a bat god whom they considered a very powerful deity. In Mexico, there was a city named Tzinacent Lan ("Bat City"). The bat was treasured medicine power to the Aztec, Toltec, Tolucan, and Mayan people.

In medieval alchemy, the meaning of the bat was similar to that of the dragon and the hermaphrodite.

Bats are fascinating creatures. It isn't, however, a good idea to allow them to roost in your house as their droppings can cause certain illnesses, but having bats nearby is a blessing if you are plagued by mosquitoes.

Superstitions: *Early Christians believed that when the devil was idle, he turned into a bat to harass people. The bat was also considered to be a familiar that lent its shape to witches.*

Some people believe that ghosts can take the form of bats; therefore, a house with bats in it is haunted.

Bats will deliberately tangle themselves in your hair and not let go until it thunders.

There is also a superstition that if you carry the dried heart of a bat in your pocket it will turn a bullet or stop you from bleeding to death. Another belief is if you wash your face in bat's blood you can see in the dark.

In Scotland, it is said that a flying bat, rising and then descending, does so near a witch's house. A certain tribe of southeastern Australia believe that to kill a bat shortens a man's life.

One flying near you is a sign that someone is trying to bewitch or betray you.

A bat hitting a building is a sure sign of rain.

Carrying a bat bone will ensure constant good luck. Carrying the right eye will make you invisible.

Magickal Attributes: The knowledge to avoid obstacles, barriers, and troublesome people. Undergoing a shamanistic death, which is learning to transform the old self into a new being. Releasing habits and personality patterns that keep you from progressing. Viewing past lives in order to learn how death occurred each time; using this knowledge to make you more comfortable with the life and death cycle of all life. Especially helpful when facing the death of a loved one or close friend.

Chant

> *Dark night flyer, lift me to higher*
> *Realms of life where loved ones go,*
> *That I might find joy mind to mind,*
> *My heart hurt less. I miss them so.*
> *Teach me that death can hurt much less*
> *If I accept it as no end,*
> *But see it true, just another view*
> *Of life continuing round a bend.*

BLACKBIRD

The name blackbird is applied to a variety of birds in the Old and New Worlds. The American blackbird is closely related to the robin. The male is black with an orange-yellow bill; the female is dark brown. Some species of blackbirds have a bright red patch on the shoulder, sometimes edged with white; they like marshy places. There is also a yellow-headed blackbird with a bright yellow head, neck, and breast.

In Greek stories, the blackbird and the thrush are often mentioned together. Although the Greeks considered the blackbird to be a destructive bird (probably because of its black color), they said it was sacred to the gods because of its sweet song.

Welsh legend says that the birds of the goddess Rhiannon were three blackbirds; they sat in the World Tree of the Otherworlds. These birds could sing any human into a sleep or trance.

Superstitions: *The Welsh say that two blackbirds sitting on a window sill or doorstep are a death omen. In other places, two such blackbirds are a good omen.*

Magickal Attributes: The learning of mystic secrets while in meditation. Learning trance. Doing deep, purposeful meditations.

Chant

> *Sing me a song of sleep*
> *That I may sink deep within.*
> *Within I seek the Sacred Center,*
> *That mystic place of age-old knowledge,*
> *Where dwell the divine powers of the universe.*
> *Sing me a song of peace*
> *While I walk the spiral inward,*
> *Inward to the cauldron-well of mighty visions,*
> *The ancient spring of renewing life,*
> *That place which silently calls me*

BLUE JAY

This New World bird in the genera *Cyanocitta* and *Aphelocoma* has mostly bright blue feathers varied with white; some have a conspicuous crest. Their usual cries can be melodious whistles or rasping shrieks, but they can also imitate the calls of certain other birds. There is an unrelated bird in India that is commonly called the blue jay, although it is a member of the roller family, Coracias benghalensis.

Superstitions: *Blue jays were said to spend every Friday with the devil, reporting all sins. A blue jay carrying twigs is taking fuel to the fires of hell.*

Magickal Attributes: Courage, warning, eloquence. Divination to check on future trouble-spots in your life.

Chant

> *Your cry of warning breaks the silence.*
> *Warn me, friend, of coming disturbances.*
> *Teach me eloquence of speech*
> *And the courage to say what is needed.*

COCK

In most cultures of the world the cockerel was a solar bird; however, in those of the Scandinavians, Celts, and in some Greek symbolism, this creature had Underworld connections. From earliest times, the cock has been considered a guardian and was one of the chief sacrifices to the gods. It was said to be a weather prophet, have the second sight, and could warn against approaching danger. To the Celts, the cock chased away ghosts and evil night spirits by its crowing at dawn.

Our expression "cocky" derives from the strutting behavior of the cock; each one thinks it is the very best.

The color often decided what aspect the cock represented. White cocks were sacred to Athene and Demeter and represented the Moon; but they were also associated with Apollo and the rising Sun because of their dawn crowing. Egyptian gods Anubis, Osiris, and the goddess Nephthys received sacrifices of white or yellow cocks. In Scandinavian legend there were two opposing cocks: Vidofnir, the golden, who sat at the top of the World Tree, and Fjalar, the red, who, although connected with the Underworld, lived in Valhalla. Fjalar's purpose was to sound the warning for the last great battle.

In Greece, the chariot of Hermes was drawn by cocks. The cockerel and eggs were forbidden to Greek women at the Winter festival of Apollo. The Romans sacrificed this bird to the Lares and kept them in the temple of Hercules. The cock was also an emblem of the Sun god Mithras. The Celts sacrificed the cock to the Mother Goddess Brigit.

China considered this bird to be the yang principle, a fortunate creature and a protection against fire. It was used in funeral rituals to ward off evil spirits. Although it symbolized courage, valor, and fidelity, the cock also represented war and aggression.

It is difficult to know if the cock on the weather vane symbolizes protection, as it did to the Celts, or if the Christians used it to mean vigilance.

Superstitions: *At one time all over Europe, medicine would only be administered at cock-crow or it was considered to be ineffective.*

At cock-crow all evil spirits and ghosts have to return to the Otherworld.

If a cock crows outside the back door, a stranger is coming.

A cock crowing as you leave for work means a good day.

If a cock stays on the roost, rain is coming.

White cocks are considered lucky; black cocks are said to work with the devil.

Magickal Attributes: The power of the word to dispel and repel negativity. Building walls of protection about you, your family and friends, pets, and property. Setting psychic guardians in place to warn you of problems.

Chant

> Cock, crow! Shatter evil!
> Ward this place, both day and night.
> Sound your warning! Repel danger!
> Build us a wall of brilliant Light.

CRANE

Cranes dwell in most parts of the world, except in South America. One member of the crane family is the tallest bird in the United States. Old World cranes have very ornamental plumes, which at one time were sought for human adornment. The crane dances on the tips of its toes, flaps its wings, and bobs its head when performing its courting dance.

The crane was held to be sacred in many ancient cultures. It was called a messenger of the gods, but also a weather prophet, as it will alight on the ground before a storm arrives. The crane symbolized the spiritual ability to enter a higher state of consciousness.

The bird was sacred to the Greeks as a creature of Apollo and an emblem of spring and light. The sacred Crane Dance, said to have first been performed by Theseus and his fellow bull-dancers, was a symbol of the beginning of a new year.

In China, the crane had great importance. It was called the intermediary between earth and heaven, a messenger of the gods to humans, and was said to carry souls to the Western Paradise at death. It represented long life, immortality, good fortune, happiness, and vigilance. In Japan, the crane had much the same importance and meaning.

At one time the crane was a common bird in Britain and Ireland. It was associated with the Scottish goddess Cailleach and the Irish god Manannan mac Lir; Manannan made his magick crane bag from its skin. With its colors of red, black, and white, the crane was a lunar bird, sacred to the Triple Goddess. To the Celts, the crane symbolized both the Sun and the Underworld. It was connected with solar, healing deities, but was also a messenger of death for Pwyll, king of the Underworld. They engraved pictures of the crane riding on the back of human-headed horses and around magick cauldrons.

Superstitions: *Cranes eat sand and small stones to give them ballast to fly in winds.*

You can tell a crane's age by its color.

Magickal Attributes: Intelligence, discipline, vigilance; magick; astral travel; learning and keeping secrets; reaching deeper mysteries and truths. Learning new types of magick. Astral traveling, especially in search of spiritual wisdom.

Chant

> *Like the crane, my spirit body stretches on its toes,*
> *Reaching for spiritual wisdom in higher realms.*
> *I dance a dance of joy and devotion to the gods.*
> *My astral body flies to meet them.*
> *I leap and dance with joy.*
> *Secrets to the deeper Mysteries open before me.*

CROW

In Native American legends, the crow could talk. Because of this, it was considered one of the wisest of birds. The sacred bird of the famous Ghost Dance was the crow.

In England, the species are called rooks. Crows are primarily black; however, on rare occasions a crow will be white. They are mischievous and fond of pranks. They are somewhat shy and suspicious. Fascinated by shiny, bright objects, they will steal things. However, they also attack other birds' eggs and the young. Crows are like noisy watch-dogs when potential danger invades their territory.

The jackdaw, *Corvus monedula,* is a small crow from Europe and northern Asia. It is black, but the sides of the head are silver-gray. Its eyes are white or luminous gray. It is a sociable bird, loving great numbers of this own species for company. The jackdaw can also be tamed as a pet and taught to talk.

A picture of two crows in ancient Egypt symbolized married happiness; for the Aryan cultures the meaning was the same, along with the idea of food and fertility. To the Hindus, the crow was an emblem of the god Varuna.

It is possible that the word crow came from Rhea Kronia, a Greek goddess and mother of time, who was a form of the Dark Mother, Mother Death.

Even though this bird was sacred to Apollo in ancient Greece, it was considered to be unlucky. It was said that the goddess Athene never allowed crows to light on the Acropolis, although they were sacred to her also. The Greeks believed, as do some people today, that if a crow perches on a roof it is an omen of death. In auguries, seeing a crow on the left was a warning of coming evil.

The Japanese also consider the crow to be a bird of ill luck, although they believe it brings messages from the gods.

A symbol of conflict, death, and ill-omens, the crow was associated with the Celtic goddesses Macha, Badb, and the Morrigan. The Irish word for crow is *badb*. This goddess, in the form of a crow, appeared to the Irish hero Cu Chulainn as a warning of his coming death. Branwen, sister of the god Bran the Blessed of Wales, was often portrayed in legend by a white crow. Later, the Celts came to suspect and dread crows as a form taken by faeries to cause problems. They said that the cawing of crows signified the approach of rain.

Krake, the shape-shifting daughter of the Valkyrie Brunnhilde, was said to have married the Danish king Ragnar Lodbrok and become the mother of the Norse-Germanic hero Sigurd (who was the same as Siegfried). Krake and Ragnar also had three prophetic daughters who created a magick banner called Raven (Hraefn).

In North America, the crow was considered to be the keeper of all sacred law, the one who knew the deep mysteries of all creation. Seeing a crow in certain situations was an omen of coming change. Spiritual crow power could lead a seeker to the gates of the supernatural.

The connection between the crow's foot sign and witchcraft began during the Middle Ages. People then said that magicians, and especially witches used this emblem to cast death spells. The description of crow's feet at the corner of the eyes may be a remnant of this superstition, symbolizing the aging process.

To the alchemist, the crow stood for the condition produced when the Elements had been separated out.

Superstitions: *The English have a rhyme about crows: one means anger; two is mirth; three a wedding; four a birth; five is heaven; six is hell; seven is the devil himself.*

To the natives of Northamptonshire, however, a single flying crow is an omen of bad luck instead of anger.

If crows make a hoarse, hollow sound, it means bad weather is coming. If a crow calls three times as it flies over a house, someone will die.

Crows or ravens gathering in trees in the dark, but never really settling, are souls in purgatory, according to the Irish.

In Russia it was believed that a witch's spirit took crow-form.

Another European saying about crows is: one for sorrow; two for mirth; three for a wedding; four for a birth.

Magickal Attributes: Thief, trickery, boldness, skill, cunning, single-mindedness; a bringer of knowledge. Prophecy. Learn from the past but don't hold onto it. Swiftness, eloquence. Shape-shifting. Letting go of past hurts. Learning to mentally shape-shift. Divination.

Chant

> *Prince of thieves, cunning and swift,*
> *Your black wings glide among the trees.*
> *Your harsh laughter breaks the silence*
> *As you perform your stealthy magick.*
> *I would learn your cunning and swift magickal ways.*

DOVE or PIGEON

The word dove is the name applied to a large number of birds of the pigeon family. Pigeons and doves belong to the family Columbidae. These birds range in size from the small sparrow-like ground doves to the now extinct dodo which was as large as a swan. The species known as doves are mostly colored in soft shades of brown, gray, and neutral. They usually have soft, low, cooing voices. The most common in the United States are the mourning dove and the ground dove.

The pigeon has a variety of colors and combination of colors: green, purple, magenta, orange, yellow, plain grays, brown, iridescent green, and violet. Although they coo, they also can make hooting, whistling, and booming sounds.

Not much different from a dove, the male pigeon will coo and strut even when it isn't mating season. It is a strong, swift flyer; some are homing-pigeons, trained to carry messages from one place to another. The ancient Romans and Greeks used the pigeon as food. The pigeon population has become so prolific they are now making a mess out of buildings and statues.

Long before the Christians adopted the dove as an emblem of spirit, ancient people considered this bird a symbol of the transition from one state of consciousness to another and the bringing of spirit down to earth. Sacred to the Great Mother, the dove represented peace, innocence, gentleness, and chastity.

In ancient Syria and Babylon, white doves were considered to be sacred messengers. At the Phoenician temple at Eryx, the dove was honored and protected as a companion of the goddess Astarte. Sacred doves were raised in her temples, their image carved on coins, jewels, and stelae. The Syrian goddess Atargatis held a scepter topped with a golden dove. The ancient Egyptians used the black dove or pigeon to symbolize widowhood. In the Minoan culture, the dove belonged to the Great Mother and was often shown along with snakes.

A statue from the Minoan civilization portrays a goddess with a crown of doves and horns. In Arcadia, a wooden statue of Demeter holding a fish in one hand and a dove in the other was found. Paphos Aphrodite of Cyprus was shown holding a dove.

In Greek mythology, doves fed the baby Zeus when Rhea, his mother, hid him from Cronus. A dove holding an olive branch was one of the emblems of Athene in her aspect as renewer of life. The dove was also sacred to Adonis, Bacchus, and Venus/Aphrodite. In particular, white doves were creatures of Aphrodite, Demeter, Irene, the Fates, and, oddly enough, the Furies. Homer said that both Aphrodite and Hera could transform themselves into doves.

The oldest oracle of Zeus was the Oracle at Dodona; there, a dove lived in a special oracular oak tree and was said to speak with a human voice. The seven major priestesses of Dodona were called Doves. These seven priestesses may have been physical representations of the legendary Seven Pleiades, or "doves." The Romans, believing that souls could inhabit doves, called their chambered burial sites catacombs (*columbaria*), which means dovecotes; these were sacred to Venus Columba.

To the Chinese, the dove represented long life, faithfulness, and orderliness. Ancient Japanese stories say that the dove is a messenger of war and belongs to the god of war, Hachiman. However, a dove carrying a sword announces the end of a war.

In the Hindu culture, Yama, the god of the dead, sometimes sent a pigeon or an owl to carry his messages instead of his two ferocious four-eyed dogs. However, the people of India called the dove *paravata*, connecting it with the goddess Parvati, and used it to symbolize lust.

Superstitions: *If a dove calls repeatedly from a certain direction, you will move someplace in that direction.*

If a dove calls near a mine shaft, miners won't go down as they believe there will be a disaster.

In Britain they say that a pillow made of pigeon feathers will prolong the life of a dying person.

The dove can recover its sight if it becomes blind.

Magickal Attributes: Communicating with friends and loved ones who are in spirit. Spiritual messenger between worlds. Peace, gentleness, love.

Chant

> *I send you, dove, with a message to those in spirit.*
> *Return to me with their words in your heart.*
> *O spiritual messenger, open a door of communication*
> *That our thoughts might flow as a river of love between worlds.*

EAGLE

The eagle is a bird of prey and feeds on small mammals, fish, reptiles, and other birds. A member of the genus *Aquila*, this bird occurs throughout the world, except on small islands far from other land. In the United States, there are two major eagle species: the golden eagle, *Aquila chrysaetos*, and the bald eagle, *Haliaetus leucocephalus*.

The eagle has very keen eyes and powerful wings. This bird can soar at great heights, yet see what is happening on the ground. It takes advantage of air currents to get where it wants to go. Armed with razor-sharp talons and beak, the eagle can swoop down on its prey at great speeds.

Since ancient times, it has been a symbol of war and courageous qualities. The eagle has long been considered a solar bird and a symbol of sky deities. It represents majesty, authority, spiritual power, victory, courage, and strength.

Ninurta, a war god of Assyria, Babylon, and Canaan, used the eagle as his emblem, as did the god Marduk. This bird was also shown with the Assyrian storm god Asshur as a symbol of lightning and helpful rain.

The eagle was the royal bird of ancient Egyptian pharaohs and the Greek Thebans. It was the only bird said to live on Olympus with the Greek deities. Originally, this bird was an emblem of Pan, who gave it to Zeus. Later, Roman emperors put the eagle on their legion standards as a symbol of bravery. When an emperor died, an eagle was released at his funeral. Among the recovered treasures of Crete are several gold pins with eagles on them; many modern coats of arms depict eagles.

Because of its connection with sky gods, the eagle was also associated with lightning, the Sun, and fire itself. Prometheus, who stole fire from heaven to give to humans, was connected with the eagle. The pediments[1] of Greek buildings were called *aetoi* ("eagles") because they were believed to deflect lightning.

In the East, the eagle was the bird of Indra. Garuda, the solar storm bird-mount of Vishnu, resembles an eagle in many ways. In the Persian religion of Mithraism, both the eagle and the hawk were symbols of Mithras, the Sun deity. To the Chinese, however, the eagle represented the warrior, carnage of war, fearlessness, and keen vision.

In the legends of Scandinavia, an eagle sat at the top of Yggdrasil, the World Tree. Odhinn once took the form of an eagle when he stole the poetic mead. Finnish tales say that the Supreme God could turn himself into an eagle. The Finnish-Ugrian people of Siberia considered holy any tree where an eagle built a nest for several years. Celtic tales all call the eagle a bird of wisdom and long life.

In North America, the eagle was considered great medicine power. To the Native Americans there were different kinds and divisions of eagles. The golden eagle had a very high rank. The most potent and magickal was the sky eagle which the Iroquois called Shadahgeyah. Among the Hopi, the eagle god was called Kwahu. According to Hopi legend, this great bird seldom came below the clouds; only the holiest of shamans ever saw it. Even the Aztecs said this bird represented celestial power and the rising Sun.

---

1   The triangular space that forms the gable of a pitched roof.

Nearly every Native American tribe had an eagle clan. They had songs to the eagle, eagle dances, eagle ceremonies, and even eagle secret societies. If an eagle was seen or dreamed of during a vision quest, the seeker gained special medicine or spirit power. That person then had the privilege of using the eagle symbol on a medicine shield. The eagle had the greatest power of all birds and was associated with the Sun. They believed it could live in both the spiritual and the Earth realms.

Alchemists used the symbol of the soaring eagle to denote the liberated spirit and a double-eagle to represent mercury. A crowned eagle shown with a lion symbolized quicksilver and sulphur.

Superstitions: *An ancient Irish legend says that Adam and Eve did not die, but changed into eagles and went to live on an island off the coast of Ireland.*

The Egyptians believed that every ten years the eagle flew into the fires of the Underworld, lost its feathers, but gained a new life.

The Welsh say that when the eagles of Snowden (an ancient sacred mountain there) fly over the plains, disease and death will follow.

A stolen eagle egg brings peace of mind. Please don't do this! Eagles are a protected species.

The eagle has each of its chicks stare at the Sun. If any do not, they are destroyed.

Magickal Attributes: Swiftness, strength, courage, wisdom, keen sight; knowledge of magick. The ability to see hidden spiritual truths. Seeing the overall pattern of life. Rising above the material in search of spiritual direction; connecting with powerful spiritual beings. Creating a stronger connection with spirit guides and teachers, deities.

Chant

> *Great wings outstretched in the wide skies,*
> *The eagle soars, majestic, bold.*
> *My heart cries out to the wise sky-traveler.*
> *He hears my plea.*
> *Illumination and truth come to me as his blessing.*

FALCON

There are many species of falcons. They are related to hawks and eagles. Falcons have long, sharp-pointed wings giving them the capability of swift flight. They occur around the world; in North America they have such names as the duck hawk, the pigeon hawk, and the sparrow hawk.

In old European falconry terms, the duck hawk would be called the peregrine, the pigeon hawk the merlin, and the sparrow hawk the kestrel. They are courageous and fierce for their small size.

As a bird of prey, the falcon feeds on much the same diet as the eagle. They have extremely sharp eyesight and can dive at 180 miles an hour. Peregrine falcons are found in all parts of the world. In European folklore, the falcon is credited with the power of healing.

The falcon or the hawk in Egyptian myth represents the god Horus and is called the King of Birds, instead of the eagle. Horus is often shown as falcon-headed, with his eyes representing the Sun and the Moon. This bird is also connected with Ra and Menthu.

The Greek goddess Circe, whose name means "she-falcon," had the falcon as one of her emblems. She was often called the death-bird (*kirkos*, or falcon). The name of her island was Aeaea, or Wailing, the same name applied to falcons. Released at a funeral, the falcon symbolized the soul's release from the earthly plane.

The falcon was also connected with magick and the shamanic ability to astral travel, as seen in the stories of Freyja's falcon-skin cape. Although other Norse deities borrowed this cape, the Goddess owned it. In some stories, Odhinn traveled about the Earth in a falcon-form.

Magickal Attributes: Magick, astral travel, healing, releasing the soul of a dying person. Sending energy and soul-healing to a dying person for an easy transition.

Chant

> High-flying falcon, bird of the Mother,
> Creature of Horus, the sharp-sighted one,
> Heal mind and body, emotions and spirit,
> Pour out a healing when this spell is done.

GOOSE

This bird is the member of a number of species of web-footed swimming birds in the family Anatidae. They are generally found in fresh and brackish waters around the world, particularly in temperate regions of the Northern Hemisphere. A few species migrate to the tropics in the Winter. They are larger than ducks, with a longer neck. The area between the eye and bill is completely feathered, unlike swans. The inside edges of the bill have tooth-like ridges for straining edible matter out of the water and mud. They usually are black, white, brown, and gray in color.

The goose as a sacred bird has a long history. One Egyptian creation myth says that the Nile Goose laid the Cosmic Egg which hatched out the god Amen. This may well be the source of the folk tale of the goose that laid the golden egg. The Egyptian hieroglyph for the World Egg and an unborn embryo were the same sign. This bird was also connected with Isis, Osiris, Horus, and, strangely enough, the evil god Set.

In Greece, the goose symbolized love and the good wife; it was an emblem of Hera. Under its meanings of wisdom, protection, and guardianship, it was associated with Apollo, Hermes, Ares, and Eros.

To the Chinese and Japanese, the goose was a messenger of good news; an emblem of inspiration, seasonal change, light, and married happiness.

This bird was taboo as food to both the Celts and the Norse. The horse goddess Epona was sometimes shown riding a goose with horns. The North Germanic goddess Holda was associated with the goose; an old children's story tells how she shakes her featherbed to make it snow. To both the Celts and Teutonic peoples, the goose was also an emblem of war gods.

Superstitions: *Rubbing a bald head with goose manure will make hair grow.*

The English believe that eating goose on Michaelmas Day (September 29) will ensure that you never lack money to pay bills.

Some old fishermen believe that the barnacles on a ship's bottom turn into geese.

Magickal Attributes: New beginnings, wisdom, inspiration, happiness. For a happy marriage and children.

Chant

> *Companion enduring, true loving and faithful,*
> *Send to my arms, great goose of the Light.*
> *Fill our lives with children, abundance, and joy,*
> *New beginnings in happiness. Turn back the night.*
> *A partnership equal in love and respect,*
> *That our growth be together, our goals keenly planned,*
> *Different, yet balancing, each life-step together,*
> *So no problems can shake us. We go hand in hand.*

GUINEA FOWL

The guinea fowl probably originated on the African coastal region of Guinea. It is part of the family Numididae, but is properly called *Numida meleagris*, the helmeted guinea fowl. It has a bony proturbance on its unfeathered head. The skin is blue and white with dark gray feathers speckled with white.

Guinea fowl are the watch-dogs of the bird world with their harsh cackling sound. For this, and other sacred reasons, the birds were kept at the Acropolis in Athens. Legend says that the sisters of Meleager were turned into guinea fowl. In ancient Greek legends they are connected with amber; Sophocles wrote that they wept amber. At the December Saturnalia, these birds were part of the gifts thrown to the people, but it is not reported whether they were alive when this was done.

Magickal Attributes: Protection, warning. Use as a spiritual watch-dog and protector.

Chant

> *Speckled watch-dog, sound a warning*
> *Whenever danger does appear.*
> *Defend my family and myself*
> *If threats and evil ones come near.*

HAWK

The hawk is related to the falcon and combined in the family Accipitridae. They are subdivided into such groups as perns, kites, buzzards, eagles, Old World vultures, and harriers. However, the name hawk usually refers to the sparrow hawks of the Old World, goshawks, sharp-shinned American hawks, and Cooper's hawks. They are found throughout the world except for antarctic regions.

A bird of prey, the hawk has very sharp eyesight, can use air currents to its advantage, and can strike swiftly. This bird has a sharp, hooked bill and strong talons. Many hawks have a variety of plumage colors which change from year to year during their early lives. Some species mate for life.

The symbolism of the hawk is much the same as that of the eagle and the falcon. As a solar bird, in Egypt it was associated with Horus, Ptah, Rehu, and Seker. When in his aspect as conductor of souls, Horus was shown with a hawk's head on a human body; this aspect was called Heru-merti. However, the hawk was also connected with Amenti in her aspect of Underworld Great Mother.

According to the Greek writer Homer, this bird was one of the messengers of Apollo because of its swiftness. Both the hawk and falcon were also associated with the goddess Circe. Although the hawk was usually associated with the Sun, a very early statue from the temple of the Moon goddess Artemis shows a priestess with a hawk on her head.

In the one of the legends of India, the hawk Gayatri brought soma from heaven for the gods. In the *Rig Veda*, the Sun is often compared to a hawk. Indra sometimes rode on a hawk. In Persian Zoroastrianism, the hawk was connected with Ahura Mazda, god of light, and Mithras, the Sun god.

In Celtic oral tradition, the Hawk of Achill is listed as the oldest creature in the world. The Celts considered the hawk to be a messenger between the Otherworlds and this existence. In magick, they said it had greater skill and strength than any of the other birds.

Superstitions: *In most of Europe the hawk is still looked upon as a symbol of good luck.*

The hawk throws its young out of the nest and won't feed them any longer when they can fly.

Magickal Attributes: Clear-sightedness; being observant. Far-memory, or recalling past lives. A message from spirit; omens and dreams. Overcoming problems. Taking advantage of an opportunity. The cry of a hawk in a meditation is a warning of upcoming situations that will require boldness and decisiveness. Courage, defense, wisdom, illumination, new life, creativity, truth, experience. Getting a larger over-view so you can make better decisions.

Chant

> Soaring, gliding, wind current riding,
> Hawk of wisdom, creativity.
> Seeking, hover, bright Sun-lover,
> Bring inspiration now to me.

HERON

The name heron is applied to a large number of small or large wading birds in the family Ardeidae; they are related to storks and ibises. These birds live in temperate and tropical areas of marshy or salt water around the world. All herons have a long, slender neck, a long, pointed bill with sharp edges, and long legs. Their plumage may be colored black, white, brown, gray, blue, chestnut, buff, or combinations of these. Although the heron is a timid bird, it will defend itself with its sharp beak if cornered.

In mystical symbolism, the heron, stork, and crane represent much the same things. They are all solar and Water birds that are said to be able to predict the weather. They represent vigilance and are valuable as destroyers of reptiles.

In Greece, the heron was sacred to Athene and Aphrodite, carrying their messages to humans. In both China and Japan, the white heron is teamed with the black crow to symbolize solar-lunar powers. Ancient Egyptians associated the heron with the rising Sun and the return of the resurrected god Osiris. It signified regeneration of life.

In the Celtic cultures the heron had many of the attributes of the crane.

Superstitions: *It is a general European belief that to shoot a heron is bad luck.*

Magickal Attributes: The ability to watch patiently for results. Dignity of movement, methodical procedure in matters. Gaining dignity and self-confidence for facing personal problems.

Chant

> *From the stately heron I learn dignity,*
> *Patience to wait for proper timing.*
> *By example I see the sense of methodic planning.*
> *One step at a time, personal problems are solved.*

HUMMINGBIRD

This beautiful iridescent bird is found only in the Americas. There are hundreds of species of hummingbirds. Except for some large species in the jungles of South America, this creature is extremely small, some no bigger than bumblebees. It is the only bird capable of backward flight; its wings can beat fifty-five times a second. It has a very thin, long beak and a long tongue, making it possible for the bird to feed while suspended in the air.

A fearless thing for its size, the hummingbird exhibits superb precision flying, especially during ferocious battles between males during the mating season. I've seen our cats creep along the side of the house rather than expose themselves to the high-speed bombing runs of humming-birds streaking between the porch railings.

The Mayans associated the hummingbird with the Black Sun and the Fifth World of their legends. Their deity Quetzalcoatl was considered to be a hummingbird god and, as the Feathered Serpent, wore its plumes. Although the feathers of this bird were used in love charms, the Aztecs had a war god, Huitzilopochtli ("the hummingbird on the left"), who wore a crown of these plumes.

Superstitions: *It is believed by many that hummingbirds migrate by hitching rides on larger birds.*

Magickal Attributes: Happiness, love, relaxation. Don't be so judgmental. Love and happiness in your life.

Chant

> Fierce tiny bird of the bright rainbow feathers,
> I see you speeding, darting, hovering.
> Like a hummingbird I am confident.
> I fear nothing, for the Gods are with me.
> I flit among the beautiful flowers of life,
> Content to do what must be done,
> And living my life to the fullest.

IBIS

The ibis is a medium to large-sized wading bird in the family *Threskiornithidae*; it is related to storks and herons. Ibis are found in the warmer climates of both the Old and New Worlds. The ibis has a long, downward curved bill. Although it usually is colored black, gray, white, or a combination of these, a few species have patches of brighter color, such as the scarlet ibis of the American tropics.

The ibis was an important symbolic creature to the ancient Egyptians. Thoth, god of the Moon and wisdom, was portrayed with an ibis-head. Thoth was the consort of Maat, goddess of truth. Because of his function as guardian of the Moon Gates, Thoth was believed to be a deity of magick, spells, writing, and record keeping. Ancient stories tell how Thoth hovered over the Egyptian people in the form of a sacred ibis, and taught them the occult arts and sciences. The ibis was also sacred to the goddess Isis.

Superstitions: *Medieval scholars thought the ibis cleaned out its bowels with its beak and was afraid of water.*

Magickal Attributes: Magick on a spiritual level. Wisdom, enlightenment. Learning magick and spellworking. Wisdom to understand and properly use the ancient deep magicks.

Chant

> Holy ibis, stalking the Nile,
> Hear my call.
> Messenger of Thoth [toe-th], guide me to ancient wisdom,
> Show me the path to take.
> Take me to the secret inner places
> Of deep Mysteries and initiations.
> Holy ibis, reveal to me the golden door
> Of forgotten spiritual knowledge.

LOVEBIRD

The name lovebird is applied to a number of small, short-tailed parrots, mostly those of the African genus *Agapornis*, but also to the Asiatic *Loriculus* and the tropical American *Forpus* and *Brotogeris*. These are what was known as Old World parrots. They are very affectionate toward their mate. The gray-headed lovebird is commonly kept as a caged pet.

Superstitions: *If one of a caged pair of lovebirds dies, the other will not live long.*

Magickal Attributes: Love, companionship, marriage. Drawing a loving companion into your life.

Chant

> Lovebirds cooing, true love wooing,
> Bring a lover to my heart.
> One so kind and tender, I will not wonder
> If he/she ever will depart.

MAGPIE

The magpie is a songbird of the crow family. It has a long, graduated tail and is pied in color. The common magpie, *Pica pica*, occurs in various forms from the British Isles to China, and from the shores of the Pacific to the Great Plains of North America.

This black and white bird collects shiny objects, as crows do. It is a cheeky, bold creature with a raucous call. It is intelligent, can be tamed and taught to talk.

In the Eastern cultures, the magpie was considered to be a bird of joy and good fortune. In the West, however, it is an ill-omened bird and a symbol of trouble between spouses.

Superstitions: *The people of Somerset, England say that you must lift your hat to a magpie or bow to him, else evil will follow you.*

Split a magpie's (crow's or jackdaw's) tongue to make it able to talk. This is untrue, and a cruel thing to do.

Magickal Attributes: Omens and prophecies; the mysteries of life and death. Divination of any kind.

Chant

> *Cheeky, bold, with raucous call,*
> *The magpie sits above the well*
> *Of inspiration and divination.*
> *Bird of power, my future tell.*

NIGHTINGALE

This name is applied to two species of thrushes in the genus *Luscinia*. *L. megarhyncha* breeds from the British Isles across Europe to southwestern Asia. The other, *L. luscinia*, has a range that does not reach western Europe. The upper part of the nightingale's body is russet brown but redder on the tail; the under parts are grayish brown and paler on the throat and belly. They are shy birds, but famous for singing in the moonlight.

This bird was associated with certain rites of Adonis and Attis, the savior-resurrected deities. To the ancient Greeks it was a symbol of the Muses. Persian literature calls it the *bulbul*.

Superstitions: *The nightingale only sings at night.* Not true; it also sings during the day.

Magickal Attributes: Inspiration, using your talents with joy. Moon magick.

Chant

> *O nightingale, who from the Moon*
> *Has learned strong magick ages old,*
> *Teach me Moon magick. Singer sweet,*
> *Teach me to weave Moon powers bold.*
> *Instruct me in the wisdom ancient*
> *That will help me ride the tides of life.*
> *Open my heart and soul to magick,*
> *To fill my days with joy, not strife.*

OSTRICH

A native of Africa, this bird is the largest of living birds and flightless. It once lived in Syria, Arabia, Mongolia, and China. This bird is listed in a separate family, Struthio camelus, but is related to the emus, rheas, and cassowaries. An adult male can stand eight feet tall and weigh as much as 300 pounds. It has two toes on each foot. The head and neck of the ostrich have only short feathers; the thighs and legs are bare. The black, white, or grayish-brown plumes of the body were esteemed as ornaments for thousands of years.

The ostrich can outrace most enemies. It has a vicious kick that can disembowel a human and some animals. It will eat almost anything.

The Semitic and Babylonian cultures considered the ostrich to be a demon, evil, and connected with the Dark Goddess Tiamat. The Arabs still regard it as a stupid bird, whose form can be usurped by a djinn.

However, in ancient Egypt the ostrich had great spiritual and religious significance. An ostrich feather symbolized the goddess Maat, deity of truth and justice; the heart of the deceased was weighed for truth against Maat's feather in the Judgment Hall of Osiris. Those who passed the test went into Osiris's presence; those who failed were cast into the Netherworld of darkness. The ostrich feather was also an emblem of the goddess Amenti and the god Shu.

The Kung Bushmen of Africa said that the eggs of this bird had supernatural power, and they performed ritual ostrich dances to honor it.

The South American ostrich, which differs from that of Africa and the East, and is not related to them, was connected with the dead. An ostrich dance was performed by several South American peoples to keep the dead from causing harm.

Superstitions: *Contrary to folk legends, the ostrich doesn't bury its head in the sand.*

In America, actors consider ostrich plumes bad luck. They won't allow either ostrich or peacock feathers in the theater.

Magickal Attributes: Spiritual truth, protection from troublesome spirits. Exorcisms.

Chant

> *Bird of Maat* [may-at], *feather of Light,*
> *I call to you!*
> *Symbol of truth that banishes night,*
> *Be my defense!*
> *Sweep away all evil power*
> *And protect me!*
> *Shelter me in this dark hour.*
> *Destroy the evil!*

OWL

A nocturnal bird of prey in the families Tytonidae (barn owls) and Strigidae, these birds are related to the goatsucker and guacharo. They are found nearly everywhere in the world. Owls have hooked beaks and curved talons. They range in size from about five inches to over two feet. They have a variety of color combination, such as black, white, gray, brown, buff, and reddish. Their eyes are quite large for seeing in the dark, and their face is surrounded by a disk of feathers. Their calls vary from cackling to low-pitched hooting.

Since ancient times, the owl has been associated with wisdom, deep learning, and the Underworld deities. Later, it came to be connected with black magick. It is a bird of prey and a night hunter. The owl is a powerful, noiseless flyer with good hearing and sight.

The owl is armed with vicious talons and beak for protection and hunting. It is so alert to its surroundings that it appears to turn its head completely around when watching something.

The owl was early on a creature of the Great Goddess. It was often combined with the goddess figure to make an owl-woman in early matriarchal cultures, such as Le Tene. Stelae, figurines, and amulets belonging to the Megalithic era of France, Spain, Portugal, and Great Britain show a goddess with great staring eyes; this figure has come to be referred to as the Eye-Goddess.[2]

In Peru and Ecuador, the owl image decorated spindle whorls along with a birth-giving goddess. In Crete, during the third millennia B.C.E., jug-vases shaped like a winged owl with female breasts were a ritual vessel; the breasts were perforated for pouring.

Originally, such Middle Eastern goddesses as Mari, Lilith, and Anath were closely connected with owls. A Sumerian relief of the goddess Lilith shows her naked except for a horned tiara; she has owl-clawed feet and is accompanied by owls. The Hebrew translation of this goddess's name is "screech owl."

---

2 This term wasn't used until after the 1957 publication of *The Eye Goddess* by O. G. S. Crawford.

As the patriarchies gained control, people began to believe the owl, and the goddesses with which it was associated, was an ill-omened bird whose form could be taken by an evil spirit. Babylonians said that hooting owls were the souls of dead mothers crying for their children. This gradually changed into the owl being an evil spirit which prowled the night and carried off children.

In Egyptian hieroglyphs, the owl signifies death, night, the black Sun in the Otherworlds.

There are differences of opinion as to whether the Chinese and Japanese considered this bird to symbolize evil and death. The Ainu of Japan, however, did call this bird "beloved deity."

Athene/Minerva had an owl as her sacred familiar; its image was cast on coins to represent the city of Athens. Homer writes that Pallas Athene was sometimes portrayed with an owl-face. The Etruscan god of night and darkness was associated with the owl and death; the Romans adopted this view of the bird, saying that it was prophetic but its hooting prophesied death and misfortune. In Latin, the owl was called *strix* (pl. *striges*), a word which later changed into the Italian word *strega* for witch.

To the Celts, in general, this bird was a sacred magickal creature, sometimes called the Night Hag and the Corpse Bird. It symbolized Underworld deities, such as the Welsh god Gwynn ap Nudd, and the Welsh Moon goddess Blodeuwedd.

The messengers of the Hindu death god Yama were usually two dogs, but occasionally he would send an owl as his messenger.

The Scottish Gaelic word *cailleach* means "owl"; this word connects it with the goddess Cailleach, who was a deity of death. The owl is identified with many Crone or Underworld goddesses in Europe and the Mediterranean area. During the Middle Ages, the owl became known as the Night Hag.

This bird was called the Night Eagle by Native Americans. Most of them believed the owl was a bird of sorcerers. However, the Cherokees held sacred both the owl and the cougar for their ability to see in the dark. They said the owl brought messages at night through dreams. This creature was the Chief of the Night to the Pawnees, who said it gave protection.

Superstitions: *Many cultures believe that to see an owl is unlucky, while others consider this bird to be a messenger and guide, particularly in spiritual affairs.*

Supposedly owls see in total darkness; the truth is they must have some light just as cats do. They are not blind during the day.

If you look into an owl's nest, you will be unhappy the rest of your life.

In Wales they say that if an owl hoots around houses, an unmarried girl has lost her virginity.

In France, if a pregnant woman hears an owl, the child will be a girl.

Magickal Attributes: Silent and swift movement; keen sight into obscure events; unmasking those who would deceive you. In meditation, often a guide to and from the Underworld. Wisdom, magick, darkness, freedom. Dreams, shape-shifting. Clairvoyance, astral projection, magick. A messenger of hidden truth, secrets, and omens. Moon magick. Wisdom to make positive changes.

Chant

> *Soft darkness of night, a time of deep magick,*
> *Your realm, great owl whose eyes see reality in the darkness.*
> *I would call up wise and deep magicks,*
> *Magicks bold and strong, creating change.*

PARROT

The parrot makes up a large number of species belonging to the family Psittacidae, which includes cockatoos, lories, macaws, and lovebirds. They live in tropical and subtropical regions. Parrots have stout hooked bills and prehensile toes. The plumage is usually in brilliant colors. They can learn to imitate human speech. A friend of ours had a parrot who learned to sing opera by listening to records. This was fine until a woman visited with a whining child. Punkie added this whining, crying sound to her repertoire along with laying her head on the perch, imitating the child's tantrums.

Kama, the Hindu god of love, had a parrot as his emblem. To the people of India this bird was prophetic and a bringer of rain. The Roman writer

Ovid talked about a parrot cult in Rome, although very little is known about it. Parrots were carried in Ptolemy's procession at Alexandria.

There are four leading Hopi clans of Native Americans. In these clans, the Bear Clan is first in importance, followed by the Parrot Clan. To the Hopis, this bird represents the South and fruitfulness. It is called the Mother of the Hopis.

To "parrot" something is to repeat a conversation, opinion, or action of another, without thinking about what you are saying or the meaning behind it.

Superstitions: *All parrots can talk.*

A parrot's beak is so strong that if dropped on the closed beak, it won't be hurt.

Magickal Attributes: Imitation, mockery, unintelligent repetition of something. Think carefully before you speak. Don't repeat gossip. Guidance and wisdom to think before you speak.

Chant

> *Talking, singing, always repeating,*
> *Every single thing you hear.*
> *Teach me to think before I speak,*
> *And bring no word-harm, O Goddess dear.*

PEACOCK

Native to the East Indies and southeastern Asia, the peacock is an unusual bird. The male has long tail-feathers with "eyes." A very vain bird, it has a disagreeably shrill cry like a person screaming. The peacock is actually a large pheasant of the genus *Pavo*. The blue peafowl, *P. eristatus*, is native to India and Sri Lanka, while the green peafowl, *P. muticus*, lives in Indo-China and Java. The males may measure seventy-eight to ninety inches from the head to the tip of their long, trailing tail.

There was a Peacock Throne in ancient Babylon, where these birds were kept as sacred creatures. Up until the overthrow of the Shah of Iran, that country also had a Peacock Throne. In Persia, the peacock specifically denoted royalty.

The largest bird in the Old World, next to the ostrich, the peacock is shown in Egyptian art as a companion of Isis. It was also sacred to the goddess Hera/Juno, and before her the Etruscan goddess Uni. The Greeks and Romans said that the "eyes" on its feathers symbolized the fifty priestesses who served each temple of this goddess. Juno's priestesses had fans of peacock feathers (*flabelli*) that they carried to denote the goddess.

The peacock was a sacred bird in China and Japan, representing dignity, rank, and beauty. As an emblem of the Ming dynasty, the peacock feather was awarded to show imperial favor and high rank.

As a Bird of Paradise (soul-bird) and a symbol of good luck, the peacock was, and still is, allowed to wander the grounds of Indian temples and royal gardens. There is an old Hindu saying that the peacock has angel's wings, a devil's voice, and a thief's walk. It is, however, considered to be a lucky bird because it warns of danger and intruders.

Sometimes the Hindu goddess Sarasvati was shown accompanied by or riding on a peacock. This was also true of the god Brahma and the goddess Lakshmi. When the god Kama was portrayed riding this bird, it represented impatient desire. The peacock is said to dance when rain is coming and to hate gold.

During the sixteenth century in Europe, liars, cheats, and traitors had to wear a peacock feather.

Superstitions: *The folk saying "strutting like a peacock" or "proud as a peacock" refers primarily to males, but can apply to women who dress in flashy clothes and act as if they are the center of everyone's admiration.*

The bad luck associated with peacock feathers originated from the peacock's status as a protected and revered creature of the Great Goddess. A great many actors believe that peacock feathers bring bad luck to the play and will not allow them in the dressing-rooms or even in the theater.

In much of England, to bring a peacock feather into the house is to bring in illness and death.

The "eye" on the feather is associated with the evil eye which can cause terrible things to happen.

The peacock's flesh is so hard it won't rot.

Magickal Attributes: Dignity, warning, self-confidence. Use the symbol of the peacock "eye" to see into the past, present, and future.

Chant

> *The peacock's eye I see before me,*
> *A door to present, future, past,*
> *A guide to divination true,*
> *A spiritual power that will last.*
> *My inner eye is like the peacock's,*
> *Open to the tide of life,*
> *Whether it be joy or sorrow,*
> *Success or change, abundance, strife.*

QUAIL

The term quail covers a number of small birds in the genus *coturnix*. They tend to live in temperate and tropical regions almost throughout the Old World, including Australia. The migratory quail, C. *coturnix*, breeds in northern Europe and winters in the tropics. The quails of the United States, such as the bobwhite and others, are only distantly related to the European quail.

A flock of quail will always have one bird as a lookout while feeding. This guard will chatter to the others, warning them of approaching danger. I've watched quail toy with my cat for long periods of time, the lookout bird telling the others where Flash was, the flock staying just beyond his reach.

The symbolism of the quail covers a wide area of the world, from Ireland to China and Japan, and from Northern Europe to Central America. It was considered to be a night bird and was associated with the Fire Phoenix by the Chinese. In some cultures, the quail symbolized Spring and good luck, while in others it meant Summer. Many times this bird was classified as erotic and phallic.

The quail was an emblem of the Greek deities Apollo and Artemis because Hera had turned their mother, Leto, into a quail. The goddess Astaeria was also changed into a quail at one time. The Romans associated it with courage and victory in battle.

Among the Phoenicians, eating quail was taboo. It was, however, sacrificed in a Spring festival to Hercules, to the god Ba'al, and to the god Melkart because he defeated the evil Typhon.

To the Hindus, this bird was a symbol of the returning Sun each year. In Hindu legends there is the story of the Asvins reviving the quail that had been swallowed by the Great Wolf of Darkness and Destruction. This probably refers to the returning Sun symbolism.

When Russia had ruling royalty, the quail was an emblem of the Tsars. However, the bird appears in early myths as a symbol of the Sun found by the Dawn Maiden.

The Mayans sacrificed the quail to certain of their gods.

Superstitions: *It was believed that quail fattened themselves on poisonous seeds. Aristotle said that they ate henbane and hellebore.*

Magickal Attributes: Good luck, courage, victory. For success in a project.

Chant

> Bring me victory, little quail.
> Grant to me success in my plans.
> Guard my steps, warning of dangers.
> Shower me with good luck and happiness.

RAVEN

This name applies to a number of species of large crows, members of the genus *Corvus*, but especially to *C. corax*. Ravens inhabit nearly every region throughout the Northern Hemisphere. The raven has jet black plumes, glossed with green and purple; it has a dismal croaking. These birds are intelligent, adaptable, ingenious, and mischievous. Ravens are bold birds, and extremely noisy when disturbed. Like crows, ravens are curious creatures and will pack off shiny objects. They will also feed on anything dead, just like a vulture.

An ambivalent bird, the raven is connected with prophecy and wisdom. They were believed to be able to find lost things; this was known as Raven's Knowledge, but the bird was also associated with darkness, death, and evil.

In China and Mithraism, it represented the Sun, while in many western cultures it symbolized death. This bird often appeared with deities of the dead, such as Odhinn's two ravens. The Danes have a legend concerning King Morvran ("Sea-Raven"), who was a son of the Underworld goddess. To the ancient Egyptians this bird signified malevolence and destruction. During the Middle Ages it was said to be a familiar of witches.

Ovid told of a legend that said the raven was at first silver in color, but turned black because of its delight in carrying evil news. Ravens were supposed to have prophesied the deaths of Cicero, Plato, and Tiberius.

In Greek myth the raven was a messenger of Apollo. It was also associated with Athene, Cronus, and Asclepias. In later Orphic art, the raven, when shown with a pine cone and a torch, symbolized death and resurrection.

The followers of Zoroaster called it a pure bird. This idea was adopted by Mithraism, which called its first grade of initiate the Raven.

Representing power and the Sun in China, this bird was one of the animals of the Twelve Terrestrial Branches. Hindu myth says that Brahma once appeared as a raven.

In Ireland, the raven was associated with the Morrigan and other battle or death goddesses. Badb, the Raven of Battle, was a goddess of war and bloodshed. The Morrigan was a raven deity who gloried in battles;

she could assume the forms of a hag, a beautiful woman, or a crow or raven. The continental Celts had a goddess Nantosuelta whose symbols were ravens and doves. The god Lugh had two magickal ravens as companions.

In Welsh, *ubran* means "raven," the name connecting it with the god, Bran the Blessed. One of the greatest heroes in Welsh legend was Owein, who had an army of magickal ravens that fought King Arthur's men. Although an important totem animal of the Celts, the raven was considered to be of dubious reputation, and they took great care when dealing with it. Ravens were scavengers, one of the birds that frequented battlefields and feasted on the dead. If a raven had any white on it, the bird was considered to be beneficial and not malevolent.

Ravens were creatures of the Norse-Germanic Valkyries, who wore their black feathers when they fulfilled their task as Choosers of the Slain. The Germans called the raven *waelceasig* ("corpse-choosing") and a Valkyrie *waelcyrge*. The skalds, Nordic poets, had a number of *kennings* (metaphors) for the raven: "blood-swan," "blood-goose." They also called dead warriors "feeders of the ravens."

To Native Americans, the raven could see everything and had the ability to find hidden things. It was considered a magickal creature, with its black coloring symbolizing spiritual paths. The raven was a shape-shifter, a bird of ceremonial magick and healing.

Superstitions: *In Cornwall, the croaking of a raven over a house means bad luck is coming. They also say that to kill a raven is a crime, for King Arthur still lives in the form of a raven.*

Sailors believe that killing a raven, like killing an albatross, brings bad luck.

Scottish deer hunters believe that hearing a raven croak before they begin hunting will bring them success.

The English believe that if the ravens desert the Tower of London, the reigning family will die and Britain will fall.

It refuses to feed its young properly until they develop the black feathers.

Magickal Attributes: Help with divination. Often represents the upset in life necessary to create something new. Wisdom, eloquence, magick. A change in consciousness. Messages from spirit; something unforeseen but special is about to occur. Magick of the Crone. Divination.

Chant

> *Wing so black it shines like Moon at midnight,*
> *O Raven strong, hear my cry!*
> *Teach me old magick, powerful, bold,*
> *O Raven, eloquent and wise.*

ROBIN

Originally, the name given in England to the redbreast. In North America, this name is applied to the thrush, *Turdus migratorius*, a species related to the Old World blackbirds. On the American robin, the top and sides of the head are black, the upper parts slate gray, the throat white streaked with black, and the breast red. It has a beautiful song.

The robin is mentioned in several cultural mythologies, but in a vague sense. In Norse legend, however, this bird was considered to be a storm creature and was sacred to the storm god Thorr.

Robins are very combative in the spring. One year we watched a robin fight his reflection in the car's hubcap for several days before he gave up.

Superstitions: *The Irish say that if you kill a robin, a large lump will grow on your hand, making it impossible for you to work.*

In Yorkshire, they believe that if you kill this bird your cows will give bloody milk. If you break one of its wings, you will break your arm.

If a robin taps on the window of a sick room, that person will die.

When you see the first robin of the year, make a wish before it flies away. Then you will have good luck for the next twelve months.

Magickal Attributes: Happiness, new beginnings. For guidance in beginning a new cycle of life.

Chant

> *The robin red is a sign of Spring,*
> *A new cycle brought in on his wings.*
> *New beginnings, hope anew,*
> *Show me the way. Point out the clue*
> *That sets my feet on the proper path*
> *To find my new-born place at last.*

SEA GULL

A number of species of web-footed sea birds of the genus *larus*; related to the terns. They live primarily in the arctic and temperate regions around the world. The adults are mostly white with patches of gray, brown, or black. A few species live inland on lakes and marshes, but most gulls stay around salt water.

The sea gull can soar on the air currents over the ocean waters with grace. However, it can also be a nuisance. The sea gull is an avid scavenger, preying on eggs and the young of other birds. It will eat almost anything. Its raucous scream is part of the atmosphere of the coastline.

Although not mentioned in the Celtic legends, the sea gull was connected with the Celtic god Manannan mac Lir and the Welsh goddess Don. Like other birds, they were considered to be messengers from the Otherworlds to humans.

Superstitions: *Some sailors believe that killing a sea gull is to court bad luck for the rest of your sailing career.*

Magickal Attributes: Spiritual messengers. Opening yourself to communication with deities.

Chant

> I rise on spirit wings.
> Like the sea gull, I soar over the waters of life.
> I glide to Otherworlds
> Where the powers of the Old Ones are strong.
> I open my heart and mind to the gods.
> Their messages are clear to me.

SPARROW

This species of small songbirds is combined in the genus *Passer* of the family Ploceidae or weaverbirds. In the United States and Canada, the name sparrow is applied to a variety of finches in the family Fringillidae. The best known species is the *P. domesticus*, or English sparrow which ranges from Britain to Burma; it was introduced into the United States in 1850.

To the ancient Greeks the sparrow was a creature of Aphrodite, goddess of love; it was also associated with Lesbia of the island of Lesbos. Probably because of its connection with love deities, the sparrow came to symbolize lust, wantonness, and fertility.

Superstitions: *The sparrow was consecrated to the Roman Penates, making it sacred. Today there is still the belief in many countries that killing this bird brings evil upon you.*

Never catch or cage a sparrow or you will be unlucky.

In several areas of Britain, the sparrow is regarded as a symbol of the friendly spirits of the household and is cherished.

Magickal Attributes: Love, desire, fertility. Getting pregnant. Bringing a love into your life.

Chant

> I wish a child, a gift of love,
> To come to me. My heart will move
> In dances of both joy and care.
> My arms are full, no longer bare.
> Promise I give to protect and bless
> A baby in my life at last.

SWALLOW

The swallow is a member of a species of songbirds in the family Hirundinidae. They live in temperate and tropical zones in both the Old and New Worlds. The swallow has a slender body, long pointed wings, and a large mouth for catching insects in flight. Their voices are twittering and unmusical. This bird is highly migratory and the most graceful and attractive of songbirds.

Although the swallow was associated with the goddess Aphrodite, the Greeks considered it unlucky. In Rome, however, where it was a symbol of Venus, the bird was regarded as lucky and a creature that carried the souls of dead children. In northern Europe, the fork-tailed swallow was a symbol of Spring and love, therefore sacred to the May Queen. In ancient Chaldea, there are carvings of a fish with the head of a swallow. These strange figures represents cyclical regeneration.

In China, this was a bird of daring, and it came to signify coming success and fidelity. The Japanese saw it as a bird of unfaithfulness.

In Native American lore, the swallow is considered closely related to the magickal Thunderbird, because it will fly before a thunderstorm arrives.

Superstitions: *It is a general belief that to kill a swallow is to bring bad luck. It is a sign of good luck if a swallow builds a nest on your house.*

In Germany, people believe this bird prevents fire and storms from damaging any house on which it has its nest.

The Irish seem to connect quite a few birds with the devil; they say that the swallow has three drops of the devil's blood in it.

European farmers say that to kill a swallow will ruin the milk yield. If you disturb their nests, the harvest will be bad.

In Germany, if a woman steps on a swallow's eggs, she will be barren.

Medieval scholars recommended swallow dung to cure blindness in children.

Magickal Attributes: Good luck, success. Changing your luck.

Chant

> *Change my luck to something new*
> *And prosperous, bird of brilliant hue.*
> *Grant success and opportunity*
> *And I shall ever grateful be.*

SWAN

There are five species of these very large, long-necked and web-footed birds in the genus *Cygnus*. They are related to geese. Three species are found in the Northern Hemisphere and two species in Australia and southern South America. Northern swans are all white. The Australian swan is black with white wing patches, while the South American bird is white with a black neck. The only species without a loud voice is the mute swan which produces only hissing sounds.

Swans pair for life. They are graceful, beautiful, and fast fliers and swimmers, but they can be very aggressive. They glide with stately dignity on the water.

To the Greeks, the swan was the bird of Apollo. According to a Greek legend, the swan sings a melody of haunting beauty just before its death, thus connecting it with Apollo, god of music. It was dedicated to the Omphalos stone at Delphi. The swan was also an emblem of the Muses and Aphrodite. They were said to pull the chariot of Venus through the air. Zeus took swan-form to satisfy his lust with Leto and Helen.

The Greek love goddess Aphrodite had three bird familiars: the dove, swan, and goose. A sixth century B.C.E. statue shows her standing on a giant swan; in one hand she carries a sacred casket, symbol of her secret knowledge of death and rebirth. In another terra cotta image, Aphrodite sits on a throne made of two swans.

Hindu deities often interchanged the goose and the swan, which represented breath and spirit. The swan was a mount for the goddess Sarasvati and sometimes Brahma. The heavenly nymphs, called the *apsaras*, were often portrayed as swans. The goddess Devi rides a swan that wears a necklace.

Several Celtic folk legends tell of the mystical sacred swan. Its feathers were used in ritual cloaks by the Bards since swans are connected with music and song. People who shape-shifted into swans were identified by gold or silver chains around their necks. Norse legend also speaks of this shape-shifting as one form which the Valkyries could take; they were called swan maidens.

As an alchemical symbol, the swan stood for mercury.

Superstitions: *Some cultures still believe that the swan sings at its death.*

It is said the swan can't hatch its eggs except in a thunderstorm.

In Scotland, if three swans fly together, it means a national disaster.

Magickal Attributes: Aid with the interpretation of dream symbols; transitions; spiritual evolution. Developing intuitive abilities; seeing into the future. If a swan is seen in meditation, pay close attention to hunches and omens. Divination on a spiritual level.

Chant

> *White bird of graceful beauty,*
> *Lift my thoughts to spiritual things.*
> *Let me not be confined by physical matters,*
> *But aware that spiritual outcomes guide me.*
> *I seek higher knowledge.*
> *Show me the way.*

TURKEY

This large bird of the class Aves in the genus *Meleagris*, species *Gallopavo*, is native to the Western Hemisphere. At least five sub-species of wild turkey have been identified, ranging from Mexico to northern New England. This bird is noted for its heavy broad breast, the red wattle that hangs from the lower part of the beak, and its black and white coloring.

The Aztecs domesticated the turkey long before the arrival of Europeans. To many

Native Americans, the turkey was known as the Give-away Eagle or the South Eagle.

Some people say that wild turkeys are intelligent, but I have my doubts. One old method for trapping wild turkeys alive was to lay down a trail of grain that led into a large box held up by a stick. The turkey would eat the grain, following the trail into the box. When it stood up, it was trapped because it wouldn't put its head down to get out.

Magickal Attributes: Symbol that a gift is coming. Asking for helpful gifts and blessings from the Gods.

Chant

Woodland bird, bring to me blessings,
The blessings and gifts of powerful Gods.
Let me receive them in thankfulness.
Teach me how to share them with others.

VULTURE

The vulture of the Old World is in a subfamily of the family Accipitridae; they are found in temperate and tropical regions of Europe, Asia, and Africa. The Old World Vulture can be colored black or brown with patches of white. Some of them reach a nine-foot wing span. The unfeathered head and neck are adorned with wattles of flesh. A non-aggressive bird, it feeds entirely on carrion. Among the Old World vultures are the lammergeier and the "Pharaoh's chicken."

The New World vulture, *Cathartes aura*, is the turkey vulture. It can be found from Canada to the Falkland Islands. This bird can be almost three feet long with a wing span up to six feet. It is brownish black, with a bright red neck and naked skin on the head; its under parts are a silvery hue. It feeds on carrion. Another of its names is the turkey buzzard. Among the New World vultures is the condor.

Although a repulsive-looking and bad-smelling bird, the vulture has long been held in high regard by ancient cultures. It was a symbol of compassion and protection, but also of destruction. Vulture claws were said to detect poisons in food and drink. This bird was considered to be prophetic, knowing beforehand the site of battles.

The vulture has been associated with the Great Mother for thousands of years in her aspect as life-giver and destroyer. In the ancient matriarchal ruins of Catal Huyuk are wall paintings of priestesses dressed in vulture costumes. The Egyptian glyph for mother was a vulture; for grandmother, a vulture carrying royal symbols. The Hebrews had the same word similarity between vulture and womb, as did the Siberian Yakuts.

As a representation of love and care, the goddess Isis is sometimes shown with vulture wings in her role as Great Mother. Mut, goddess of maternity and the sky, was often portrayed with the head of a vulture or wearing a vulture headdress. Hathor and Nekhebet could also take vulture form. In the funeral rites of Osiris, four vulture feathers were attached to each corner of the coffin. Nekhebet and Mut, both vulture goddesses, were said to guard mummies and protect the dead.

The name "necropolis" (city of the dead) comes from Nekhebet, the Egyptian vulture goddess. The Greeks associated this city with their goddess Aphrodite Eileithyia, and the Romans with Juno.

The early Arabs had a vulture god named Nasr. The king of the birds in West Africa was Fene-Ma-So, the Vulture Spirit.

This bird was associated with the Greek deities Pallas, Ares, and Apollo, and was sometimes mentioned as the vehicle of Saturn. Athene changed into a vulture in *The Odyssey*. Pictures of the Harpies show them as having women's heads and breasts, but the feet of vultures. The Harpies were also called the Keres (Fates) of Death.

Superstitions: *Vultures do not copulate, but the female reproduce without male assistance.*

Vultures can live for 100 years.

Magickal Attributes: Cycle of death and rebirth. Prophecy. Deep love of the Mother Goddess. Asking for understanding and wisdom concerning the death of a loved one.

Chant

> *Gathering bird of the Dark Goddess,*
> *Teach me not to fear physical death.*
> *Ease the sorrow in my heart and mind.*
> *Let me understand the hidden wisdom of the Goddess.*

WOODPECKER

A non-singing bird of the family Pieidae, woodpeckers are related to honey guides, toucans, and jacamars. They have a straight, hard bill and powerful neck for hammering, and a long, sticky tongue to lap up insects. Their stiff tail feathers help them keep their balance as they hang on trees. The males all have an area of bright red or yellow somewhere on their heads. Their call is harsh and shrill.

A bird of both the Old and New Worlds, except for Australia, New Zealand, and the oceanic islands, the woodpecker was known to the Romans as the bird of the god Mars. It is constantly digging in wood for bugs. Its powerful neck muscles and persistence make it possible for this bird to carve out holes in trees for nests. Its sharp claws enable it to walk up and down trees without a problem.

Indo-European mythology lists the woodpecker as a bird of fire and lightning, a prophetic bird who has magickal powers. It was also considered to be one of the guardians of kings and trees.

In Greece and Rome this bird was connected with Ares/Mars, Zeus/Jupiter, Silvenus, and Triptolemus. In most of their symbols, the woodpecker represented war, destruction, sudden attacks, and storms.

The Germans called it the Little King in the West and the King of the Birds. However, legend says it won the contest of which could fly higher with an eagle by deceit; it rode on the eagle's back until the big bird was exhausted, then flew on by itself to gain the victory. Sometimes the image of a woodpecker replaced the dove as a sign of spirit, but it was also called a witch bird.

The Druids read foretellings from its chirping, just as they did from the wren's. The direction from which it called was of great prophetic importance to the Celts. The Welsh Bard Taliesin called it one of his helping birds. The bird was titled the Lady of Heaven's Hen in Scotland; to kill it was extremely unlucky. Because it was associated with the Underworld and the Winter Solstice, it was only killed in England and France at the time of the Winter Solstice.

In Japan the woodpecker was known as a lucky bird that brought good fortune to hunters; people honored it with a salute when it was seen.

The woodpecker often gives a shrill cry when a storm is approaching. In this manner, said Native Americans, the bird spoke to thunder.

Superstitions: *The yellowhammer* (a species of woodpecker) *is an ill-omened bird that is a servant of the devil. The devil makes the marks on its eggs.*

A nail will not stay in any tree where the woodpecker builds its nest.

Magickal Attributes: Warning of approaching trouble. Good luck. If seen in meditation, trouble is near. Prophecy. Divination for checking a situation for problems.

Chant

> Hammer, pound, a warning sound
> Alerts me to potential strife.
> At your call I see it all
> And plan protection for my life.

WREN

A large number of species of the family Troglodytidae, wrens range in size from four inches up to eight inches. They are related to mockingbirds and thrashers. All wrens are found in the New World, except for one species in the temperate zones of the Northern Hemisphere. They have a long slender bill, a chunky body, and short wings and tail. Their coloring is a combination of browns, grays, black, and white. They prefer forests and thickets. They are very energetic and some are extremely pugnacious.

To me, wrens are the most fascinating birds, next to hummingbirds. Consider yourself fortunate indeed if a wren nests in your garden, for its melodious, bubbling song is one of the most beautiful there is.

The wren will build its nest in tiny spaces that do not meet the requirements of other birds. It will also dive-bomb intruders to its territory when nesting. Its little bobbing movements when it chirps and sings are an expression of the joy of life.

This was a very sacred bird to the Celtic Druids. They practiced a kind of divination from its musical notes. On the Isle of Man, the wren was a sacred bird well before the arrival of the Christians, while the people of Devonshire still call it Bran's sparrow, signifying its ancient connection with prophecy and the deity Bran who prophesied.

Superstitions: *If you kill a wren or destroy their nests, you will break a bone soon.*

The French say if you disturb a wren's nest you will get pimples.

Wren feathers are said to keep you from drowning.

Magickal Attributes: A messenger from the gods. Prophecy. Living life to the fullest. Protecting yourself when necessary.

Chant

> *Tiny wren of wondrous song,*
> *Druid bird of magick sharing,*
> *Give to me your prophecies,*
> *True divinations with me sharing.*
> *Guide my intuition to*
> *Dreams of future, readings true.*

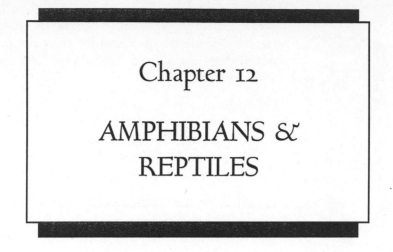

Chapter 12

AMPHIBIANS &
REPTILES

Snakes, toads, and other such creatures are perhaps the least popular of animals in people's minds. However, they do have their places and uses in animal magick and as familiars. At some time in your development, you will meet one or more of these creatures in your dreams, astral travels, or meditation. Their appearance will be important, so try to understand why they have appeared and what they have to offer you.

ADDER

Any member of the Old World family Viperidae, but especially the species of *Vipera*, which includes the only poisonous snakes found in Europe and northern Asia. The northern viper or adder is the only venomous snake in England. It seldom exceeds two feet long and has a light zigzag pattern down the back. Fatalities from its bite are rare as its poison is fairly weak; it can, however, make one very ill.

A very deadly viper is the *daboia*, or Russell's viper, of southeastern Asia and the East Indies; this snake can reach over five feet in length and is vicious if aroused. Three African vipers, the puff adder (*Bitis arietans*),

the rhinoceros viper (*B. nasicornis*), and the gaboon viper (*B. gabonica*), are noted for their flattened bodies, triangular-shaped heads, long fangs, and virulent poison.

Although there were no snakes or adders in Ireland, the Celts there knew of them. The Druids in Wales called themselves *Nadredd*, "serpent." In the Scottish Highlands, the adder symbolized the goddess Cailleach's dark powers.

The adder, or any snake, can hide in the shortest grass from danger or large opponents. Although it will usually retreat if possible, the adder is noted for its striking ability in self-defense.

Superstitions: The Celtic English have some very unusual ideas about adders. *An adder skin hung from the rafters will prevent fire; a skin hung by the chimney will bring luck. The skin will draw thorns out of the body. Seen by the front door, the adder is a death omen.*

Adders gather in Cornwall at Summer Solstice eve and in Wales on Beltane eve.

The Gypsies say that killing the adder that bit you and rubbing its body on the bite will cure you of the venom.

Medieval scholars had some very strange ideas about the breeding habits of adders. *The male spit semen into the female's mouth and she bit off his head. The young chewed their way out of their mother at birth.*

Magickal Attributes: Shedding something in favor of something better. Wisdom, cunning, reincarnation. When needing to get rid of a person, situation, or attitude that is holding you back.

Chant

> I watch you shed the old for new,
> Little adder, as you renew your skin.
> Like you, I shed old things for new,
> Another cycle to begin.

CHAMELEON

This unique species of lizard can change its coloring in order to blend into the surroundings. This color change is influenced by light, temperature, and emotional agitation. Examples of lizards that can change color are the *Gekkonidae, Iguanidae, Agamidae,* and *Chamaeleontidae.* The chameleon's eyes move independently of each other. (See Lizard, pages 204-205.)

The changing color of the chameleon symbolized inconstancy of life and the uncertainty of fortune, while its eyes were said to see into both the past and the future. African Bushmen considered this creature to be the bringer of rain.

Magickal Attributes Hiding by changing colors. Weather influences. Adopting protective coloration to stay out of trouble; learning to use invisibility.

Chant

> *Like the chameleon I go quietly.*
> *I fade into the surroundings.*
> *I gather my protection about me*
> *And become invisible.*

COBRA

Although snakes as a species are listed later in this chapter, there were specific types of snakes which were considered sacred and revered; I have listed these separately. The cobra is one such snake. Cobras are found in Africa, India, and other warm countries of Asia and the Near East. These large poisonous snakes of the family Elapidae can rear the front part of their bodies, flatten the neck, and produce a "hood" of skin just below the head. There are seven species in Africa and Asia in the genus *Naja;* two African species in the genus *Pseudohaje,* two African water cobras *Boulengerina,*

199

the South African spitting cobra *Hemachatus haemachatus*, and the king cobra of southeastern Asia *Ophiophagus hannah*. All the species have hollow, non-folding fangs in the upper jaw. The most aggressive is the deadly king cobra which can get up to 18 feet long.

The Indian or spectacled cobra has a terrifying hood of skin which can expand to four times the diameter of its body. It can also raise a third or more of its body upright. Cobras can hiss loudly. Although some cobras spit venom, which is intensely irritating to the skin or can cause blindness if it gets in the eyes, they kill by biting.

The Egyptian hieroglyph for goddess was the image of a cobra. Neith sometimes appeared as a golden cobra. Isis (her Egyptian name was Au Set) wore a crown of horns twined with serpents.

The raised cobra image is well known from the pictures of the ancient crown of Egypt. The cobra was set over the forehead of the pharaoh to show his royalty, divinity, and connection with the Great Goddess.

The goddess Ua Zit (known to the Greeks as Buto) took the form of a cobra. Buto (also known as Per-Uatchet and Iusaset) was one of the oldest goddesses in Egypt. Her image was seen in the uraeus, which was worn by Ra and the pharaohs to denote royal power and wisdom through the Goddess.

Magickal Attributes: Spiritual wisdom from the Goddess. Protecting yourself from religious persecution.

Chant

> *Lift your head, great sacred serpent,*
> *You who are a servant of the Goddess.*
> *Strike fear into the hearts of all persecutors.*
> *Let those who hate my spiritual path*
> *Be cast down by their own actions.*

CROCODILE

There are fourteen species of true crocodiles, members of the genus *Crocodilus*. Included in this species also are two gavials, one each in India and Malaysia. True crocodiles have sharply tapering heads which expose a tooth on either side of the lower jaw. These creatures are descendants of ancestors very much like them who lived with the dinosaurs. A few have been known to reach 23 feet in length. They like to float in water with just their nostrils, eyes, and ears above the surface. They have a powerful tail, webbed feet, and strong jaws.

To distinguish between an alligator and a crocodile, certain physical characteristics can be observed. The alligator's snout is wider and more rounded than that of the crocodile. Crocodiles are found in rivers, lakes, and oceans throughout most of the tropic regions, as well as in warmer, moist temperate zones. Like alligators, all crocodiles must live in water, except for brief forays onto land; they breathe air. Those crocodiles with longer, more slender snouts live in India and the Malay region. They are known as Gavials, a corruption of the Hindu name *gharial*.

The Mayans considered the image of a crocodile to be an object of fun, such as the hobby horse in English festivals. However, in the rest of the world, the crocodile has had dual symbolism from the earliest times. It is both feared and revered in most countries in which it lives.

In ancient Egypt, the crocodile was connected with Set, the god of evil, and Sebek, who was shown with a crocodile-head. Although Sebek was the son of Neith and an ancient solar god, he was associated with Set and brutality. Since the crocodile can see even when its eyes are covered by its nictitating membrane, the Egyptians said it symbolized seeing reason clearly. They linked this creature with fury and evil, but also believed that it had access to great knowledge.

Superstitions: *The people of India say that crocodiles make a moaning and sighing noise like a human in distress to attract victims. Crocodiles are also said to cry tears over the victim's head when they have devoured the body.*

Therefore, the expression "to cry crocodile tears" means to pretend you are sorry for something you did when you really aren't.

Magickal Attributes: Deceit, treachery. Lying in wait to get revenge. Waiting patiently to see the truth behind a veiled issue. Protecting yourself from deceitful and manipulating people.

Chant

> *I wait beside the never-ending river*
> *Of spiritual energy and life.*
> *Truth reflected on its surface helps me*
> *To avoid all manipulation and strife.*

FROG

These creatures are of the aquatic Amphibia, which have no tails. The true frog belongs to the family Ranidae, which includes the common frog of Europe (*Rana temporaria*) and the bullfrog of North America (*Rana catesbeiana*). True frogs are most diverse in Africa where the largest of them is nearly a foot long. A native of Cuba, the smallest frog is less than half an inch long. True frogs are aquatic and have smooth skins and webbed feet. Some tree frogs in Africa have feet with suction disks on their toes. The "hairy frogs" of West Africa develop hairlike growths on their bodies during breeding season.

The frog has been a Goddess symbol of rebirth since the earliest Neolithic times. It has been made into figurines, painted on walls and ceramics, and engraved on stone.

The Egyptians had a frog goddess Heket, who was called the midwife of the world, and who protected mothers and newborn children. She was  portrayed either as a frog itself or with the head of a frog. The amulet of the frog was often buried with mummies; on it was engraved "I am the Resurrection." The frog was also a symbol of the Great Mothers, Isis and Hathor.

In China, the Frog Spirit, called Ch'ing-Wa Sheng, was worshiped both as a healer and as a deity who brought prosperity in business. The frog was a Chinese lunar symbol; a frog pictured in a well meant a person who had only limited understanding.

The Greeks and Romans considered this creature to be both an emblem of Aphrodite (representing licentiousness), and a symbol of fertility and harmony between lovers. It was also a companion of the nymphs. Hecate is associated with frogs in very ancient lore.

Around the world, the frog had a variety of meanings. In the *Rig Veda* of India, frogs were invoked as deities in their own right. However, the Zoroastrians believed them to be an evil creature of their demon god Ahriman. To the Celts, the frog was Lord of the Earth and represented healing Water.

In many parts of the world, the frog or its image was used in rain charms. An ancient Babylonian cylinder, used as a fertility charm, shows nine frogs. The frog was also cited as one of the witches' familiars.

One Winter we heard a frog singing away in the plant room. We finally decided it must be hidden in the large fern. Since the frog's presence didn't disturb us, we left him there. When Spring came and the frogs outside began to sing their mating calls, we no longer heard our visitor. We couldn't understand where it had gone, but when Summer ended we discovered its clever exit point. The cat door was flush at the bottom with the floor in the plant room. The frog simply backed up to the door and pushed until it could go in or out.

Superstitions: *Pliny the Elder said that frogs attracted friends to your house along with good luck.*

It is still considered to be a reliable weather-predictor as it will croak when the barometer goes down. Croaking during the day is an omen of rain.

If a frog comes into your house by itself, it symbolizes good luck arriving.

The ornamental cloth closing for garments (called a frog) may be a remnant of an old French custom of embroidering frogs on clothes for good luck.

In many places it is considered unlucky to kill a frog; you could lose your luck.

Handling frogs and toads is said to give you warts.

If a dog eats a live frog, it will be unable to bark.

Magickal Attributes: A symbol of initiation and transformation. Cleaning out negativities and distractions and replacing them with positive energy. Joy in a new cycle of life. Being reborn after a period of seeming-death, when undergoing an initiation of transformation. Beginning a new life cycle by dispensing with negative thoughts and deeds.

Chant

> Your singing marks the season
> Of new life and new beginning,
> A time of wonder and of joy,
> A time of rebirth and of Light.
> Like the tiny frog in Spring renewing,
> I joyfully face my new beginning.
> I boldly stand upon the threshold,
> And leave confusion for the Light.

LIZARD

Related to crocodiles and snakes, the lizard family (Sauria or Lacertilia) is found in various parts of the world, except in extremely cold regions. In the western hemisphere they range from Canada to Tierra del Fuego in South America, including the West Indies. In the eastern hemisphere, they are found from Siberia to Africa and Australia. There are more than 3,100 species of these reptiles.

Generally, lizards have a slender body covered by loose skin and fine scales. They shed their skin in patches, at regular intervals. Most of them have four legs with five toes on each foot; an exception is the family of legless lizards—the worm lizards. Unlike a snake, the lower jaw is fused and cannot be opened too wide. They are basically terrestrial animals, but many are very good swimmers.

Although most lizards are less than a foot in length, the monitor lizards (the largest of the species) can be over nine feet long. The frilled lizards expand a fringe of skin around their necks to frighten away attackers. The horned toad has spiny scales and will squirt blood from its eyes when frightened. The gila monster and the beaded lizard are the only poisonous members of this species; they are found in the desert areas of Utah, Nevada, New Mexico, Arizona, and Mexico.

No lizard is truly a water-living creature, although they may enter the water and can swim. They like to bask in the Sun as they are reptiles and are cold-blooded. All lizards are able to grow a new tail if they lose it in an accident. They hear reasonably well and see as well as many mammals.

The myths of Egypt and Greece portrayed the lizard as signifying wisdom and good fortune. This creature was an emblem of both Hermes and Sarapis. The Zoroastrians classified it as an animal of the evil Ahriman.

The lizard appeared in Roman art as a symbol of death and rebirth. Sometimes it took the place of snakes as the genii of a house. If lizards lived under a house, they were fed on milk and crumbs. Their appearance was greeted with happiness, for it meant that good luck was coming.

Among the Polynesians, Moko (King of the Lizards) was worshiped as a god and the protector of fishing, the prime source of food for these people.

There is a type of small lizard known as the alligator lizard which has a powerful gripping action in its jaws. One of our cats found out about this when he accidentally sat on one. The lizard clamped down on the cat's tail and got quite a ride before he fell off.

Superstitions: *This creature had a dual symbolism in Europe. Although it was believed to be a sinister being, it was used in certain love charms. However, many Europeans believe that if a lizard crosses the bride's path on the way to get married she will never be happy.*

Magickal Attributes: Dreams, mental creations. Stop running from your fears and face them. Asking for guidance in facing difficult situations that make you afraid. Understanding dreams.

Chant

> *The world of dreams, that nightly place,*
> *Is formed of symbols, great and small.*
> *O lizard, help me understand*
> *Those symbols that my mind recalls*
> *From other lives and knowledge past*
> *When once I knew what they all meant.*
> *Teach me dream symbols once again,*
> *O little lizard, Goddess-sent.*

SCORPION

Technically, the scorpion is not a reptile, although it is an invertebrate; it is an arthropod (order Scorpionida of the class Arachnida) and more closely related to spiders. A scorpion has four pairs of legs, a pair of pincer-like front feet, and bears live young. From before the days of the ancient Greeks and Egyptians, the scorpion has been much feared. They are more numerous in the tropics, but do extend into Canada in western North America.

From the shining black, eight-inch species that infest tropical jungles, to the thin, pale, 1-inch ones that live in sandy wastes, all scorpions have an abdomen ending in a tail-like section that is armed with a curved stinger at the tip. This tip is like a poison-filled syringe, with some scorpions more deadly than others; a few species have poison glands also in their jaws. Arching over the back, this tail waves in all directions. The scorpion usually hunts by night, hiding by day under stones or loose bark.

The ancient Sumerians believed that scorpions or Scorpion-Men were guardians of the Gateway of the Sun, the Mountains of the East, and the Twin Gates. This creature was associated with various aspects of Ishtar (as Ishara Tamtim, the scorpion-tailed Mother), Nanna, and the Phrygian Sabazius. Myth tells how the hero Gilgamesh had to make his way through the Scorpion-Men to the house of the Scorpion Goddess, Siduri Sabitu.

To both the Zoroastrians and the Egyptians, the Scorpion was an embodiment of evil. A desert animal, it accompanied the Egyptian god Set. However, the scorpion was also connected with the Egyptian goddess Selket who was pictured with a scorpion on her head or as a woman with a scorpion-body; she was known as a protector of the dead. Myth tells of seven scorpions that went with Isis on her search for Osiris. The scorpion goddess is mentioned in the *Book of the Dead* as being an extremely ancient deity.

Mithraism had a slightly different spiritual explanation of the scorpion. Their Dadophori, who were twins with upward and downward pointing torches, were called the Bull and the Scorpion. These twins symbolized life and death, the rising and setting Sun.

In Central and South America, several cultures spoke of Mother Scorpion, who lived at the end of the Milky Way; she received the souls of the deceased. The ancient civilizations of Babylon, India, Greece, Egypt, and the Mayas all knew of the same constellation of Scorpio and associated it with the scorpion.

Superstitions: *If you hold a scorpion on your palm, it can't sting you.*

Magickal Attributes: Revenge, dark magick. Sending dark magick and negativities back to the makers.

Chant

> Scuttling in the shadows,
> Poisonous sting raised in defense,
> Like the scorpion I strike only to protect myself.
> Beware, trouble-makers! I am not defenseless.

SNAKES

Snakes are reptiles, cold-blooded and requiring heat to bring them to an active stage. They are found around the world, except for the colder regions. There are about 2,500 species of the suborder Serpentes or Ophidia. About 250 snakes are poisonous, but only about half this number have sufficient venom, sharp enough fangs, or are large enough to threaten humans. They have flexible backbones, loosely connected jaws, and no legs or movable eyelids. They are covered with small scales.

Snakes or serpents were very early symbols of the Great Mother Goddesses. Serpents had dual spiritual meanings, even when shown singular: life and death, solar and lunar, good and evil, healing and poison. Because it sheds its skin, this creature became a symbol of reincarnation and immortality. The snake was considered to be the embodiment of all potentials of a physical, material, and spiritual nature. When specifically shown with Mother Goddesses, it was a mediator between worlds and represented esoteric secrets, deep wisdom, true intuition, and the mystic mysteries. Although the snake was sometimes used to represent the death aspect of the Goddess, this creature was never considered to be evil in the Mediterranean and Europe as it was in Near Eastern and Indo-European myths.

The Egyptian Isis sometimes carried or was accompanied by snakes. Thoth, like the Greek Hermes, could change into a serpent; a serpent was said to guard the hidden Book of Thoth. Serpents were also creatures of Set. Statues of the Phrygian god Sabazius show him holding a snake; his priest carried a golden image of this creature. It was considered to be a form of the Canaanite god Bel.

Apep was pictured as a huge snake that lived deep in the Nile. He was called the Great Serpent of Tuat (the Underworld). As the demon enemy of the Sun, Apep tried to periodically swallow it, causing eclipses. The Egyptians said that the Underworld was actually the interior of Apep's body.

A benevolent serpent which protected the Sun god Ra was the huge speckled snake called Kheti, also known as the Spitting Serpent. It was said he had seven undulations of his body and belched fire into the faces of Ra's enemies.

Egypt has a small desert snake with a horny knob above each eye which was said to ward off the evil eye. The Greeks called this reptile the *cerastes*.

The Persian Zoroastrians thought the snake to be an evil animal of Ahriman, but the followers of Mithras believed it to be beneficent. A snake was often shown beside the horse of Mithras in a capacity of protection.

The Babylonian goddess Kadi of Der, who was a serpent with a woman's head and breasts, may have been the same deity as Kadru of India. The Akkadian Ninhursag was called Mistress of Serpents; she was the dark twin of Lamia or Lamashtu of Babylon. Atargatis, who became Dea Syria in Rome, was connected with snakes. Her images were encircled by a serpent with seven eggs tucked into its great coils.

In many Greek, Roman, and Cretan households certain snakes were kept as sacred pets. To these cultures, serpents were closely connected with the Savior deities of the Mystery cults and deities of healing. Certain brown harmless snakes were kept in the healing temples of Asclepias, son of Apollo and god of medicine. His daughter Hygeia is often shown holding boa constrictors.

When associated with Greek Underworld deities, the serpent represented the spirits of the dead. Snakes were pictured on the chariot wheels of the goddess Persephone. When symbolizing Apollo's vengeful aspect, it meant darkness. In the Garden of Hesperides, the goddess Hera had a sacred life-giving apple tree which was guarded by Ladon, a huge serpent.

A caged serpent, representing wisdom, guarded Athene's temple at Athens. According to Herodotus, Athene's snake founded the temple at this site. Originally, the serpent-hair of Medusa, the Graiae, and the Erinyes signified the powers of enchantment, guile, and magick connected with true wisdom. An ivory plaque from Sparta shows a winged Hecate with serpents coiling toward her arms.

The goddess Gaea founded the Delphic Oracle long before Apollo took it over. There she was called Gaea Pelope, the female serpent. The priestesses who served her and this temple, even later under Apollo, were given the title of Pythonesses, which means serpent-priestesses.

One of the most strikingly beautiful statues to be found in the ruins of the Double Axe shrine in ancient Knossos on the island of Crete is the woman holding serpents in each hand or with them twining about her arms. Some of these statues have snakes as arms, or serpents clasping their waists and in their headdresses. These statues were either of the Cretan Mother Goddess or of her priestesses. Several of these statues have been found in buildings, other than temples, pointing to the symbolism of protection.

This particular symbolism was used by the Romans who associated the snake with the *penates* who guarded the *penus* (food storage room). The Slavs and Russians had Domovoj, who was said to live under the threshold or behind the oven; his other names were Ded or Dedushka, meaning "grandfather, ancestor." They believed this snake-deity shed his skin every year.

The caduceus, which was a staff or wand intertwined with two snakes, was carried by deities, physicians, and messengers (such as Hermes). The two snakes symbolized opposites: healing and poison, binding and loosing, sleep and awakening, good and evil, peace and upset.

The Nagas were very important in Hindu mythology. They were portrayed either as human-headed snakes or as cobras. They lived in beautiful Underworld palaces filled with flowers and gems. The Hindus said they had semi-divine powers and controlled the rain clouds. In Hindu art, the Nagas symbolized cosmic power and the Shakti. They were considered to be guardians of treasures (both material and spiritual) and the keepers of ancient mystical knowledge. It was said that the serpent-goddess Kadru was the mother of the Nagas. As rain deities, the Nagas were associated with the rainbow, which tribes of northern India called Buddhi Nagin ("old female snake").

Krishna is often shown dancing on the head of Kaliya, the serpent king. Kaliya may have been a form of the goddess Kali who wore a crown and garland of snakes. The god Indra killed the dragon-snake Ahi ("the throttler"), a three-headed creature who had dammed up the waters. Ananta the Infinite gently cradles all the gods in their sleep between incarnations; Ananta was first listed as female, then changed to a male.

In Japan, the trickster, trouble-making god Susanoo is sometimes portrayed as a snake. There was also a lesser known snake god, Uga-Jin, who resembled the Aztec Quetzalcoatl. The Chinese consider serpents to be destructive, deceitful, and cunning. However, their ancient deities Nu Kua and her brother Fu Xi had half-snake, half-human forms.

Among the Celtic clans the goddess Brigit had a snake as her emblem even though there were no snakes in Ireland. Stone carvings of the Picts in Scotland show a Snake Goddess with snake-legs and hair. The Nordic peoples had the story of the Midgard Serpent which surrounded the world and held its tail in its mouth. The Greek version of this World Serpent was Oceanos; the Russians called it Koshchei, the Deathless. Even Koshi, the Japanese dragon of the sea tides, may be a version of this creature.

In the Serbian cultures, the Vila were shape-shifting spirits that could assume the form of serpents or swans.

The Aztecs and Toltecs had several deities connected with serpents. Quetzalcoatl, the Feathered Serpent, was a combined bird-snake entity; one of his images shows him with a serpent body and a human head. The Mayans of Yucatan called this deity Kulkulcan. Coatlicue, the Snake Woman and Earth Mother, wore a skirt of serpents. The Mexican serpent goddess was Coyolxauhqui; her images show her with a serpent-girdle, arms and legs twined with snakes, and a snake in her feathery crown. A snake-skin drum and a scepter of serpents were used by the war god Huitzilopochtli. As intermediaries between the gods and humans, snakes were companions of the rain and wind deities.

In Australia, the native people had a deity called Julunggul or the Great Rainbow Snake. She was said to have come out of the sea. Sometimes Julunggul was described as female, sometimes as male.

Native Americans believed that all snakes had great power; however, the ones with a deadly bite were the most powerful.

Medieval alchemists said that the Apophis-snake (their name for the Hermetic Ouroboros) symbolized a hidden serpent-spirit who knew the secret of the Philosopher's Stone.

Know your snakes before you pick up one. Even non-poisonous snakes have teeth and can bite.

Superstitions: *An old superstition, not true of course, is that a snake will not die until the Sun goes down.*

People in North Lincolnshire say that if you wear a snakeskin around your head you can cure a headache. An old Cornish tale says that no snake will approach anything made of ash wood.

A ring made in the shape of a snake is said to bring long life and good health to its owner.

Central Europeans believed that if a woman pulled out one of her hairs at a certain Moon sign she could turn it into a snake by placing it in water. Another similar belief is that if a horse hair is dropped into water it will become a snake.

Certain snakes, called hoop snakes, take their tail in their mouth and destroy trees, animals, and people, by stinging them with the tail.

Snakes have bad eyesight and can't see forward.

If a snake swallows the spit of someone who has fasted, it will die.

Magickal Attributes: Psychic energy, creative power, immortality. Transmute your life into higher levels. Wisdom, understanding, connection with spirit. Facing your fears of spiritual initiations and life problems; moving on to higher goals.

Chant

> Coiling, turning, deep knowledge burning,
> Sacred serpent, lead me on
> To the initiate's fire on planes much higher.
> I yearn to grow, O Goddess-one.

TOAD

True toads are terrestrial, tail-less amphibians of the family Bufonidae. They have squat bodies and short forelegs, and are found in almost all parts of the world. The toad differs from the frog in that it breeds in water but spends most of its time on land, sometimes miles from permanent pools. Its skin is usually rough and moist, but not slippery.

Toads, like frogs, don't cause warts on humans. The so-called warts on a toad are actually poison glands scattered over the upper surface of its body to discourage attackers. Getting this poison (bufotenine) into the eyes, the mouth, or a cut can cause intense irritation.

The toad, like many other misunderstood creatures once connected with the Goddess, had a dual symbolism attached to it. As a lunar reptile, it represented resurrection, but also evil, loathsomeness, and death. It was also a death symbol to Polynesians and the Aztecs. In the ancient art of alchemy, the toad signified the dark side of Nature.

Hecate of the Mediterranean area was sometimes called Baubo, which means "toad." Many European names given to the toad link it with the Goddess as witch and prophetess: *hexe*, German; *fata*, Italian; *czarownica*, Polish; *bosorka*, Ukranian; *gatalinka*, Serbo-Croatian; *mantis*, Greek.

To the Celts, the toad symbolized evil power. It was an emblem of the Greek god Sabazius and the Zoroastrian Ahriman.

In China, however, they said that a three-legged toad lived on the Moon. To them this creature meant long life, wealth, and money making. It was also a creature of the Immortal Liu-hai. In Japan they had a wizard toad named Gama.

In the ancient cultures of Mexico, the toad symbolized the Earth; the toadstool was connected with the sacred hallucinogenic mushroom which was said to give enlightenment. When the Toad God was shown sitting under a toadstool, it symbolized the Mushroom God of Mexico.

Superstitions: *Still today, many European country people believe that the toad is an omen of pregnancy.*

Handling a toad or frog is said to give you warts.

The midwife toad of Europe and the British toad, popularly called the Natterjack, were both thought to be favorite familiars to witches. For this reason, during the sixteenth century in England, toads were burned as creatures of the devil.

It was, however, thought to be lucky to possess and wear a toad stone ring; supposedly, this "stone" will sweat and change color if it is near poison. The Scots believed that a toad stone would prevent the burning of a house or the sinking of a boat.

Magickal Attributes: Long life, prosperity, new beginnings, good luck. Beginning new projects. Changing your luck.

Chant

> I change my luck to all things new.
> I have a precious stone, like you,
> The stone of spirit, mind, and soul
> That leads me to the proper goal.

TURTLE or TORTOISE

The tortoise can be a land-dwelling or land-living pond chelonian and a vegetarian. Tortoises are members of the family Testudinidae, which have unwebbed feet with stubby toes. The hind feet are often elephant-like. They have a plated nose and a high-domed shell. They vary greatly in their shapes and colors.

Turtles are reptiles, *Testudinata* or *Chelonia*. There remain about 300 species in twelve families. They tend to spend their time in and around water. They are slow-moving and have tough, horny shells protecting their bodies. Turtles have powerful jaws with sharp-edged horny ridges instead of teeth. All tortoises and turtles breath air and deposit their eggs in holes in the Earth.

To the Hindus, the tortoise is a lunar creature. Their myths tell of a giant tortoise upon whose back stands an elephant who in turn supports the world. It is also a creature of Prajapati, the Creator, who was also called Lord of Creatures.

The Chinese also believed the tortoise supported the world, and was an attendant of the world-architect P'an Ku. This creature symbolized strength, endurance, and long life, and was called the Black Warrior. Other Chinese deities were connected with the tortoise, such as Wu Hsien, called the Transcendent Tortoise, and Hsi Wang-Mu, Golden Mother of the Tortoise.

In Japanese legend, the Cosmic Mountains were said to be supported by a tortoise. Among the Ainu of Japan, however, this creature was associated with the god of the sea and was considered to be his messenger.

In Arcadia, the tortoise was connected with the god Pan, while in Greece and Rome it was a companion of Aphrodite/Venus and Hermes/Mercury. It was sacred to Ea-Oannes in Sumeria. To the people of West Africa the tortoise symbolized feminine power and fertility. The Nigerians say the turtle represents the female sex organs.

The images of turtles appear on Mayan stelae but we do not know much about their symbolism in that culture. To the Aztecs, this creature signified treachery and cowardly but boastful people.

Native Americans associate the turtle with the Elements of Earth and Water. It symbolizes the energy of the Goddess, the give-and-take cycle necessary for productive life. Its shell is a physical shield and, therefore, a psychic and spiritual shield.

The turtle symbolized material existence or the *massa confusa* in alchemy. It represented natural evolution, slow and methodical.

Superstitions: *The tortoise protects itself from venomous snake bites by eating marjoram.*

If the right foot of a tortoise is carried on a ship, that ship will not be able to move very fast.

Magickal Attributes: Patience, long life, perseverance. Slow down; enjoy life more; allow your ideas time to develop properly. Visualize the shell as a spiritual shield to protect yourself from the negative thoughts of others. Learning to relax and enjoy life. Developing new ideas. Psychically protecting yourself.

Chant

> *Perseverance has the turtle*
> *As he patiently travels along.*
> *In his slowness he misses nothing,*
> *For he hears Mother Earth's song.*
> *Patience, old wisdom, I'll learn from you,*
> *Deep forest secrets and Earth magick true.*

Chapter 13

AQUATIC CREATURES

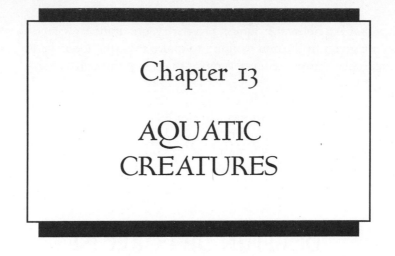

This chapter discusses creatures who live in water of some kind. Symbolically, water represents emotions in one form or another. The appearance of any aquatic creature in your dreams, astral travels, or meditations will signal approaching help with emotional issues in your life, or the fact that you are avoiding working on such issues. Be attentive and thoughtful when an aquatic creature appears to you as a familiar.

CARP

The carp, *Cyprinus carpio*, is native to fresh waters in Asia, but was introduced into Europe and North America. It is a food fish in both the Orient and Europe. The largest carp ever recorded was from South Africa and weighed over eighty-three pounds. The goldfish is a member of the carp family.

The carp is an important symbol in both China and Japan. To the Chinese, it signifies literary eminence and perseverance in the face of difficulties. It is a Japanese symbol of courage, endurance, dignity, good fortune, and submitting to necessary fate.

Magickal Attributes: Courage, prosperity, endurance. Accepting what you are given in life and working to make it better. Courage to tackle difficult circumstances. Perseverance to endure through a trying time.

Chant

> The goldfish lives its life with confidence,
> Never believing in negativity.
> Like the goldfish, I trust in the Gods.
> I shall endure and be successful.

DOLPHIN OR PORPOISE

Dolphins and porpoises are a smaller species of Cetacae, an order of aquatic mammals which includes whales. Dolphins can be distinguished from porpoises by the beak which projects forward from the head. Types of dolphins are: the bottle-nosed, the common, and the spotted. Types of porpoises are: the common and the white-vented. The vast majority of dolphins and porpoises are marine animals, although there are a few living in rivers and fresh water.

The dolphin, with its antics and friendliness, probably attracted the attention of the first men to sail in boats. Dolphins make a wide variety of audible sounds and are able to communicate with each other in this way. The common dolphin is known as the Arrow of the Sea, sometimes traveling at a speed of thirty knots.

The Sumerians knew of the dolphin and said it was connected with Astarte and Ishtar. The ancient Egyptians thought of this creature as a symbol of Isis.

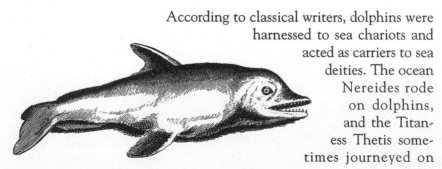

According to classical writers, dolphins were harnessed to sea chariots and acted as carriers to sea deities. The ocean Nereides rode on dolphins, and the Titaness Thetis sometimes journeyed on them naked. Dolphins were called the King of Fishes and the Arrow of the Sea. Their usual symbolic meaning was power and swiftness, but they were also considered to be the guides of souls into the Underworld.

Dolphins were sculpted on the walls of Apollo's temple at Delphi. In his aspect of Apollo Delphinos, this god could take the form of this creature. The Greek word *delphinos* means both dolphin and womb, and is seen in the title Delphi, or World Center. When painted on funeral urns, the dolphin symbolized the passing of the soul from one world to another.

The dolphin was an emblem of Minoan sea power, so powerful in the Mediterranean at one time. These sea creatures even appear on Celtic coins and in their art, usually ridden by a male figure. For some reason, they were associated with well worship. Dolphins were known to the coastal Native Americans as very powerful and magickal creatures. Because these animals breathe air, but live in the water, they were considered to be keepers of the sacred breath of life.

Superstitions: *Dolphins will rescue drowning swimmers by pushing them back to shore; this is one superstition that has some truth behind it.*

Dolphins or porpoises swimming along with a ship or playing in its vicinity are a prediction of good weather and good luck on the voyage.

River dolphins cut up the bellies of crocodiles with their fins.

Magickal Attributes: The sea, wisdom, eloquence, freedom, magick, change, discovery, truth, communication, trust, balance, harmony. Create a rhythm in your life. Learn to release intense emotions through breathing. Water Element magick, especially for releasing negative or debilitating emotions.

Chant

> Leaping, flashing through the water,
> Free as wind upon the sea,
> Beautiful dolphins, magick brothers,
> Give me balance, harmony.

EEL

The eel, *Anguilla bostoniensis*, is hatched in the sea, lives most of its life in fresh water, and returns to the ocean to spawn. It has a snake-like body with a long dorsal fin. When mature, eels can reach four to five feet in length.

Sacred eels have been known to various cultures around the world.

 Sometimes they play an important part in mythology. The Phoenicians kept them in the sanctuary of their war god; these eels wore gold ornaments. Sacred eels are also mentioned in ancient Greek writings.

The Celts have a legend of two Druids who were at first friends. Through a shape-shifting competition these men became enemies. Eventually they each turned into an eel which was then swallowed by cows belonging to two rival clans. This led to the birth of magickal bulls and the Battle of Cooley.

Superstitions: *You can cure a craving for alcohol by drowning an eel in liquor, then giving the drink to the alcoholic.*

You can kill an eel, especially a sea eel, at once with a whip by hitting it on the tail.

Magickal Attributes: Be electrifying; being able to slip out of a bad situation. When needing to get out of a sticky situation that could cause anger and upset.

Chant

> *With a twist and a slip, the eel is free,*
> *Back to its life without a care.*
> *Like the eel I turn, opportunity see,*
> *And free myself because I dare.*
> *No false guilt can hold me or hinder my path.*
> *No threats shall bar my way.*
> *With a twist and a slip, I free myself*
> *To open the door to a brand new day.*

FISH

At the rites of such lunar love and fertility goddesses as Atargatis, Ishtar, Derceto, Isis, and Aphrodite, it was common for the initiates to eat sacred fish. These fish, which were kept in special ponds on the temple grounds, were served on Fridays, a day sacred to these goddesses, as well as to the northern Freyja. A mermaid form was taken by such goddesses as Atargatis, Aphrodite, and Derceto. In Rome the sign of a fish was originally a symbol of the love deity Venus.

The Ephesian Great Goddess often had a fish or fish amulet hung over her genitals. The pointed oval is a yoni sign and is called the *vesica piscis*, or Vessel of the Fish. In Greek, *delphos* meant both fish and womb.

In ancient Middle Eastern cultures, the fish was sometimes a personification of a deity. Statues of the Philistine god Dagon show him as half-fish, half-man. The Greek Poseidon was sometimes pictured with a fish-tail as a symbol of his dominion over the power of the seas.

The Middle Eastern goddess Atargatis had a shrine on the island of Delos. Her temple there was surrounded by fish-filled ponds and trees of doves. The sacred fish at Hieropolis in Egypt wore gold ornaments, a sign of their sacredness. In the aspect of Hat-Mehit, Isis was the Great Fish of the Abyss. When she was shown with a fish as a crown, it meant victory over death.

Part of the Greek festival of Thesmophoria in honor of Demeter was the Haloa, a rite where fish were used as religious symbols.

Fish, particularly salmon and trout, had several mystical meanings to the Celts. They were connected with sacred wells and springs. The Celts believed that eating fish, and salmon and trout especially, would give wisdom, healing, and the ability to prophesy.

To the Chinese, the fish represented abundance and was a symbol of Kuan Yin, goddess of fertility and children. It also meant wealth, harmony, and regeneration. Kwannon of Japan was connected with fish, where the creature symbolized love.

Superstitions: *The first fish must be thrown back as payment to the sea and water deities. If you don't, you won't have any luck fishing.*

In Scotland, if the fish won't bite, they throw a fisherman into the water and then haul him out like a fish.

Magickal Attributes: Abundance, prosperity, children. Harmony in your life. A loving companion. Divination and prophecy. Getting pregnant. Bringing a companion into your life.

Chant

> Fish of prophecy, show me my future.
> Open my mind to true foreseeing.
> Reveal all possibilities
> And help me to make good choices.

OCTOPUS

The octopus, of the genus *Octopoda*, is found in all temperate and warm seas. Sometimes it is called the devil-fish. There about fifty species of octopi ranging in size from one inch to twenty-eight feet. They all have eight arms armed with two rows of suction disks, large prominent eyes, and jaws that are sharp and beak-like. The octopus can rapidly move itself from one place to another by forcing jets of water through its body. The octopus can change colors rapidly if alarmed. Most of these creatures are no larger than an orange, but one from the Pacific Ocean was measured at twenty-eight feet across the tentacles.

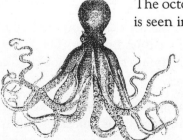

The octopus has been painted on Cretan jars and is seen in many examples of ancient Aegean art. To the Greeks and Minoans, this creature symbolized the sacred spiral of the Goddess and was related to the spider web. As a creature of the Great Mother, it represented Moon phases, feminine powers, and the cycle of life and

222

death. However, it was sometimes used to represent faithlessness after the patriarchal societies took over.

In the art of the Celts and Scandinavians, the octopus is always shown with its arms straight out, not curved as in Mediterranean art. It was an ambivalent creature to these cultures, symbolizing the cycle of life and death, but also the dark, malevolent power of total destruction.

In Japanese lore, it is called Umi Bozu, god of the sea. Because of its firm grip, it represents love. The Samoan held the octopus to be a sacred creature. Hit was an octopus goddess of Micronesia.

Magickal Attributes: Understanding the cycle of life and death. Destruction of negative things. destroying negative barriers. Removing people who are deliberately and harmfully obstructing you, not by destroying them but by moving them on to other places.

Chant

> The sacred spiral gently turns
> And casts its mighty powers about
> Me in a strong protective shield
> And puts my enemies to rout.
> The power turns. It gathers in
> And changes negative to wise,
> Then sends the energy to me
> As reformed power in positive guise.

SALMON

There are two classes of fish belonging to the Salmonidae family: the Atlantic salmon (*Salmo salar*) and the Pacific salmon (*Oncor-hynchus*). This family also includes the trout and char. Salmon are found in the northern latitudes.

The salmon is depicted as a sacred creature primarily in Celtic and Norse cultures. It was especially sacred to the Celts and figures in several of

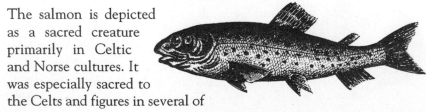

their myths. Usually the inhabitant of a sacred well, the salmon was eaten or consulted for wisdom and prophecy. Any time a Celtic hero eats a salmon, it symbolizes his gaining wisdom and supreme knowledge. This fish was also a creature of the Celtic god Nodens.

Scandinavian stories tell of the trouble-maker, Loki, changing himself into a salmon when he tried to escape from Thorr after he had caused much commotion and upset at a gathering of the gods. It did Loki no good, for the gods captured him and chained him to a great rock. There he must stay, poison dripping on his face, until Doomsday comes.

Magickal Attributes: Wisdom, divination, spiritual knowledge. Help in divination. Seeking wisdom and spiritual understanding through meditation.

Chant

> O salmon of wisdom, guardian of the sacred well,
> Guide me to the spiritual path of ancient wisdom.
> Help me to wisely choose the spiritual food and drink
> That will open my mind and soul to higher knowledge and experience.

SEAL

Seals are large aquatic mammals, with prominent flippers and short, dense fur. They are found in all the oceans of the world. The best known are the sea lions (*Zalophus californianus*) and the Alaskan fur seal (*Callorhinus alascanus*). These members of the Otariidae family have small external ears and front limbs that are as large as those behind.

The ancient Romans believed that a seal skin could protect against thunder storms and lightning strikes. Several European myths and faery tales tell of seal-people who could lay aside their skins temporarily and live on land. Some Scottish and Welsh families claim seal-ancestors. The Mackays of Scotland are known as *sliochd an roin* (descendants of the seal); one of the old lairds tricked a seal-woman into marrying him by hiding her cowl or skin. When she finally managed to find it again, she returned to the sea, leaving behind her husband and a child.

Magickal Attributes: Protection. When faced with changing the life completely. When facing a separation or divorce. Protection from malicious gossip or physical danger.

Chant

> Grant me courage and wisdom to separate myself from
>   troublesome people.
> Show me how to slide easily through the waters of life,
> How to wisely choose companions and revel in the joys of living.

WHALE

Whales are the largest sea mammals in the order *cetacea*. They range in size from twenty to 100 feet long. The toothless whales are: the blue, the finback, the sei, the piked, the humpback, the gray, the right, and the bowhead. They eat small shrimps by straining them out of the water. Toothed whales are: the sperm, the bottlenose, and the killer. The sperm and bottlenose feed on squid and fish, while the killer whale will eat seals, fish, porpoises, large sea birds, and occasionally other whales.

One widespread myth is the story of a hero being swallowed by a whale, then spit out on land at a later date. This action represents death and rebirth. It may also be a symbolic telling of the initiation process for certain ancient Mystery Religions; the initiate was enclosed in a dark place for three days before being brought forth into the light of the temple. One of the first recorded sea goddesses connected with this swallowing story was the Babylonian Derceto, whose name means "The Whale of Der." She swallowed, then gave birth to the

225

god Ea-Oannes. One version of the story of the hero Ilmarinen of Finland says he was temporarily swallowed by a giant fish. The same theme is seen in the Polynesian tale of the hero Nganaoa.

The whale also denotes the waters of life and the regeneration process, whether that is by rebirth back into the physical or awakening in a heavenly realm.

In such vastly separated cultures as the Arabs, the Russians, and the Arctic peoples there were stories of sailors landing on what they thought was an island and which turned out to be a giant whale. The Slavonic cultures have a myth of four whales supporting the Earth. The Norse believed that whales had magick powers and were often the vehicles of witches. In Japan, the Ainu said that the chief god of the sea rode on a whale. Even parts of the Polynesian culture honored whales.

Whales were known to the coastal Native Americans. Even though they were hunted by some tribes as food, they were considered powerful, magickal beings. Whales were thought to be record keepers for the Earth.

Superstitions: *To see a whale is a sign of good luck, unless it is in a place where it hasn't been seen before. Then it is a sign of misfortune.*

Magickal Attributes: The sea, music, long life, family, friends, trust. Developing psychic and telepathic abilities. Using sound and music to balance and heal. Learning new magick. Working with Element magick.

Chant

> *Graceful music, powerful, bold,*
> *Rise up from the oceans cold*
> *As the whales sing out their song*
> *To all creatures who belong*
> *To the Earth and sky and sea.*
> *Lend your joyfulness to me!*

Chapter 14

SPIDERS &
INSECTS

 Spiders are not technically insects, but I have included them among insects in general because of their long-standing traditional connections with the practice of magick.

ANT

The ant is a member of the Hymenoptera family which includes bees and wasps. This insect has a slender waist with conspicuous enlargements of the upper and lower body. Most ants are wingless, except for certain of their number which grow wings for breeding in the air. Basically, there are three castes of ants in a nest: queen, male, and worker. The workers are further divided into the soldiers and the gatherers. Most nests contain thousands of ants; however, the Pharaoh's ants, which are constantly on the move, may have less than a hundred individuals and as many as ten queens.

Universally, the ant symbolizes work, thrift, and forethought. The Chinese call it the "righteous insect" and say it signifies virtue, orderliness, and submission to authority. However, they have a god, Wang-ta Hsien, whom they invoke against the insects and white ants that destroy rice

crops. In the legends of China, Persia, India, and Greece, huge ants guard treasures. Ants were also symbols of the Greek goddess Demeter. As creatures of the goddess Ceres, ants were used in a kind of foretelling ritual. In India, they are said to represent the pettiness of all living things.

Superstitions: *The Cornish think it unlucky to destroy an ant colony.*

If ants are especially busy, bad weather is near.

Cornish tin miners once believed that if you place a piece of tin in an ant hill at a certain Moon sign, it would turn to silver.

If you kill the first ant you see in the Spring, you will triumph over your enemies.

If ants build a nest near your door, you will have security and riches in the future.

Ants never sleep.

Magickal Attributes: Patience, stamina, planning. Working with a group. Planning and building with a plan in your life. Energy and determination needed to complete work. Building and storing energy for a later project.

Chant

> Building, storing, patiently working,
> Shaping my life with an ultimate plan,
> Determination, completing my goals,
> Give the confidence to know that I can.

BEES

The word bee is applied to about twenty families of the Hymenoptera. The term is usually associated with the making of honey. The honeybee, *Apis mellifica*, builds wax cones in which it stores honey and raises its young. It is native to Europe, Asia, and Africa and has been introduced into the Western Hemisphere. However, there are other bees in Asia and Australia. The bumblebee, a large bee which will bore into wood to build a nest, is a familiar insect in many parts of the world.

The Italian honeybee is gentle in temperament and is now the most widely used in the United States. It ranges from dark to golden in color. There are three castes in each bee colony: the queen, the workers, and the drones.

In the early part of the Egyptian civilization, the symbol for royalty in Lower Egypt meant "he who belongs to the bee." Bees were called the tears of the Sun god Ra, and represented birth, death, and resurrection.

Honey was one of the few preservatives known to the ancient cultures. In religious rites honey was used as a symbol of preservation after death. The Finnish *Kalevala* tells how Lemminkainen was restored to life by magick honey from Mehilainen, the Bee.

The Hindu gods Vishnu, Krishna, and Indra are called *madhava*, the "nectar-born ones," in the *Rig Veda*. Vishnu is often symbolized by a blue bee sitting on a lotus, while Krishna has a blue bee on his forehead.

In Minoan Crete the bee and the bull had similar mystical meanings. Seals and gemstones often showed a bee on one side and a bull on the other. An onyx gem was found in Knossos which shows the Goddess with the head and eyes of a bee and on her head double bull horns with a labyrs between them.

The sacredness of the bee has a long history in Greece. Aristotle, Pliny, and others wrote that good souls could come back as bees. To the Greeks, the bee symbolized industry, prosperity, purity, and immortality. The writer Porphyry said that bees were the souls of Aphrodite's priestesses (nymphs); this was considered to be especially true of those who served her temple at Eryx where a golden honeycomb was her symbol.

Bees were lunar creatures when connected with the goddesses Demeter, Cybele, Artemis/Diana, and Rhea. With the goddess Demeter as the Queen Bee, her priestesses were called Melissae, or the Bees. The name Melissa was once the title of a priestess of the Great Mother. Some records list the priestess at Delphi as the Delphic Bee. Even in the Eleusinian Mysteries, which were in honor of Demeter, the officials were known as Bees. The title, Melissae, on occasion carried over to the priestesses of Apollo, probably because bees were said to have erected some of the temples at Delphi.

These insects are shown on statues of Artemis. In the Ephesian temple of Artemis, this title was also used for the priestesses, while the eunuch priests were called *essenes* (drones, King Bees), according to the ancient writer, Pausanias.

The Greek myths tell how both Zeus and Dionysus were fed by bees when they were babies. Legend says that Dionysus made the first hives and introduced the use of honey to the people; he was offered honey-cakes at his shrines. Both Pan and Priapus were gods who protected and kept bees.

To see a swarm of bees in China was considered lucky. To the Romans, however, a swarm meant misfortune, defeat in battle, or death. The Koran says that bees symbolize wisdom, harmlessness, and the faithful. In the Celtic cultures, bees were said to have a secret wisdom that came directly from the Otherworlds. Even the Aztecs made reference to a Bee God.

Superstitions: *Bee venom, now used in the form of a cream, is a very ancient remedy for joint diseases, such as arthritis.*

Celtic country folk still say that you must tell the bees if someone in the family dies, or they will fly away. The same applies to a marriage. If a bee flies into the house, a stranger is coming.

Stolen bees will not thrive, but die. In Wales, to give a hive to someone will bring good luck, but they will not sell bees. However, it is permissible to barter for a hive.

Supposedly bees hum loudly on Christmas Eve.

It is considered to be unlucky to kill a bee because they are called The Little Servants of God; this designation of the bee as a "servant" originated with the Goddess religions.

A bee flying into your house means a visitor is coming.

Supposedly, any girl who is a virgin can pass through a swarm of bees without getting stung.

The saying "busy as a bee" refers to this insect's constant movement and work when the weather is good.

Medieval scholars believed that bees were born from the dead bodies of cows and calves. These blood maggots were said to be the early stages of the bee. They also believed that bees were ruled by kings.

Magickal Attributes: Concentration necessary to carry out a task. Planning and saving for the future. Prosperity. Astral traveling to the realm of the Goddess to better understand the cycle of reincarnation. Talking to a deceased person. Helping an Earth-bound spirit move on to its proper place.

Chant

> You have lost your way, Earth spirit.
> Tell me what you still seek,
> What keeps you bound to this place.
> I will call upon your loved ones in spirit.
> They will guide you to realms of peace and healing.
> Follow them to the pathway of Light.

BEETLE or SCARAB BEETLE

This name has been given to members of the family Scarabaeidae of the order Coleoptera. The most famous of these beetles, *Scarabaeus sacer*, is in Egypt. It is about an inch long and can live for more than two years.

The Scarab Beetle has become widely known through the beliefs of the ancient Egyptians, who revered it as a symbol of the Sun. It is also called the dung beetle. This little insect rolls a ball of dung to cover the egg it has placed inside. It was an emblem of the Egyptian god Khepera, the god of creation, the Sun, and immortality. The image of the *scarabaeus* beetle was a common amulet buried with the dead as a source of new life for the heart in the next world. These sacred beetles were carved on all kinds of amulets and seals. Large images of them were worshiped in temples.

During the Middle Ages, the alchemists drew the scarab beetle in diagrams of the double spiral, which they said led to the center of the universe.

Superstitions: *The Scots say that if a beetle enters a room while the family is seated, it means bad luck; however, you get even worse luck if you kill it.*

If a beetle walks over your shoe, it is a death omen.

Many parts of Europe say that a beetle can bring on a terrible storm.

The sound of a deathwatch beetle is a signal of approaching death in the family.

Magickal Attributes: Vitality, new life. Learning to pace yourself through the seasonal changes of the year. Learning about past lives. Seeking spiritual enlightenment.

Chant

> Open the door to lives long gone.
> Show me the door with the spiritual key,
> The door to my past, to the lives that I lived.
> My spiritual pattern I need to see.

BUTTERFLY

The name butterfly is given to a large group of Lepidoptera, which includes moths. These insects are found in a variety of colors, shapes, and sizes around the world. Most of them fly only during the daylight hours and usually feed on the nectar of flowers; moths fly at night. Colorful dust-like scales coat the wings. They have a knob, or enlargement, at the tip of their antennae; this physical trait distinguishes them from moths.

The butterfly is a Chinese symbol of immortality, leisure, and joy; if shown with a chrysanthemum, it depicts beauty in old age; with a plum, long life. A jade butterfly was believed by the Chinese to be an emblem of love. In Japan this insect represents much the same thing, with a pair of butterflies meaning married happiness. However, it can symbolize a false lover or vain woman. The Japanese say that a pure white butterfly can contain the soul of someone who has died.

The labyrs, or double-axe, of the Bronze Age and Crete may well symbolize a butterfly. This axe probably came from the original hourglass-shape of the Goddess, who symbolized death and regeneration. The Greek, Germanic, and Slavonic words *mora*, *mara*, and *morava* mean both "nightmare" and "butterfly." The Death Goddess of

Lithuania (More) and of Ireland (Maro or Mara) may well be connected with this Mediterranean interpretation.

In Greek art, the butterfly symbolized the psyche, or soul, and represented immortality. The Horae, who were goddesses of the seasons, were sometimes shown with butterfly wings.

In such widely-separated places as Cornwall, Mexico, and Siberia, the white butterfly is said to be a spirit of the dead. The Celts firmly believed that the soul could occupy either a butterfly or a fly.

Certain Native Americans believed that the butterfly had power over the whirlwind, causing it to appear and disappear by the flapping of its wings. Xochiquetzal, the love goddess of ancient Mexico, was pictured as a human-headed moth or butterfly.

Superstitions: *In Serbia they say that if you kill a butterfly, you kill a witch.*

The people of Devonshire believed that if you killed the first butterfly you saw each year you would have good luck.

In Scotland, a golden butterfly near a dying person was considered to be a good omen of eternal happiness; much the same was believed in Ireland.

If the first butterfly you see in the year is yellow, you will become ill.

Three butterflies on a leaf are unlucky. A butterfly flying at night is an omen of death.

If a black moth flies into a house, someone will die. However, if it flies at you from the darkness, an important letter is on the way.

Magickal Attributes: Reincarnation, magick, beauty, love. Transformation of the personality and life. Understanding where you are in the cycle of your life and using it to the fullest. Divination concerning future events that have a bearing on your cycle of life and rebirth.

Chant

> *Beautiful creature, wings lit by the Sun,*
> *Help me to know when this life is done*
> *A new life awaits from the Spirit above,*
> *My soul shall renew through the magick of love.*

DRAGONFLY

There are about a thousand different kinds of this insect, which is a member of the suborder Anisoptera of the order Odonata. They all have large heads, composed mostly of eyes. Its two huge compound eyes give it an exotic appearance. The dragonfly has a long, slender body and four large, strong wings.

The dragonfly is also called the Devil's Darning Needle, the Bee Butcher, and the Mosquito Hawk. It is one of the most beautiful of all insects and harmless to humans and animals, regardless of some of the gruesome folklore connected with it. However, it does eat large quantities of insects, particularly mosquitoes, both as an adult and as a nymph. It doesn't sting or attack horses.

The dragonfly shares much of the same symbolism as that of the butterfly. It is the national emblem of Japan, which is sometimes called the Island of the Dragonfly, *Akitsu-Shima*. Japanese art and poetry make frequent use of this insect. However, it can also represent irresponsibility and unreliability. The Chinese say that the dragonfly symbolizes Summer, weakness, and instability.

There are Native American legends that say the dragonfly was once a dragon and had scales like those on the dragonfly's wings. However, Coyote tricked it into changing it form, and it couldn't change back. They say it represents swiftness, illusion, and change.

Superstitions: *Dragonflies are believed to sew together the lips of people who sleep outside overnight. They are said to attack snakes and sting horses.*

If a dragonfly hovers over a fisherman, he will have good fishing luck.

Magickal Attributes: Dreams, illusions. Mystic messages of enlightenment from spirit. Breaking down illusions in order to transform your life. Change is coming. Understanding dreams. Opening yourself to messages from the gods. Seeing the truth in any situation or person.

Chant

> *A key to my dreams, an eye for the truth,*
> *An ear open to spirit for messages bold,*
> *Will break down illusions and transform my life,*
> *So I remake myself in a positive mold.*

SPIDERS

This is the most common member of the class Arachnida and is related to scorpions. There are extremely few places in the world where one doesn't find some kind of spider. There are nearly 100,000 species, with over 2,000 in the United States alone. They range in size from an eighth-inch up to the huge tarantulas.

A spider is in a class by itself; it has four pairs of legs. The head and thorax are fused together. The abdomen is unsegmented, round, and soft. It spins its silk for webs out through spinnerets on the underside of the abdomen. Most spiders have four pairs of simple eyes on the top of the head. Nearly all spiders have fangs and poison glands; in some the venom is more potent than in others. While all can produce silken strands of one kind or another, only a few spin complicated and beautiful orb webs.

The only spider I can tolerate in my house is the wolf spider. This hairy, active spider with strong legs doesn't spin a web but runs down its prey. It usually hunts at night but can be out and about during the day. They are playful creatures. If you tap next to them with a pencil, they will jump forward and backward, alternately attacking and retreating. I watched a whole colony of them hatch out one year in my plant room. The tiny black specks fanned out across the ceiling and within a day's time completely vacated the house, although I don't know how they got outside.

This is one of the most powerful creatures in all myth and symbolism in both the Old and New Worlds; it represents the Great Terrible Mother in her fate-weaver aspect. Neith was the Weaver of the World in Egypt;

in Babylon it was Ishtar and Atargatis; in Greece, Athene and the Fates; in Norse myth, the Norns and Holda. One Greek tale tells how the goddess Athene turned the human Arachne into a spider because of her arrogance over her spinning and weaving.

The Hindus say that the spider weaves life itself from its own body, but is also the creator of illusion, or *maya*. Barbara Walker suggests that the eight-armed deities of India and Odhinn's eight-legged horse may be associated with the spider.

The Japanese have two spider goddesses: Spider Woman, who can ensnare careless travelers, and the Goblin Spider, who can change shape to harm people.

The Ashanti of Africa say that the Great Spider is God. In many African tales, the spider is a trickster deity. This idea was brought to Jamaica in the form of Anansi, the Great Spider.

Many Native American tribes had a spider deity. To the Plains people, this was Inktomi, the Trickster Spider, a shape-shifter who brought culture to their people. The Southwestern Pueblo tribes speak of Spider Woman, who created the universe; they refer to her as Kokyangwuti, Tsitsicinako, Sussistanako, Thought Woman, or Thinking Woman. Spider Grandmother is the Kiowa heroine/goddess who brought light to the world. Native Americans say that the spider's web connects it with the four Elements. They believe although it is a small creature, it is cunning and intelligent, tricking other insects into its webs. They called spider power the female energy for the creative force of life.

There are a number of poisonous spiders whose bite can be debilitating and sometimes fatal to humans. I see nothing wrong with getting rid of spiders indoors since one can't always tell which is which until you've been bitten.

Superstitions: *Many folk tales around the world still portray the spider as lucky, a creature who can spin money, but who also is crafty and cunning.*

The dance called the tarantella was originally the specified cure for the bite of the tarantula spider.

Some people believe that if you kill a spider it will rain.

A cobweb is said to stop bleeding when laid on a wound. This really works if the cut isn't too deep!

In the United States, if a girl finds a cobweb on her door, her boy friend is seeing another girl.

If a spider falls on you from the ceiling, it is good luck. If you find one crawling on your clothes, money is coming. This is especially true if it is the little red "money spider."

If you see a spider spinning its web, you will get new clothes.

There is an old saying: If you wish to live and thrive, let the spider run alive.

In Britain and many parts of Europe it was once believed that swallowing a piece of web, eating a crushed spider, or wearing a bag of live spiders around the neck would cure whooping cough, gout, ague, and asthma.

Magickal Attributes: wisdom, creativity, new life. Being industrious. Be cautious: you are involved in a tempting but entangling situation. Bringing in divine inspiration and creativity. Beginning a new project or becoming pregnant.

Chant

> *Webs of beauty and purpose,*
> *Dew-gemmed and rainbow-wrapped,*
> *The spider never questions its creative ability.*
> *O Deities of Earth and sky, the four directions,*
> *Help me to be creative with such confidence.*

Chapter 15

MYTHICAL CREATURES

 Although mythical creatures exist only in the inner dimensions of the mind, that does not make them any less powerful as familiars. Several of the following creatures are of a malevolent nature and should be used with extreme caution. Working with mythical creatures is really no different than working with other astral familiars.

BASILISK

The basilisk, or cockatrice, was not a large creature, but its glance and breath were considered deadly. Its name comes from the Greek and means "little king serpent," or King of Small Serpents. It had the head of a cock with a three-pointed crest, glittering yellow toad-eyes, the body of a snake, the talons of a cock, and a sting in its tail. Ancient writers said it hissed like a snake and could split rocks with its breath. To smell its breath, be touched by its tail, or look into its eyes was said to kill a person or at least drive them insane.

Medieval writers got carried away when describing the origin of the basilisk; they said it came from a yolk-less egg laid by a cock and

hatched by a toad in a pile of manure. They said that the only two ways to destroy a basilisk were to let it see itself in a mirror or to set a weasel (probably a mongoose) on it.

Although one hears more about basilisks in Western lore, there is mention of them in the East. There the creature was said to be a mixture of cock, snake, and toad.

Legends refer to the basilisk as a creator of wastelands, which it presumably causes by its deadly breath; there in the wastelands, it keeps and guards treasure.

Magickal Attributes: Revenge, retribution, protection. Setting up a reflective protection to return dark magick.

Chant

> In a mirror, bright not dark,
> An awesome figure reflects its form
> Into a barrier, protective, fierce.
> I stand behind it safe from harm.
> No threats can reach me, here behind.
> No magick reaches to my heart.
> The mirror sends evil back to source.
> O evil powers, now depart!

CENTAUR

The centaur was known to various cultures in the Middle East, but we are acquainted with it primarily through Greek lore. Centaurs were always portrayed as male; they had the upper body, head, and arms of a man and the lower body and legs of a horse.

One legend said they came from the sexual union of the Greek Centaurus and the Magnesian mares. In the Hindu pantheon were the Asvins and the Gandharvas, or horse-gods; the Indo-Europeans may have brought this idea of man-horse beings with them when they traveled through Greece. The area of central Asia had the belief in man-horse wizards also. Assyrian seals show both the centaur and the winged horse.

Hellenic myths say the centaur Cheiron was the son of a god and was skilled in hunting, medicine, music, and divination. The wild, shaggy Greek centaurs were considered to be great wizards, shape-shifters, and well-versed in occult lore. They taught their skills to the gods and special heroes. Another name for centaurs was Magnetes, or "great ones," which comes from the Magnesian mares.

Another Greek tradition said that the centaurs were the offspring of Demeter; in Crete, they supposedly came from Leukippe, the White Mare Goddess. The horse-masked priestesses of the Pirene fountain were called the Pegae, connecting them with Pegasus who dug the spring of the Muses. The Greeks also called these priestesses the man-eating mares.

Magickal Attributes: Healing magick, shape-shifting, music, the arts, divination. Inspiration for an artistic talent.

Chant

> *Healing, shape-shifting, magickal lifting*
> *Of spirit to spiritual realms of delight.*
> *Consciousness higher meets spiritual fire*
> *And changes my powers from weakness to might.*

DRAGON

The dragon in one form or another was known to the majority of world cultures in both the Old and New Worlds. It was one of the early symbols of the Great Mother Goddess of the matriarchies. Until the arrival of patriarchal societies, the dragon was considered to be a sacred, benevolent creature; its serpent body symbolized matter and life-giving water of creation, its wings spirit and the sacred breath of life.

It was used as an emblem for divinity and royalty in Babylon, Egypt, China, Japan, Greece, and Rome. The Chinese Manchu dynasty, the Phoenicians, and the Saxons all showed it as enthroned, a symbol of the power of the ruler. The Chinese dragon symbolized the masculine yang power, very high spiritual power, and the emperor himself. This connection with imperial power carried over into England and Wales.

The dragon was known as the King of Larger Serpents to medieval writers. Dragons and bulls in the Western world were fought by such Sun-heroes as Mithras, Siegfried, Hercules, Jason, Horus, and Apollo.

In Hindu myth, Vitra, the Dragon of the Waters, was killed by Indra so that the waters could be released upon the Earth. The dragon was also an emblem of Aruna and Soma.

There were two major categories of physical appearance of dragons: those of the East and those of the West.

The Oriental or Chinese dragon looked terrible and fierce, but was a symbol of prosperity, rain, wisdom, and hidden secrets. Oriental dragons did not have wings, but were shaped more like huge serpents with four legs. The early Chinese worshiped the dragon, and at one time had its image on national flags. Using the symbol of the five-toed imperial dragon was reserved for emperors. The guardian of the mansions of the gods was the Chinese Celestial Dragon, T'ien Lung; he also prevented the deities from falling out of their heavenly realm. Oriental heroes did not hunt the dragon, as did Western heroes. The Oriental dragons were said to leave their mountain caves or watery homes in the Spring to bring the fertilizing rains.

Both the Chinese and Japanese believe that dragons can turn themselves into birds. The three-clawed dragon of Japan symbolized the Mikado, the imperial and spiritual power. Most Japanese dragons were said to live in lakes and springs.

Ancient Western writers wrote all kinds of terrifying things about the Western dragons. These creatures were built like enormous lizards with wings; their bodies were thicker than those of Oriental dragons. Their throats and back legs were like those of an eagle, the grasping front legs like those of a reptile, and a tail that ended in an arrow-point. Western dragons were considered to be enemies of humans, and heroes were always hunting them down and killing them. Under the circumstances, it's no wonder that Western dragons stopped trying to get along with humans. They liked to live in dark caves, a few of them in water. They breathed fire, and their breath was supposed to spread plagues.

The dragon in alchemy had a number of meanings. If several dragons were shown fighting each other, it meant separating out the Elements, or psychic disintegration. A dragon biting its tail symbolized cyclic processes and time; this particular dragon was known to the Gnostics as Ouroboros. A winged dragon represented a volatile Element, while the wingless dragon stood for a fixed Element.

In spiritual definitions, the dragon represents the supernatural, infinity itself, and the spiritual powers of change and transformation.

Magickal Attributes: Protection, instruction in the spiritual, Element magick. Using the spiritual to transform life. Protection. Adding extra power to magick.

Chant

> Dragons strong and dragons bright,
> Dragons full of wisdom old,
> Teach to me the spiritual light.
> Let me walk with knowledge bold.
> Dragon fire, lift me higher!

GRIFFIN

The griffin (sometimes spelled gryphon or griffon) was enormous, with the head, claws, and wings of an eagle, and the back parts of a lion. Its tail was long and serpentine. A Sun symbol, this creature was said to build its nest in the mountains and line it with gold. It symbolized the combination of Earth and sky. The griffin was known throughout the Near and Middle East, including Greece. It was sometimes shown lying down, other times sitting on its haunches. The Mesopotamian griffin had a crested head, while that of the Greeks was pictured with a mane of spiral curls.

Among the Greeks the griffin was consecrated to the goddess Nemesis and the god Apollo in their vengeful aspects. The Babylonians and Persians had similar creatures with wings, eagle-head, goat-beard, lion-body. The description is much the same for the Hebrew cherubim, the Arabian roc, Garuda of India, and the winged bulls of Assyria.

As the guardian to the pathway to spiritual enlightenment, this creature was usually shown next to a Tree of Life or a similar symbol. The griffin symbolized the seasons and guarded the Sun, the sacred Golden Apples, and treasures. It is one of the oldest and most popular symbols in heraldry.

Medieval scholars wrote that the griffin was especially hostile to horses.

Magickal Attributes: Understanding the relationship between psychic energy and cosmic force. Spiritual enlightenment.

Chant

> *The griffin in its mighty form*
> *Stands at the gates between the worlds,*
> *And ushers in the seekers of*
> *Initiation, enlightenment.*
> *The wisdom-filled Doorkeeper*
> *Guards us from the dark sides of ourselves*

Until we gain the strength and knowledge
To bring the dark into submission.
Guard and guide me, O great griffin!

PEGASUS

Pegasus (from Greek and Roman mythology) was a beautiful white horse with wings. Legend says that the Fountain of Hippocrene (the Moon-Horse well or spring) on Mount Helicon, and which belonged to the Muses, was created when Pegasus struck the ground there with his hoof. Pegasus supposedly sprang into being from the blood of Medusa when Perseus cut off her head.

However, there are other stories of the creation of Pegasus. One says that he rose from the menstrual blood of the Moon goddess Medusa. Another says he was born of the goddess Demeter when she was raped by Poseidon; this assumes that Pegasus and the magickal horse Arion were the same being. Very early records tell of a female Pegasus named Aganippe, which is actually another name for Demeter in her destroying aspect of the Nightmare. Pegasus was also sacred to the people of Carthage.

However, the idea of Pegasus may have originated in Egypt where the ancient shrine of Osiris at Abydos held a sacred spring called Pega. This cult may have branched off later to Corinth, where the sacred spring of Pirene was tended by the water-priestesses known as the Pegae.

During the Middle Ages, there appeared in the bestiaries a similar creature called a hippogryph.

Magickal Attributes: Poetic inspiration; learning astral travel. Changing evil into good. Riding Pegasus in meditation or astral travel to Otherworlds can help bring poetic inspiration. Fame, eloquence.

Chant

> *Through time-clouds I fly to days gone by.*
> *Physical limits are all left behind.*
> *The future and past, all in my grasp,*
> *For Pegasus shows me the key's in my mind.*
> *Horse of poetry, Light,*
> *Inspirational height,*
> *Your companion I'll be,*
> *New lands shall I see.*

PHOENIX

The phoenix is known in various forms, and by various names, around the world, as a symbol of resurrection. Although it was sometimes said to be about the size of an eagle, it had certain characteristics of the pheasant. It was said to live most of its life in a secret, sacred garden and fed on air. When it reached a thousand years old, legend says the phoenix flew to a special place and built a funeral nest of sweet-smelling woods and resins in a tall palm tree. In fact, the Greek word for phoenix and palm tree are the same. When the nest was set ablaze by the force of the Sun, the phoenix stayed in the nest and was destroyed. After nine days, a new phoenix rose from the ashes.

The Egyptian phoenix was often identified with the bennu bird, a heron sacred to Osiris and Ra, and a symbol of the Sun and resurrection. In Mesopotamian art, the phoenix may have originally been the horned and winged solar disk. The Greek word *Kerkes* (falcon) was applied to the phoenix and connects it with the goddess Circe.

Traditions from Turkey call this creature the *Kerkes*; the Persians knew it as the *Simurgh*. The Simurgh, written about in the *Shah-Nameh*, had lion claws, peacock plumes, snake tails, and a griffin head.

Such Greek and Roman writers as Tacitus, Ovid, Pliny, Herodotus, and Hesiod all referred to the phoenix either as the Arabian

Bird or the Egyptian Bird. An extremely gentle creature, it was said to weep tears of incense, while its blood was balsam.

It was the emperor of birds in China and a lunar-solar symbol. The phoenix represented the empress, while the dragon represented the emperor. As one of the Chinese Sacred Creatures, the phoenix had five colors, symbolizing the five Chinese virtues. It was called the *Feng-huang*, or fire-bird. To the Japanese, the phoenix was the *Ho-Ho*, which reappeared on Earth to open each new era, then returned to heaven. It was a solar symbol in Japan.

Alchemists used the phoenix to symbolize the color red and the successful completion of a process.

Magickal Attributes: Rebirth, renewal, spiritual growth. Call upon the phoenix for strength and renewed energy when facing or undergoing trials of life.

Chant

> *Out of ashes, new beginnings,*
> *Out of fire comes new power,*
> *Out of darkness, new day dawning,*
> *Phoenix, help me in this trying hour.*

SATYR

The Greek satyrs were horned deities of wild nature and followed the gods Pan, Silvanus, Faunus, Dionysus, and Bacchus. Sometimes satyrs (Roman, Sileni) were described as young men with the ears and tail of a horse; other times as having the body, arms, and sex organs of men and the legs, hooves, and tails of goats. They loved music, dancing, women, and wine.

Pan was known to the Greeks as the "Little God," the Horned God of Nature, or the goat-foot god; he was a frequent companion of the god Dionysus. Pan was one of the oldest of Greek deities and the Positive Life Force of the world. In his light aspect, Pan symbolized the woodlands and the wild creatures, healing, gardening, plants and animals, music and dancing, soothsaying, and lovemaking. However, he had a dark side in which he caused the wild and unreasoning terror sometimes experienced in lonely woodlands and mountains.

The Greeks identified the Egyptian Amen-Ra with Pan and called his holy city of Chemmis by the Greek name Panopolis, "city of Pan." The word "panoply," meaning elaborate religious ceremonies, may have originated with this name.

The Roman version of a satyr was called a faun. This was a woodland spirit, half-man, half-goat, with twisted ram-horns, pointed ears, and a goat tail. As companions of the god Faunus, fauns lived in the wild forests.

The Slavic-Russian cultures had a wood spirit called the Leshi, which resembled the satyrs; the Leshi were said sometimes to have human shape with the horns, ears, and legs of a goat.

Aldrovandus, a medieval writer, stated that there were an infinite number of satyrs in Ireland.

Magickal Attributes: Music, dancing, lovemaking. Lustful and untamed emotions. Use absolutely no drugs, alcohol, or stimulants when calling on the satyrs and Pan!

Chant

> Ancient Pan of Arcadian woods,
> I feel your wisdom, hear your words.
> I seek instruction and desire
> To turn emotion to spiritual fire.
> Great ancient Pan,
> Show me how I can!

SPHINX

The sphinx is known through the surviving, but badly eroded, Egyptian monument near the pyramids. However, there were two kinds of sphinxes: the Egyptian and the Greek. The Egyptian sphinx had the head of a man and the body of a lion. It symbolized the four Elements and Spirit, and all the science of the past. Barbara Walker suggests that the sphinx may symbolize the Egyptian goddess Hathor in her lioness aspect.

The generic Greek creature had the head and breasts of a woman, the body of a lion, and wings. However, the Theban sphinx described in legend had the head and breasts of a woman, the body of a dog, the claws of a lion, tail of a dragon, and wings of a bird. The Greeks associated her with initiation and death. Jung compared this creature to the archetypal Terrible Mother. The Babylonian sphinx, symbolizing the goddess Astarte, was female like that of the Greeks. The Hittites carved in rock images of lion bodies with human heads.

A mysterious magickal being, the sphinx was said to possess the deepest secrets of the universe, but remained eternally silent.

Magickal Attributes: Initiation, end of a cycle, Element magick. Meeting the Dark Mother; instruction from Her.

Chant

> I spiral inward to the Center,
> The hidden sacred space of the Dark Mother.
> She awaits beside Her cauldron of rebirth
> With open arms and comforting words.
> The silent sphinx sits beside Her,
> All ancient knowledge in its keeping.
> The Wise One is the ultimate wisdom of life.
> She answers all who call to Her.
> None pass through death without Her.
> No one re-enters life, but with Her blessing.
> From Her hands come all cycles, physical or material.
> I await Her wise words.

UNICORN

The unicorn has long been a favorite mythical creature in both the Western world and the Orient. This creature has been depicted and supposedly seen in such places as China, Mongolia, Persia, Babylon, Assyria, Chaldea, Palestine, Egypt, Africa, Poland, Scandinavia, Florida, along the Canadian border, and in many other places around the world.

According to Barbara Walker, the unicorn may have originated in the seasonal animal symbols of Egypt and Babylonia. In Babylonia there was a dragon-beast that had a horse-like body, lion's front legs, a long neck, and a flat head with a single horn on the center of the nose.

Pliny wrote that the unicorn lived in India, while Herodotus said it existed in Libya. Ethiopia claimed to have unicorns living in the Upper Nile regions. The Tibetans wrote of seeing unicorns there, and the Arabs knew this animal well.

The Western and Oriental unicorn were similar in nature, but differ in description. The Chinese unicorn was called *Ch'i-lin*, or *Ky-lin*, and could have either one or two horns. This creature was said to have the head of a dragon, the tail of an ox, and a stag's body. Its skin was red, yellow, blue, white, and black; when it made a noise, it sounded like bells. Chinese legend says this unicorn lived for a thousand years; they considered it to be the noblest of animals. As an emblem of high birth and good character, it was a symbol of high-ranking army officers. The Japanese creature called the *Ki-rin* is exactly the same mythical being.

In Greek and Roman art, the goddess Artemis/Diana was often shown in a chariot being pulled by eight unicorns. This connection with Moon goddesses was seen in art as far back as the Sumero-Semitic civilizations.

The Western creature had the head and body of a horse, the hind legs of an antelope or stag, the whiskers of a goat, the tail of a lion, and a long spiral horn in the middle of its forehead. Sometimes the horn was said to be straight instead. Medieval writers left detailed descriptions of the unicorn. Vertomannus, Albertus Magnus, and Strabo said that it had split hooves like those of a goat.

There are many stories of the unicorn being hunted for its horn (the Alicorn), which was considered to detect and be an antidote for poisons. The unicorn lived in the forests and was so swift no one could catch it. In order to trap it, a beautiful young virgin was set as bait; the unicorn would come to her willingly.

Medieval alchemists considered the unicorn to be of an ambivalent nature and used it to symbolize the *Monstrum Hermaphroditum*. Western cultures believed that the unicorn was a lunar animal, gentle and wise, while some the Middle Eastern and Eastern cultures said it was fierce and had great strength. They also said it was no larger than a goat. They believed that the unicorn killed elephants by goring them in the stomach.

Magickal Attributes: Good will, fame, prosperity, gentleness, purity, strength of mind. Individual power that is unlimited. For wisdom with success. Developing personal power.

Chant

> *A child of the unicorn, that would I be.*
> *Your goodness and wisdom reflected in me.*
> *Let me seek for the good things that brighten my name,*
> *For gentleness, purity, abundance, and fame.*
> *Let me know that my power is forever unbound,*
> *That what's given in love circles right back around.*

WINGED BULL

The massive figure of the winged bull can still be seen in Assyrian and Sumero-Semitic sculpture. The Assyrians called this being the Shedim, or Shedu. They carved his image in stone as guardian of the gates and doors of their temples and palaces. The winged bull had a crowned man's head and the body of a bull with wings.

The Cretan minotaur is another form of the man-bull. Supposedly, this creature was born from the union of Parsiphae and the Minoan sacred bull. The minotaur signifies the animal passions of humans that can rage out of control if not balanced by spiritual understanding.

Magickal Attributes: Supernatural strength; protection. Protection without revenge, but through spiritual strength.

Chant

Ancient winged bull, your form is a powerful symbol
Of the physical in which we live and the spiritual toward which
*   we reach.*
Winged bull standing firm upon the Earth
With feathered wings to raise you toward spirit,
Show me the way to control the emotions and physical desires.
Teach me the secrets of going beyond what is seen and felt
To what is unseen and experienced in a greater reality.

WYVERN

The wyvern, a creature of the Western world, resembles the dragon in some aspects, but is a separate magickal creature. It had a head like a dragon, body like a serpent, a barbed tail, wings, strong talons, but only two rear legs, like those of eagles. Seeing it brought great fear, for it symbolized war, viciousness, and pestilence. The wyvern was more aggressive than the dragon. To the Saxons it was the *Wivere*, a winged serpent.

Magickal Attributes: Revenge, retribution. Creating protective barriers of fear as a defense.

Chant

The winged serpent hunts the night,
Its great wings silent in its flight.
It casts its shadow o'er the Moon,
My mighty guardian wyvern. Soon
All those who wish me woe shall know
The winged serpent is their foe.

PART IV

APPENDIX
BIBLIOGRAPHY
INDEX

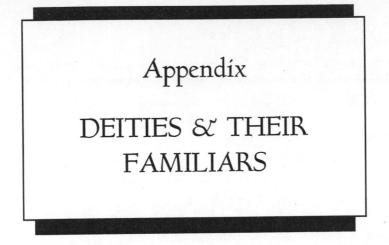

Appendix

DEITIES & THEIR FAMILIARS

Addad/Iskur (Canaan, Babylonia, Assyria, Syria, Mesopotamia; god): bull, lion-dragon

Aditi (India; goddess): cow

Adonis (Middle East; god): dove, nightingale, boar

Aganippe (Greece, Crete; goddess): Pegasus

Agni (India; god): bull, goat, ram

Agunua (Solomon Islands; god): serpent

Ahriman (Persia; god): serpent, cats, jackal, wolf, frog, lizard, toad

Ahura Mazda (Middle East; god): hawk

Amaru (Inca; goddess): dragon

Amen/Amen Ra (Egypt; god): ram with curled horns, goose, satyr, frog

Amenti (Egypt; goddess): hawk, ostrich, dog, hippo

Anahita (Middle East; goddess): horse

Anait (Phoenicia, Canaan, Ur; goddess): lion, dog

Anansi (West Africa; god): spider

Anath (Middle East; goddess): owl

Andraste (Celtic; goddess): hare

Angus mac Og (Ireland; god): bird

Anubis (Egypt; god): cock, jackal

Apesh (Egypt; god): tortoise

Aphrodite (Greece; goddess): heron, lovebird, swan, dove, sparrow, swallow, vulture, boar, deer, hare, sheep, frog, turtle, tortoise, fish, bee

Apollo (Greece; god): cock, crane, crow, goose, horse, raven, hawk, quail, swan, vulture, lion, wolf, stag, mouse, snake, dolphin, bee, dragon, griffin

Apsaras (India; goddesses): swan

Arawn (Wales; god): dog, pig

Ares (Greece; god): goose, vulture, woodpecker, wolf, boar

Artemis (Greece; goddess): wild animals, dog, stag, guinea fowl, hawk, quail, horse, cats, wolf, antelope, bear, bull, deer, goat, bee, unicorn

Asclepius (Greece; god): pale brown snake, raven

Asherah (Middle East; goddess): cow

Ashoreth (Middle East; goddess): dog

Asshur (Assyria, Babylonia; god): bull, snake-dragon, white horse, eagle

Astaeria (Greece; goddess): quail

Astarte (Babylonia, Assyria, Phoenicia; goddess): dove, pigeon, horse, bull, dog, antelope, cow, dolphin

Asvins, the (India; gods): horse, bird, centaur

Atargatis (Syria, Canaan, Mesopotamia, Philistines; goddess): dove, pigeon, fish, snake, spider

Athene (Greece; goddess): cock, owl, crow, ox, horse, dove, heron, intertwined snakes, guinea fowl, raven, vulture, dog, deer, goat, spider

Attis (Middle East; god): nightingale, lion, ram

Audhumla (Norse; goddess): cow

Auf (Egypt; god): ram

Aulanerk (Eskimo; god): sea creatures

Ba'al (Middle East; god): quail, bull

Ba'alat (Phoenicia; goddess): cobra

Ba'al Gad (Middle East; god): goat

Ba'al-Hammon (Carthage; god): ram

Baba Yaga (Slavonic; goddess): snake

Bacchus (Rome; god): dove, panther, satyr, centaur, elephant, satyr, pig

Badb (Ireland; goddess): crow, raven

Ba-Neb-Tetet (Egypt; god): ram

Bast (Egypt; goddess): cats, lynx

Behanzin (West Africa; god): fish

Bel (Ireland; god. Middle East; god): cattle, bull, snake

Belit-ili (Middle East; goddess): dog

Benten (Japan; goddess): dragon, white snake

Biliku (Micronesia; goddess): spider

Blodeuwedd (Wales; goddess): owl

Brahma (India; god): swan, peacock, raven

Bran the Blessed (Wales; god): raven, wren

Branwen (Wales; goddess): crow

Brigit (Wales, goddess): cock, boar, ewe, snake

Buto (Egypt; goddess): cobra, vulture, shrew-mouse

Cailleach (Scotland; goddess): crane, owl, adder

Callisto (Greece; goddess): bear

Camael (Angelic): leopard

Cassiel (Angelic): dragon

Centon Totochtin (Aztec; gods): rabbit

Ceres (Rome; goddess): pig, ant

Cernunnos/Herne the Hunter/the Horned God (Celtic; god): wild animals, ram, stag, bull, horned serpent, flocks, goat, bear, wolf, otter

Cerridwen (Wales; goddess): sow

Chac (Maya; god): serpent

Chandra (India; god): antelope, hare

Chang Kwo-lao (China; god): donkey

Ch'ang-O (China; goddess): hare

Chantico (Aztec; goddess): red serpent

Cheiron (Greece; god): centaur

Ch'ing-Wa Sheng (China; goddess): frog

Chu Pa-chieh (China; god): pig

Circe (Greece; goddess): falcon, sow, phoenix

Cit Chac Coh (Maya; god): dog

Coatlicue (Aztec; goddess): snake

Cocidius (Celtic; god): stag

Coyolxauhqui (Mexico; goddess): snake

Coyote (Many Native American tribes; god): coyote

Cronus (Greece; god): raven, ass

Cybele (Greece, Phrygia; goddess): bees, lion, wild animals, dog

Dagon (Philistines; god): fish, serpent

Daikoku (Japan; god): white rat

Damkina/Damgalnuna (Mesopotamia; goddess): lion

Danh (Dahomey Africa; god): snake

Dea Artia (Celtic; goddess): bear

Dea Syria (Rome; goddess): snake

Demeter (Greece; goddess): cock, dove, pig, fish, ant, centaur

Derceto (Babylonia; goddess): whale, fish

Devi (India; goddess): swan

Diana (Rome; goddess): cats, wild animals, dog, stag, antelope, deer, bee, unicorn

Diiwica (Slavonic; goddess): wild animals, horse, hounds

Dionysus (Greece; god): bull, centaur, satyr, cheetah, lion, leopard, panther, tiger, fox, ass, fawn, elephant, goat, ram, bee

Don (Celtic; goddess): sea gull

Dumuzi (Middle East; god): bull

Durga (India; goddess): lion, tiger, buffalo

Dylan (Wales; god): silver fish

Ea/Enki/Ea-Oannes (Mesopotamia, Babylonia, Sumeria; god): goat, fish, turtle, tortoise, frog, antelope, ram

Eingana (Australia; goddess): snake

Ek Chuah (Maya; god): scorpion

El (Canaan, Phoenicia; god): bull

Enki (Middle East; god): lion, fox, bull

Enlil (Mesopotamia; god): snake-dragon

Enmesarra (Mesopotamia; god): pigeon

Enodia (Thessaly; goddess): dog

Eos (Greece; goddess): Pegasus

Eostra (Germany; goddess): hare

Epona (Britain, Gaul; goddess): horse, goose, dog

Erh-lang (China; god): dog

Erinyes (Greece; goddesses): serpent

Eros (Greece; god): goose, hare

Europa (Greece; goddess): cow

Fates (Greece; goddesses): dove, spider

Faunus (Rome; god): goat, bees, flocks, wild animals, satyr

Fene-Ma-So (West Africa; god): vulture

Feronia (Rome; goddess): wolf

Flidais (Ireland; goddess): wild animals, deer

Freyja (Norse; goddess): falcon, cats, horse, boar, bear, sow, hare

Freyr (Norse; god): boar, horse

Furies/Erinyes/Eumenides (Greece; goddesses): dove, snake

Fu Xi (China; god): snake

Gaea (Greece; goddess): snake

Gama (Japan; god): toad

Gandharvas (India; god): horse, centaur

Ganesha (India; god): elephant, rat

Gauri (India; goddess): cow

Gefion (Norse; goddess): ox

Goblin Spider (Japan; goddess): spider

Graiae (Greece; goddesses): snake

Great Spider (Africa; god): spider

Gucumatz (Maya; god): snake

Gula (Babylonia, Kassites; goddess): dog

Gwynn ap Nudd (Celtic; god): owl

Hachiman (Japan; god): dove

Hanuman (India; god): monkey

Hapi (Egypt; god): ape

Harpies (Greece; goddesses): vulture

Hathor (Egypt; goddess): cow, cat, frog, vulture, sphinx, lion

Hay-Tau (Phoenicia; god): bull

Hecate (Greece, Thrace; goddess): snake, dragon, dog, frog, toad

Heimdall (Norse; god): ram

Heket (Egypt; goddess): frog

Hel (Norse; goddess): wolf

Hera (Greece; goddess): peacock, cow, dove, goose, cattle, sheep, snake

Hermes (Greece; god): cock, sheep, cow, goose, hare, lamb, lizard, tortoise, turtle

Heru-Merti (Egypt; god): hawk

Hit (Micronesia; goddess): octopus

Holda/Bertha (North Germanic; goddess): goat, hounds, goose, hare, spider

Horae (Greece; goddesses): butterfly

Horus (Egypt; god): falcon, hawk, cats, goose, antelope, dragon, wolf

Hsi Wang-Mu (China; goddess): tortoise

Huang Ch'u-Ping (China; god): sheep

Huehuecoyotl (Aztec; god): coyote

Huitzilopochtli (Aztec; god): hummingbird, snake

Hygeia (Greece; goddess): snake

Igaluk (Eskimo; god): sea creatures

Inanna (Canaan, Phoenicia, Sumeria, Uruk, Babylonia; goddess): lion, hunting dog, serpent

Inari (Japan; goddess/god): fox

Indra (India; god): eagle, hawk, white elephant, horse, hunting dogs, bull, cobra, snake, bee, dragon

Inktomi (Native American; god): spider

Io (Greece; goddess): cow

Irene (Greece; goddess): dove

Ishtar (Mesopotamia, Babylonia, Assyria, Sumeria, Arabia, Phoenicia, Canaan; goddess): lion, serpent, dragon, dove, cow, calf, scorpion, hedgehog, dolphin, fish

Isis (Egypt; goddess): cow, cats, goose, swallow, peacock, vulture, antelope, deer, cobra, snake, scorpion, dolphin, fish, dog

Ison/Obask Nsi (West Africa; goddess): tortoise

Itzamna (Maya; god): lizard, jaguar

Itzpaplotl (Aztec; goddess): butterfly

Iwazaru (Japan; god): monkey

Jok (Uganda, Zaire; god): black goat

Julunggul (Australia; goddess): snake

Juno (Rome; goddess): peacock, vulture

Jupiter (Rome; god): eagle, woodpecker

Kadi (Babylon; goddess): snake

Kadu (India; goddess): snake, cobra

Kali (India; goddess): snake, cow

Kama (India; god): bees, parrot

Karttikeya (India; god): peacock

Kauri (India; goddess): cow

Khepera (Egypt; god): scarab beetle, Mendes ram

Khnemu (Egypt; god): ram with long wavy horns

Kikazaru (Japan; god): monkey

Koevasi (Melanesia; goddess): snake

Kokyangwuti (Native American; goddess): spider

Krishna (India; god): elephant, cobra, snake, bee

Kuan Yin (China; goddess): white horse, fish

Kul/Kul-Jungk (Finnish; god/goddess): fish

Kulkulcan (Maya; god): serpent

Kwannon (Japan; god): white horse, fish

Lakshmi (India; goddess): peacock

Lamia/Lamashtu/Lamastu (Babylon; goddess): snake, donkey

Lao Tzu (China; god): buffalo

Leib-Olmai (Finnish; god): bear

Leshi (Slavonic-Russian; gods/goddesses): goat, satyr

Leukippe (Crete; goddess): white mare, centaur

Leza (Dahomey Africa; god): chameleon

Liberty (Rome; goddess): cats

Lilith (Middle East; goddess): owl

Liu-hai (China; god): toad

Llud (Ireland, Wales; god): dog, sea creatures

Loki (Norse; god): horse, salmon, wolf

Lugh (Ireland, Wales; god): raven, white stag, hounds

Lu-Hsing (China; god): deer

Lupa (Rome; goddess): wolf

Maat (Egypt; goddess): ostrich, lynx

Macha (Ireland; goddess): crow, raven

Manannan mac Lir (Ireland; god): crane, pig, horse, sea gull, cow

Marduk (Mesopotamia; god): eagle, snake-dragon, lion, antelope

Mari (Middle East; goddess): owl

Marici (India; goddess): sow

Mars (Rome; god): woodpecker, horse, wolf, boar, sheep

Mayauel (Aztec; goddess): snake, tortoise

Medusa (Greece; goddess): snake, Pegasus

Mehilainen (Finnish-Ugrian; god): bee

Meilikki (Finnish; goddess): wild animals, bear

Melkart (Middle East; god): quail

Menthu (Egypt; god): falcon, bull

Mercury (Rome; god): turtle, tortoise

Meztli (Aztec; god): sea snail, butterfly

Michabo (Algonquin; god): hare

Min (Egypt; god): white bull

Minerva (Rome; goddess): owl, horse, ox, snake

Mithras (Persia; god): eagle, cock, hawk, raven, bull, lion, dog, horse, snake, dragon

Mizaru (Japan; god): monkey

Moerae (Greece; goddesses): dog

Moko (Polynesia; god): lizard

Morrigan (Ireland, Wales, Britain; goddess): crow, raven

Muses (Greece; goddesses): nightingale, swan, Pegasus

Mut (Egypt; goddess): vulture, cow, cat, lioness

Nabu (Mesopotamia, Sumeria; god): serpent-headed dragon

Nanna/Nanaya (Sumeria; goddess): fish, serpent, scorpion

Nantosuelta (Celtic; goddess): raven

Nasr (Arabia; god): vulture

Ndengei (Fiji; god): serpent

Neith (Egypt; goddess): vulture, golden cobra, spider

Nekhebet (Egypt; goddess): vulture, serpent, lion

Nemesis (Greece; goddess): griffin

Nephthys (Egypt; goddess): cock

Neptune (Rome; god): horse, bull

Nergal (Babylonia; god): lion

Nereids (Greece; goddesses): sea creatures, dolphin

Nereus (Greece; god): sea creatures

Nergal (Middle East; god): lion

Nerthus (Norse; goddess): cow

Nganaoa (Polynesia; god): whale

Ningilin (Mesopotamia; goddess): mongoose

Ningirsu (Middle East; god): lion

Ninhursag (Mesopotamia; goddess): cow, calf, snake

Ninlil/Mullissu/Belitis (Mesopotamia; goddess): lion

Ninurta (Mesopotamia; god): eagle, lion, lion-dragon

Niu Wang (China; god): oxen

Njord (Norse; god): sea creatures

Nodens (Celtic; god): dog

Norns (Norse; goddesses): spider

Nu Kua (China; goddess): snake

Nut (Egypt; goddess): cow

Nymphs (Greece; goddesses): flocks, wild animals

Oceanos (Greece; god): snake

Odhinn (Norse; god): eagle, falcon, raven, wolf, horse, dog, bear

Ogugu (West Africa; god): monkey

Osiris (Egypt; god): cock, ostrich, hawk, goose, heron, phoenix, vulture, leopard, antelope, bull, Mendes ram, Pegasus, phoenix, dog

Ovinnik (Slavonic; god): black cat

O-Wata-Tsumi (Japan; god): sea creatures

Pales (Rome; god/goddess): ass

Pallas (Greece; goddess): vulture

Pan (Greece; god): eagle, flocks, bees, wild animals, leopard, panther, goat, ram, turtle, tortoise, satyr

P'an Ku (China; god): tortoise

Parvati (India; goddess): dove

Pasht (Egypt; goddess): cats

Persephone (Greece; goddess): bat, pig, snake

Perun (Slavonic; god): cock, goat, bear, bull

Poseidon (Greece; god): sea creatures, horse, bull, fish

Prajapati (India; god): tortoise

Priapus (Greece; god): ass, bees

Prithivi (India; goddess): cow

Proserpina (Rome; goddess): bat, pig

Ptah (Egypt; god): hawk, Apis bull

P'u Hsien (China; god): white elephant

Pwyll pen Annwn (Wales; god): crane, pig

Quetzalcoatl (Aztec; god): hummingbird, dog, snake

Ra (Egypt; god): falcon, hawk, Mendes ram, bee, phoenix, sphinx, cat, ass

Ravana (India; god): ass

Raven (Many Native American tribes; god): raven

Renenet (Egypt; goddess): serpent, lion

Rhea (Greece; goddess): crow, bee

Rhiannon (Wales; goddess): bird, blackbird, white horse

Ribhus, the (India; gods): horse

Rudra (India; god): wild animals, bull, cattle, boar

Sabazius (Crete, Phrygia; god): ram, scorpion, snake, toad

Sakkan (Mesopotamia; god): lion, cheetah, wolf, jackal, hyena, wild cattle, oryx, gazelle, wild pig, wild cat, lynx, beaver, mongoose, deer, wild goat, ibex, wild sheep, leopard, bear

Sarama (India; goddess): dog

Sarapis (Egypt; god): bull

Sarasvati (India; goddess): peacock, swan

Saturn (Rome; god): guinea fowl, vulture, ass

Satyr (Greece; gods): goat

Sebek (Egypt; god): crocodile

Sedna (Eskimo; goddess): sea creatures, seal

Seker (Egypt; god): hawk

Sekhmet (Egypt; goddess): lion, lioness, cobra

Selket (Egypt; goddess): scorpion

Set (Egypt; god): dog, ass, antelope, hippo, boar, crocodile, scorpion, goose, black pig, turtle, desert animals, snake, wolf

Shadrafa (Phoenicia; god): lion

Shamash/Utu (Mesopotamia; god): horse, bull-man

Shasti (India; goddess): cats

Shiva (India; god): antelope, bull

Shiva (India; god): serpent, elephant, tiger

Shou-Hsing (China; god): bat, stag

Shu (Egypt; god): ostrich, Mendes ram

Shui-Khan (China; god): tortoise

Siduri Sabitu (Middle East; goddess): scorpion

Silvanus (Rome; god): woodpecker, wolf, sheep, satyr

Sinn (Mesopotamia; god): bull, lion-dragon, bull

Soma (India; god): antelope

Spider Grandmother (Native American; goddess): spider

Spider Woman (Japan, Native American; goddess): spider

Surya (India; god): mare

Susanoo (Japan; god): snake

Sussistanako (Native American; goddess): spider

Svantovit (Slavonic; god): white horse

Svarog (Slavonic; god): white horse

Tammuz (Middle East; god): boar

Tangaroa (Polynesia; god): fish, reptiles

Tanuki (Japan; god): badger

Ta-Urt (Egypt; goddess): hippo

Tekkeitsertok (Eskimo; god): deer

Tellus Mater (Rome; goddess): pig

Temu (Egypt; god): serpent, sphinx

Terminus (Rome; god): sheep

Thetis (Greece; goddess): dolphin

Thinking Woman (Native American; goddess): spider

Thorr (Norse; god): goat, robin, bear

Thoth (Egypt; god): ape, ibis, snake

Thought Woman (Native American; goddess): spider

Thunder Bird (Many Native American tribes; gods): eagle, hawk

Tiamat (Mesopotamia, Babylonia; goddess): dragon, serpent, ostrich, bird, horned snake, snake-dragon, bull-man

Tlazolteotl (Aztec; goddess): red snake

Triptolemus (Greek; god): woodpecker

Tsai Shen (China; god): carp, cock, tiger

Tsitsicinako (Native American; goddess): spider

Twen-Ch'ang (China; god): crane

Typhon (Greece; god): ass

Uga-Jin (Japan; god): snake

Umi Bozu (Japan; god): octopus

Uni (Etruscan; goddess): peacock

Urcaguary (Inca; god): serpent with deer's head

Uso-Dori (Japan; goddess): bullfinch

Uttu (Mesopotamia; goddess): spider

Vajnavrahi (India; goddess): sow

Valkyries (Norse; goddesses): horse, raven, wolf, swan

Vana (India; god): buffalo

Varuna (India; god): crow, snake, white horse

Vayu (India; god): deer

Venus (Rome; goddess): lovebird, heron, dove, swallow, turtle, tortoise

Vishnu (India; god): eagle, boar, bee

Visvakarma (India; god): horse

Volos (Slavonic; god): horned animals, cattle, horse

Waelsi/Waels (Wales; god): horse

Weyland/Wayland (North Germanic; god): horse

Wepwawet (Egypt; god): wolf

Wishpoosh (Nez Perce; god): beaver

Wu Hsien (China; god): tortoise

Xochiquetzal (Mexico; goddess): butterfly

Xolotl (Aztec; god): dog

Yama (India; god): dove, owl, pigeon, brindled watchdogs, bull

Zeus (Greece; god): dove, eagle, swan, woodpecker, wolf, bull, sheep, ram, bee

Zorya (Slavic-Russian; goddesses): dog

Zosim (Slavonic; god): bees.

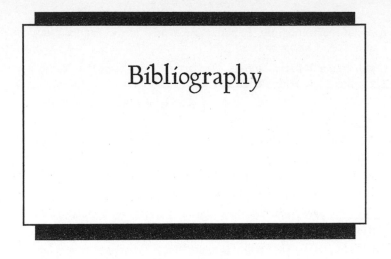

Bibliography

Black, Jeremy and Anthony Green. *Gods, Demons & Symbols of Ancient Mesopotamia*. Austin, TX: University of Texas Press, 1992.

Cirlot, J. E. *A Dictionary of Symbols*. New York: Philosophical Library, 1962.

Conway, D. J. *The Ancient & Shining Ones*. St. Paul, MN: Llewellyn Publications, 1993.

_____. *By Oak, Ash & Thorn: Modern Celtic Shamanism*. St. Paul, MN: Llewellyn Publications, 1995.

Cooper, J. C. *Symbolic & Mythological Animals*. UK: Aquarian/Thorsons, 1992.

Eichler, Lillian. *The Customs of Mankind*. New York: Nelson Doubleday, 1924.

Gimbutas, Marija. *The Language of the Goddess*. San Francisco: HarperCollins, 1991.

Johnson, Buffie. *Lady of the Beasts: Ancient Images of the Goddess & Her Sacred Animals*. San Francisco: Harper & Row, 1981.

Jung, C. G. Translated by R. F. C. Hull. *The Archetypes & the Collective Unconscious*. Princeton, NJ: Princeton University Press, 1990.

Lum, Peter. *Fabulous Beasts*. New York: Pantheon Books, 1951.

Potter, Carole. *Knock on Wood & Other Superstitions*. New York: Bonanza Books, 1983.

Radford, Edwin and Mona A. Radford. *Encyclopaedia of Superstitions*. New York: Philosophical Library, 1949.

Shapiro, Robert and Julie Rapkin. *Awakening to the Animal Kingdom*. San Rafael, CA: Cassandra Press, 1988.

Shepard, Paul and Barry Sanders. *The Sacred Paw: The Bear in Nature, Myth, & Literature*. New York: Penguin, 1985.

Thompson, C. J. S. *The Mysteries & Secrets of Magic*. New York: Barnes & Noble, 1993.

Valiente, Doreen. *An ABC of Witchcraft Past & Present*. New York: St. Martin's Press, 1973.

Walker, Barbara G. *The Woman's Dictionary of Symbols & Sacred Objects*. San Francisco: Harper & Row, 1988.

_____. *The Woman's Encyclopedia of Myths & Secrets*. San Francisco: Harper & Row, 1983.

White, T. H., trans. *The Book of Beasts: Being a Translation from a Latin Bestiary of the 12th Century*. New York: Dover, 1984.

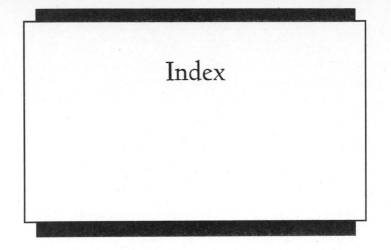

Index

Acropolis, 158, 167
Adder, 197–198, 259
Aditi, 113, 257
Adonis, 109, 161, 174, 257
Africa, 75, 78–79, 87, 90, 92, 97, 101, 108, 112,
   116, 118–119, 123, 126–127, 130, 135–137,
   174–175, 191–192, 199, 202, 204, 214, 217,
   228, 236, 250, 257, 259–264, 266
Aganippe, 245, 257
Agni, 112, 123, 142, 257
Ahi, 210
Ahriman, 72, 92, 128, 203, 205, 208, 213, 257
Ahura Mazda, 168, 257
Albertus Magnus, 251
Alchemy, 81, 88, 150, 152, 212, 215, 243
Alligator, 201, 205
Amazon, 77, 128
Amen-Ra, 142, 248
Amenti, 85, 126, 168, 175, 257
Anansi, 236, 257
Ananta, 210
Anath, 176, 257
Andraste, 138, 258
Anglo-Saxon, 110
Ant, 227–228, 259–260
Antelope, 97–99, 123, 251, 258, 260–261, 263,
   265, 267–269
Anubis, 38–39, 92, 155, 258

Apaturia, 123
Ape, 99–100, 262, 269
Apep, 208
Aphrodite, 109, 116, 138, 161, 169, 187–189,
   192, 203, 214, 221, 229, 258
Apollo, 81, 94, 117, 128, 132, 155–156, 158,
   166, 168, 182–183, 189, 192, 209, 219, 229,
   242, 244, 258
Apsaras, 189, 258
Arabs, 79, 81, 123, 174, 192, 226, 250
Arawn, 86, 111, 258
Ares, 94, 109, 166, 192–193, 258
Aristotle, 125, 182, 229
Artemis, 72, 86, 94, 98, 104–105, 114, 116,
   123, 168, 182, 229, 250, 258
Arthur, 87, 105, 111, 184
Asclepias, 183, 209
Ashtoreth, 85
Asia, 72, 75, 80, 82–83, 90, 93, 97–98, 104,
   106–108, 112, 117, 123, 127, 136–137, 149,
   158, 173, 179, 191, 197, 199–200, 217, 228,
   241
Asia Minor, 72, 80, 98
Ass, 90, 101–102, 127, 260, 267–268, 270
Asshur, 163, 258
Assyria, 75, 80, 163, 244, 250, 257–258, 263
Astaeria, 182, 258
Astarte, 85, 98, 113, 161, 218, 249, 258

Astral, 4–12, 16–18, 20–21, 23–24, 28, 33, 35, 40–43, 53–54, 68, 70, 79, 83, 92, 95, 106, 130, 132, 157, 165, 178, 197, 217, 231, 239, 245

Astral familiars, 4, 7, 10–11, 17, 20, 23–24, 43, 70, 239

Asvins, 182, 240, 258

Atargatis, 161, 209, 221, 236, 258

Athene, 32–33, 86, 116, 123, 155, 158, 161, 169, 177, 183, 192, 209, 236, 258

Attis, 81, 142, 174, 258

Au Set, 200

Audhumla, 114, 258

Aurochs, 112, 135

Australia, 71, 102, 125, 147, 152, 181, 189, 193, 204, 211, 228, 261, 263

Aztecs, 77, 163, 170, 190, 211–212, 215, 230

Ba'al, 113, 123, 182, 258–259

Baboon, 99

Babylon, 80, 85, 142, 161, 163, 180, 207, 209, 236, 242, 250, 263–264

Bacchant, 116

Bacchus, 120, 161, 247, 259

Badger, 102–103, 269

Basilisk, 62–63, 147, 239–240

Bassareus, 91

Bast, 72, 259

Bat, 71, 151–152, 267–268

Bear, 8, 76, 87, 94, 103–106, 129, 140–141, 148, 179, 258–261, 264–269, 272

Beaver, 106–107, 268, 270

Bees, 227–230, 260–261, 264, 267, 270

Beetle, 231–232, 264

Berbers, 87

Berserker, 105

Bird of Paradise, 180

Bison, 107–108

Blackbird, 153, 267

Blodeuwedd, 177, 259

Blue jay, 154

Boar, 108–112, 257–259, 261, 265, 268–270

Brahma, 180, 183, 189, 259

Bran, 86, 159, 184, 195, 259

Branwen, 159, 259

Brigit, 10, 111, 142, 146, 155, 210, 259

Britain, 15, 72, 74, 93, 95, 105, 135, 139, 157, 162, 176, 184, 187, 237, 261, 265

Brunnhilde, 159

Buddhists, 87, 109, 120, 152

Buffalo, 107–108, 135, 261, 264, 270

Buffalo Woman, 108

Bull, 87, 107, 112–115, 131, 135, 207, 229, 252, 257–263, 265–268, 270

Buto, 200, 259

Butterfly, 232–234, 262–263, 265, 270

Caduceus, 210

Cailleach, 157, 177, 198, 259

Callisto, 6, 105, 259

Canada, 76, 82, 98, 104, 107–108, 131, 140, 148, 187, 191, 204, 206

Carp, 217, 269

Carthage, 119, 245, 259

Cat, 5, 7, 10–11, 15–16, 22, 55–56, 68, 71–79, 81–83, 111, 130, 133, 138, 144, 146, 181, 203, 205, 262, 265, 267–268

Celestial Dog, 87

Celestial Stag, 117

Celtic, 72, 86, 88, 105, 111–112, 114, 117, 127, 132, 142, 144, 150, 158, 163, 168, 170, 186, 190, 195, 198, 210, 219, 223– 224, 230, 258–260, 262, 265–266, 271

Centaur, 240–241, 258–260, 262, 264

Central America, 77, 182

Cerberus, 86

Ceres, 109, 228, 259

Cernunnos, 94, 117, 135, 259

Cerridwen, 111, 259

Ch'i-lin, 250

Chaldea, 80, 188, 250

Chameleon, 199, 264

Chandra, 98, 138, 260

Cheetah, 68, 75, 98, 260, 268

Cheiron, 241, 260

China, 83, 90–91, 100, 104, 110, 117, 125, 128–129, 138, 141, 151, 155, 157, 169, 173–174, 180, 182–183, 188, 202, 213, 217, 228, 230, 242, 247, 250, 260–261, 263–264, 266–270

Circe, 109, 165, 168, 246, 260

Coatlicue, 211, 260

Cobra, 130, 199–200, 259, 263–264, 266, 268

Cocidius, 117, 260

Cock, 81, 147, 155–156, 239–240, 258–260, 262, 265–267, 269

Cornelius Agrippa, 16

Cornwall, 81, 184, 198, 233

Cougar, 76, 148, 177

Cow, 112–116, 119, 126, 131, 257–258, 261–267

Coyolxauhqui, 211, 260

Coyote, 82, 85, 89, 234, 260, 263

Crane, 128, 156–157, 169–170, 258–259, 265, 267, 269

Crete, 55, 58, 80, 109, 113–114, 142, 163, 176, 209, 229, 232, 241, 257, 264, 268

Crocodile, 201–202, 268

Cronus, 101, 161, 183, 260

Crow, 156, 158–159, 169, 173, 184, 258–259, 265, 267, 270

Cwn Annwn, 86

Cybele, 81, 86, 229, 260

Daemon, 16

Dagon, 221, 260

Daikoku, 144, 260

Dea Artia, 105, 260

Deer, 9, 58–59, 116–118, 121, 131, 184, 258, 260–261, 263–264, 268–270

Delphi, 94, 117, 189, 219, 229

Demeter, 109, 155, 161, 221, 228–229, 241, 245, 260

Derceto, 221, 225, 260

Devi, 189, 260

Diana, 16, 72, 86, 98, 115–116, 229, 250, 260

Dionysus, 75, 79, 83, 91, 101, 114, 116, 120, 123, 142, 230, 247, 260

Djinn, 174

Dolphin, 218–219, 258, 263, 266, 269

Donkey, 101–102, 260, 264

Dormarth, 86

Dove, 120, 160–162, 189, 193, 257–263, 267, 270

Dragon, 10, 48, 62–63, 117, 128, 150, 152, 210, 234, 242–243, 247, 249–250, 253, 257–259, 262–263, 265, 269

Dragonfly, 57–58, 234

Druids, 194–195, 198, 220

Dumuzi, 113, 261

Durga, 81, 83, 108, 261

Ea-Oannes, 98, 142, 214, 226, 261

Eagle, 150, 162–165, 168, 177, 191, 193, 243–244, 246, 258, 263, 265–267, 269–270

Eel, 220

Egypt, 15, 59, 72, 75, 79–80, 85, 101, 113, 130, 135, 142, 144, 158, 168, 174, 200–201, 205, 207–208, 221, 229, 231, 235, 242, 245, 250, 257–259, 262–270

Elemental, 5, 138

Elements, 43–44, 84, 135, 159, 215, 236, 243, 249

Elephant, 118–120, 214, 259–260, 262–264, 267–268

Eleusinia, 109

Elk, 116, 121, 131

Enki, 80, 91, 113, 261

Eostra, 138, 261

Epona, 86, 128, 166, 261

Erh-lang, 87, 261

Erinyes, 209, 261

Erl King, 86

Eros, 138, 166, 261

Euripides, 149

Europe, 4, 15, 72, 74, 78, 82–83, 86, 88, 90, 93, 95, 104, 106–108, 112, 122–123, 125, 127, 131, 135–137, 139, 144, 146–147, 156, 158, 168, 173, 177, 180–182, 188, 191, 197, 202, 205, 208, 213, 217, 228, 231, 237

Eye-Goddess, 176

Falcon, 29–31, 165, 168, 246, 260–261, 263, 265–267

Fates, 33, 161, 192, 236, 261

Faunus, 123, 247–248, 261

Fene-Ma-So, 192, 261

Feronia, 94, 261

Ferret, 122

Finland, 104, 226

Fish, 11, 21, 104, 161–162, 188, 217, 221–226, 258–261, 263–265, 267, 269

Five Animals, 147

Flidais, 117, 261

Fox, 7, 64–65, 82, 85, 90–92, 103, 260–261, 263

France, 108, 176, 178, 194

Freyja, 29–31, 73, 105, 110, 112, 128, 138, 165, 221, 261

Freyr, 110–111, 128, 261

Frog, 66, 202–204, 212–213, 257–258, 260–262

Fu Xi, 210, 261

Furies, 161, 261

Gabriel Hounds, 87

Gaea, 209, 261

Gama, 213, 262

Gandharvas, 240, 262

Ganesha, 119–120, 144, 262

Gayatri, 168

Genie, 5

Germany, 94, 117, 129, 131, 133, 188, 261

Goat, 98, 123–124, 248, 251, 257–264, 267–269

Goblin Spider, 236, 262

Goose, 166–167, 189, 257–258, 261–263, 267–268

Gorilla, 99

Graiae, 209, 262

Great Goddess, 94, 116, 176, 181, 200, 221

Great Hare, 138

Great Mother, 80, 85, 98, 111, 113–115, 125, 143, 151, 160–161, 168, 192, 208, 222, 229, 242

Great Spider, 236, 262

Greece, 79–80, 91, 98, 114, 125, 127, 135, 142, 155, 158, 166, 169, 193, 205, 207, 214, 228–229, 236, 241–242, 244, 257–263, 265–270

Griffin, 244–246, 258, 266

Grizzly, 104

Guinea fowl, 167, 258, 268

Gula, 85, 262

Gullinbursti, 110

Hachiman, 161, 262

Hanuman, 99, 262

Hapi, 99, 262

Hare, 137–140, 258, 260–262, 265

Harpies, 192, 262

Hathor, 113, 192, 202, 249, 262

Hawk, 163, 165, 168–169, 234, 257–258, 262–263, 265, 267–269

Hawk of Achill, 168

Healers, 4, 7, 21

Hecate, 86, 203, 209, 212, 262

Hedgehog, 125–126, 263

Heimdall, 110, 142, 262

Heket, 202, 262

Hel, 14, 86, 94, 262

Hera, 114, 141, 161, 166, 180, 182, 209, 262

Hermes, 83, 116, 138, 142, 155, 166, 205, 208, 210, 214, 262

Heron, 169–170, 246, 258, 267, 270

Hildisvini, 110

Hindu, 72, 92, 98–100, 102, 108, 110, 112–113, 119, 123, 161, 177–178, 180, 182–183, 189, 201, 210, 229, 240, 242

Hippopotamus, 126

Hittites, 80, 117, 249

Ho-Ho, 247

Holda, 138, 166, 236, 262

Horned God, 117, 142, 247, 259

Horse, 10, 36, 41, 57, 101, 126–129, 166, 201, 208, 211, 236, 240–241, 245–247, 251, 257–258, 260–270

Horus, 98, 165–166, 168, 242, 263

Hsi Wang-Mu, 214, 263

Huang Ch'u-Ping, 141, 263

Huitzilopochtli, 170, 211, 263

Hummingbird, 170–171, 263, 267

Hygeia, 209, 263

Ibis, 59–60, 171–172, 269

Ibo, 79

Ilmarinen, 226

Inanna, 80, 113, 263

Inari, 91, 263

India, 14, 78–81, 83, 87, 92–93, 97–99, 101, 104, 107, 113, 117, 119, 128, 130, 142, 154, 161, 168, 178–179, 199, 201, 203, 207–208, 210, 228, 236, 244, 250, 257–265, 267–270

Indra, 87, 112, 119, 163, 168, 210, 229, 242, 263

Inktomi, 236, 263

Irish elk, 116, 121

Ishtar, 80, 113, 125, 206, 218, 221, 236, 263

Isis, 92, 98, 113, 116–117, 166, 171, 180, 192, 200, 202, 207–208, 218, 221, 263

Italy, 114

Jackal, 38–39, 85, 92–93, 257–258, 268

Jackdaw, 158, 173

Jaguar, 77–78, 263

Japan, 73, 91, 100, 103–104, 110, 117, 134, 140, 152, 157, 169, 177, 180, 182, 194, 210, 213–214, 217, 222, 226, 232, 234, 242–243, 247, 259–260, 262–265, 267, 269–270

Julunggul, 211, 263

Juno, 180, 192, 263

Kadi, 208, 263

Kadru, 208, 210

Kalevala, 104, 229

Kali, 92, 112–113, 210, 264

Kaliya, 210

Kama, 178, 180, 264

Khepera, 142, 231, 264

Kheti, 208

Khnemu, 142, 264

Ki-rin, 250

King Morvran, 183

Korea, 125

Krake, 159

Krishna, 119, 210, 229, 264

Kuan Yin, 127, 221, 264

Kulkulcan, 211, 264

Kwannon, 127, 222, 264

Labyrs, 114, 229, 232

Lakshmi, 113, 180, 264

Lamia, 209, 264

Lammergeier, 191

Lao Tzu, 108, 264

Lemminkainen, 229

Leopard, 22–23, 75–79, 83, 116, 259–260, 267–268

Leshi, 248, 264

Leto, 182, 189

Leukippe, 128, 241, 264

Lilith, 176, 264

Lion, 21, 74, 76–83, 85, 92, 116, 164, 244, 246, 249–251, 257–258, 260–263, 265–268

Lion-Dog, 87
Lithuania, 121, 233
Liu-hai, 213, 264
Lizard, 199, 204–206, 257, 262–263, 265
Loki, 94, 224, 264
Lovebird, 172, 258, 270
Lu-Hsing, 117, 264
Lugh, 184, 264
Lunar, 72, 86, 98, 103, 105, 109, 111, 113–114, 142, 157, 203, 208, 212, 214, 221, 229, 251
Lynx, 76, 82–83, 259, 265, 268
Maat, 92, 171, 174–175, 265
Macha, 158, 265
Madagascar, 71, 102, 125
Maenads, 116
Magickal power, 7, 117
Magpie, 173
Malay, 78, 83, 104, 119, 201
Malta, 109
Manannan mac Lir, 110, 114, 157, 186, 265
Manchuria, 125, 131
Marduk, 80, 98, 123, 163, 265
Marici, 109, 265
Mars, 94, 109, 141, 193, 265
Mascots, 14
Masks, 14, 21, 95, 102, 110
Mayas, 77, 207
Medb, 146
Meditation, 10–12, 18–20, 22–23, 27–31, 33, 35–36, 38–41, 45, 54, 67–68, 88, 118, 153, 169, 178, 190, 194, 197, 224, 245
Medusa, 209, 245, 265
Melkart, 182, 265
Merlin, 111, 165
Mesopotamia, 21, 113, 257–258, 260–261, 263, 265–266, 268–271
Mexico, 76–77, 82, 93, 98, 109, 151–152, 190, 205, 213, 233, 260, 270
Middle East, 80, 85, 113, 123, 130, 240, 244, 257–259, 261, 264–266, 268–269
Minerva, 177, 265
Minos, 114
Mithraism, 81, 87, 163, 183, 207
Mithras, 114, 128, 155, 163, 168, 208, 242, 265
Mohammed, 16
Moko, 205, 265
Mongoose, 130, 240, 266, 268
Monkey, 99–100, 262–266
Moon Hare, 138
Moose, 131
Morrigan, 158, 183, 265

Mountain lion, 76
Mouse, 7, 64, 132–133, 258
Muses, 174, 189, 241, 245, 265
Mut, 192, 265
Mycenae, 80, 125
Nadredd, 198
Nagas, 210
Nandi, 112
Nanna, 206, 265
Nasr, 192, 266
Native Americans, 4, 76, 82, 89, 95, 103, 108, 118, 121, 134–136, 138, 140, 163, 177, 179, 184, 191, 194, 211, 215, 219, 226, 233, 236
Neith, 200–201, 235, 266
Nekhebet, 192, 266
Nemesis, 244, 266
Nephthys, 92, 155, 266
Nereides, 218
Nergal, 80, 266
Nerthus, 114, 266
Nganaoa, 226, 266
Nightingale, 173–174, 257–258, 265
Ningilin, 130, 266
Ninhursag, 113, 208, 266
Ninurta, 80, 163, 266
Niu Wang, 135, 266
Nodens, 86, 224, 266
Norns, 33–34, 236, 266
Norse, 29, 73, 86–87, 102, 105, 110, 123, 128, 142, 165–166, 185, 190, 223, 226, 236, 258, 261–262, 264, 266, 269–270
Nu Kua, 210, 266
Nut, 113, 266
Oceanos, 210, 266
October Horse, 128
Octopus, 222–223, 262, 270
Odhinn, 14, 86, 94, 105, 128, 163, 165, 183, 236, 266
Ogugu, 100, 266
Onager, 101
Opossum, 133–134
Orangutan, 99
Orc Triath, 111
Orphic, 116, 183
Osiris, 79–80, 92, 98–99, 113, 142, 155, 166, 170, 175, 192, 207, 245–246, 267
Ostrich, 174–175, 180, 257, 265, 267–269
Otter, 94, 134–135, 259
Ovid, 179, 183, 246
Owein, 184

Owl, 40, 71, 76, 161, 176–178, 257–259, 262, 264–265, 270
Oxen, 135–136, 266
P'an Ku, 214, 267
Pacific, 108, 111, 149, 173, 222–223
Pallas, 148, 177, 192, 267
Pan, 79, 123, 142, 163, 214, 230, 247–248, 267
Panther, 8, 74, 76, 78–79, 259–260, 267
Paracelsus, 5
Parrot, 10, 178–179, 264
Parvati, 161, 267
Pasht, 72, 267
Peacock, 175, 179–181, 246, 259, 262–264, 268, 270
Peacock Throne, 180
Pedu, 128
Pegasus, 41–42, 241, 245–246, 257, 261, 265, 267
Persephone, 109, 209, 267
Persia, 80, 90, 127, 180, 228, 250, 257, 265
Phoenix, 63–64, 128, 182, 246–247, 260, 267
Physical familiars, 4, 7, 16–17
Pig Faery, 110
Pigeon, 16, 160–162, 165, 258, 261, 270
Pliny the Elder, 132, 203
Polynesia, 76, 265–266, 269
Porcupine, 125, 136–137
Porpoise, 218
Poseidon, 221, 245, 267
Power Animals, 4
Prajapati, 214, 267
Priapus, 101, 230, 267
Priestesses, 21, 33, 86, 91, 128, 161, 180, 192, 209, 229, 241
Prithivi, 113, 267
Prometheus, 163
Ptah, 113, 168, 267
Puma, 76
Pwyll, 111, 157, 267
Quail, 181–182, 258, 265
Quetzalcoatl, 87, 170, 210–211, 267
Rabbit, 137–139, 259
Raccoon, 140
Radha, 119
Ragnar, 159
Rainbow Snake, 211
Ram, 141–143, 257–262, 264, 267–268, 270
Rat, 143–144, 260, 262
Ratatosk, 146
Ravana, 102, 267

Raven, 159, 183–185, 258–260, 264–267, 270
Rhea, 158, 161, 229, 267
Rhiannon, 128, 153, 267
Rig Veda, 168, 203, 229
Rituals, 21, 24, 43–45, 47, 49, 51, 53, 55, 57, 59, 61, 63, 65, 70, 92, 109, 114, 117, 120, 138, 142, 150, 155
Robin, 153, 185, 269
Roman, 16, 72, 92, 94, 101, 116, 120, 135, 138, 142, 149, 163, 178, 187, 205, 209, 245–248, 250
Rudra, 110, 268
Russia, 90, 121, 159, 182
Sabazius, 132, 142, 206, 208, 213, 268
Salmon, 221, 223–224, 264
Sarama, 87, 268
Sarapis, 113, 205, 268
Sarasvati, 180, 189, 268
Saturnalia, 167
Satyr, 247–248, 257, 259–261, 264, 267–268
Scandinavia, 127, 129, 163, 250
Scarab beetle, 231, 264
Sceolan, 86
Scorpion, 206–207, 261, 263, 265, 268
Scotland, 71–72, 93, 111, 115, 124, 133, 138–139, 143, 152, 190, 194, 210, 222, 224, 233, 259
Sea gull, 186, 260, 265
Seal, 117, 224, 268
Sebek, 201, 268
Sekhmet, 80, 268
Selket, 207, 268
Set, 20, 38, 44, 48, 50, 52, 54–55, 57, 60, 62, 65, 93, 98, 101, 103, 110–111, 126, 134, 166, 200–201, 207–208, 240, 246, 251, 268
Shamanism, 4, 271
Shape-shifting, 21–23, 29, 73, 78, 103, 159–160, 178, 190, 210, 220, 241
Shasti, 72, 268
Shedim, 252
Sheep, 97, 141–143, 258, 262–263, 265, 268–270
Shiva, 83, 92, 98, 112, 119, 268
Shou-Hsien, 117
Shou-Hsing, 151, 268
Siberia, 78, 83, 90, 104, 108, 123, 125, 131, 149, 163, 204, 233
Siegfried, 94, 150, 159, 242
Silvanus, 94, 141, 247, 268
Simurgh, 246
Sinn, 113, 268

Skunk, 144–145

Slavic, 87, 128

Sleipnir, 128

Snakes, 3, 10–11, 31, 118, 125, 130, 161, 197–199, 204–205, 207–211, 234, 258

Snow leopard, 78

Socrates, 16

Solar, 72, 80, 86, 98, 113, 128, 142, 155, 157, 162–163, 168–169, 201, 208, 246–247

Soma, 98, 168, 242, 269

South America, 133, 137, 156, 170, 189, 204, 207

Sow, 50, 73, 108–112, 259–261, 265, 270

Spain, 130, 138, 176

Sparrow, 165, 168, 187, 195, 258

Sphinx, 249, 262, 267, 269

Spider Woman, 236, 269

Spiders, 10–11, 33, 206, 227, 229, 231, 233, 235–237

Squirrel, 146

Staffs, 121

Stag, 116–118, 250–251, 258–260, 264, 268

Stork, 169

Sumeria, 80, 98, 123, 214, 261, 263, 265

Surya, 128, 269

Susanoo, 210, 269

Swallow, 188, 208, 258, 263, 270

Swan, 160, 189–190, 258–260, 265, 268, 270

Symbolic images, 15

Syr, 110

T'ien Kou, 87

T'ien Lung, 243

Ta-Urt, 126–127, 269

Tammuz, 109, 269

Tanuki, 103, 269

Tellus Mater, 109, 269

Thesmophoria, 109, 221

Thetis, 218, 269

Thorr, 105, 123, 185, 224, 269

Thoth, 59–61, 93, 99, 171–172, 208, 269

Tiamat, 174, 269

Tibet, 80, 101

Tiger, 77–78, 83–84, 116, 260–261, 268–269

Toad, 66, 205, 212–213, 240, 257, 262, 264, 268

Toltecs, 77, 211

Tortoise, 214–215, 258, 261–263, 265, 267–268, 270

Tree of Life, 244

Trickster, 89, 91, 134–135, 138, 210, 236

Tsai Shen, 84, 269

Turkey, 80, 94, 190–191, 246

Turtle, 214–215, 258, 261–262, 265, 267–268, 270

Twrch Trwyth, 111

Typhon, 101, 182, 270

Uga-Jin, 210, 270

Umi Bozu, 223, 270

Underground Panthers, 76

Uni, 180, 270

Unicorn, 36–38, 92, 250–251, 258, 260

Valkyries, 94, 128, 184, 190, 270

Vana, 108, 270

Varuna, 158, 270

Vayu, 117, 270

Venus, 161, 188–189, 214, 221, 270

Vesta, 128

Vila, 210

Viper, 197–198

Vishnu, 110, 163, 229, 270

Vulture, 183, 191–192, 258–259, 261–263, 265–268

Wales, 73, 86, 91, 124, 129, 139, 159, 178, 198, 230, 242, 258–259, 261, 264–265, 267, 270

Weasel, 102, 122, 130, 147–148, 240

Wepwawet, 94, 270

Western Hemisphere, 76–77, 82, 93, 125, 190, 204, 228

Whale, 35–36, 225–226, 260, 266

Wild Hunt, 86–87

Winged bull, 252

Winter Solstice, 110, 194

Witch, 3, 14–16, 73, 87–88, 125, 139, 152, 159, 177, 193, 212, 233

Wolf, 36, 43–48, 50, 53, 71, 85, 87–95, 148, 182, 235, 257–259, 261–266, 268, 270

Wolverine, 148

Woodpecker, 193–194, 258, 263, 265, 268–270

Wren, 194–195, 259

Wu Hsien, 214, 270

Wyvern, 253

Xochiquetzal, 233, 270

Xolotl, 87, 270

Yama, 87, 112, 161, 177, 270

Yggdrasil, 163

Yule, 110, 123

Zeus, 94, 105, 114, 116, 132, 141–142, 161, 163, 189, 193, 230, 270

Zoroaster, 72, 92, 94, 183

Zorya, 87, 270

On the following pages you will find listed, with their current prices, some of the books now available on related subjects. Your book dealer stocks most of these and will stock new titles in the Llewellyn series as they become available. We urge your patronage.

TO GET A FREE CATALOG

You are invited to write for our bimonthly news magazine/catalog, *Llewellyn's New Worlds of Mind and Spirit*. A sample copy is free, and it will continue coming to you at no cost as long as you are an active mail customer. Or you may subscribe for just $10 in the United States and Canada ($20 overseas, first class mail). Many bookstores also have *New Worlds* available to their customers. Ask for it.

In *New Worlds* you will find news and features about new books, tapes and services; announcements of meetings and seminars; helpful articles; author interviews and much more. Write to:

Llewellyn's New Worlds of Mind and Spirit
P.O. Box 64383-168, St. Paul, MN 55164-0383, U.S.A.

TO ORDER BOOKS AND TAPES

If your book store does not carry the titles described on the following pages, you may order them directly from Llewellyn by sending the full price in U.S. funds, plus postage and handling (see below).

Credit card orders: VISA, MasterCard, American Express are accepted. Call us toll-free within the United States and Canada at 1-800-THE-MOON.

Special Group Discount: Because there is a great deal of interest in group discussion and study of the subject matter of this book, we offer a 20% quantity discount to group leaders or agents. Our Special Quantity Price for a minimum order of five copies of *Animal Magick* is $55.80 cash-with-order. Include postage and handling charges noted below.

Postage and Handling: Include $4 postage and handling for orders $15 and under; $5 for orders *over* $15. There are no postage and handling charges for orders over $100. Postage and handling rates are subject to change. We ship UPS whenever possible within the continental United States; delivery is guaranteed. Please provide your street address as UPS does not deliver to P.O. boxes. Orders shipped to Alaska, Hawaii, Canada, Mexico and Puerto Rico will be sent via first class mail. Allow 4-6 weeks for delivery. **International orders:** Airmail – add retail price of each book and $5 for each non-book item (audiotapes, etc.); Surface mail – add $1 per item.

Minnesota residents add 7% sales tax.

Mail orders to:
Llewellyn Worldwide, P.O. Box 64383-168, St. Paul, MN 55164-0383,
U.S.A.

For customer service, call (612) 291-1970.

Prices subject to change without notice.

THE ANCIENT & SHINING ONES
World Myth, Magic & Religion
by D. J. Conway

The Ancient & Shining Ones is a comprehensive reference guide to the myths and deities from ancient religions around the world. Now you can easily find the information you need to develop your own rituals and worship using the Gods/Goddesses with which you resonate most strongly. More than just a mythological dictionary, *The Ancient & Shining Ones* explains the magickal aspects of each deity and explores such practices as Witchcraft, Ceremonial Magick, Shamanism and the Qabala.

Most people are too vague in appealing for help from the Cosmic Beings—they either end up contacting the wrong energy source, or they are unable to make any contact at all, and their petitions go unanswered. In order to touch the power of the universe, we must re-educate ourselves about the Ancient Ones. The ancient pools of energy created and fed by centuries of belief and worship in the deities still exist. These energies can bring peace of mind, spiritual illumination and contentment.

0-87542-170-9, 448 pgs., 7 x 10, 300 illus., softcover   **$17.95**

CELTIC MAGIC
by D. J. Conway

Many people, not all of Irish descent, have a great interest in the ancient Celts and the Celtic pantheon, and *Celtic Magic* is the map they need for exploring this ancient and fascinating magical culture.

Celtic Magic is for the reader who is either a beginner or intermediate in the field of magic. It provides an extensive "how-to" of practical spell-working. There are many books on the market dealing with the Celts and their beliefs, but none guide the reader to a practical application of magical knowledge for use in everyday life. There is also an in-depth discussion of Celtic deities and the Celtic way of life and worship, so that an intermediate practitioner can expand upon the spellwork to build a series of magical rituals. Presented in an easy-to-understand format, *Celtic Magic* is for anyone searching for new spells that can be worked immediately, without elaborate or rare materials, and with minimal time and preparation.

0-87542-136-9, 240 pgs., mass market, illus.   **$3.95**

NORSE MAGIC
by D. J. Conway

The Norse: adventurous Viking wanderers, daring warriors, worshippers of the Aesir and the Vanir. Like the Celtic tribes, the Northmen had strong ties with the Earth and Elements, the Gods and the "little people."

Norse Magic is an active magic, only for participants, not bystanders. It is a magic of pride in oneself and the courage to face whatever comes. It interests those who believe in shaping their own future, those who believe that practicing spellwork is preferable to sitting around passively waiting for changes to come.

The book leads the beginner step by step through the spells. The in-depth discussion of Norse deities and the Norse way of life and worship set the intermediate student on the path to developing his or her own active rituals. *Norse Magic* is a compelling and easy-to-read introduction to the Norse religion and Teutonic mythology. The magical techniques are refreshingly direct and simple, with a strong feminine and goddess orientation.

0-87542-137-7, 240 pgs., mass market, illus.   **$4.99**

BY OAK, ASH & THORN
Modern Celtic Shamanism
by D. J. Conway

Many spiritual seekers are interested in shamanism because it is a spiritual path that can be followed in conjunction with any religion or other spiritual belief without conflict. Shamanism has not only been practiced by Native American and African cultures—for centuries, it was practiced by the Europeans, including the Celts.

By Oak, Ash and Thorn presents a workable, modern form of Celtic shamanism that will help anyone raise his or her spiritual awareness. Here, in simple, practical terms, you will learn to follow specific exercises and apply techniques that will develop your spiritual awareness and ties with the natural world: shape-shifting, divination by the Celtic Ogham alphabet, Celtic shamanic tools, traveling to and using magick in the three realms of the Celtic otherworlds, empowering the self, journeying through meditation and more.

1–56718–166-X, 320 pp., 6 x 9, illus., softcover $12.95

MAIDEN, MOTHER, CRONE
The Myth and Reality of the Triple Goddess
by D. J. Conway

The Triple Goddess is with every one of us each day of our lives. In our inner journeys toward spiritual evolution, each woman and man goes through the stages of Maiden (infant to puberty), Mother (adult and parent) and Crone (aging elder). Maiden, Mother, Crone is a guide to the myths and interpretations of the Great Goddess archetype and her three faces, so that we may better understand and more peacefully accept the cycle of birth and death.

Learning to interpret the symbolic language of the myths is important to spiritual growth. Through learning the true meaning of the ancient symbols, through facing the cycles of life, and by following the meditations and simple rituals provided in this book, women and men alike can translate these ancient teachings into personal revelations. Not all goddesses can be conveniently divided into the clear aspects of Maiden, Mother and Crone. This book covers these as well, including the Fates, the Muses, Valkyries and others.

0-87542-171-7, 240 pgs., 6 x 9, softcover $12.95

DANCING WITH DRAGONS
Invoke Their Ageless Wisdom & Power
D. J. Conway

You can access one of the most potent life forces in the astral universe: the wise and magickal dragon. Dragons do exist! They inhabit the astral plane that interpenetrates our physical world. Now, Dancing with Dragons makes a vast and wonderful hoard of dragon magick and power available to you.

Dancing with Dragons is a ritual textbook that will teach you to call, befriend, and utilize the wisdom of these powerful mythical creatures for increased spiritual fulfillment, knowledge, health, and happiness. Here you will find complete, practical information for working with dragons: spells and rituals ranging from simple to advanced workings; designing ritual tools to aid you in using dragon energy; channeling power using the lines of dragon's breath (energy lines that run through the Earth); and using the true language of dragons in ritual and spell-casting with herbs, oils, stones, and candles.

ISBN: 1-56718-165-1, 320 pp., 7 x 10, illus., softbound $14.95

Prices subject to change without notice.